CONTEMPORARY ISRAEL

JEWISH STUDIES IN THE 21ST CENTURY

General Editor: Frederick E. Greenspahn

The Hebrew Bible: New Insights and Scholarship
Edited by Frederick E. Greenspahn

Women and Judaism: New Insights and Scholarship
Edited by Frederick E. Greenspahn

Jewish Mysticism and Kabbalah: New Insights and Scholarship
Edited by Frederick E. Greenspahn

Contemporary Israel: New Insights and Scholarship
Edited by Frederick E. Greenspahn

Contemporary Israel

New Insights and Scholarship

Edited by Frederick E. Greenspahn

NEW YORK UNIVERSITY PRESS
New York

NEW YORK UNIVERSITY PRESS
New York
www.nyupress.org

Library of Congress Cataloging-in-Publication Data
Names: Greenspahn, Frederick E., 1946– editor. | Saposnik, Arieh Bruce, 1966–
Contesting Israel : narratives in scholarship and beyond. Container of (work):
Title: Contemporary Israel : new insights and scholarship /
edited by Frederick E. Greenspahn.
Description: New York ; London : New York University, [2017] | Series: Jewish studies in the 21st century | Includes bibliographical references and index.
Identifiers: LCCN 2016010228 | ISBN 978-1-4798-9680-6 (cl : alk. paper) |
ISBN 978-1-4798-2894-4 (pb : alk. paper)
Subjects: LCSH: Israel—History—1993- | Israel—Social conditions—21st century. |
National characteristics, Israeli.
Classification: LCC DS128.2 .C66 2017 | DDC 956.9405—dc23
LC record available at http://lccn.loc.gov/2016010228

New York University Press books are printed on acid-free paper, and their binding materials are chosen for strength and durability. We strive to use environmentally responsible suppliers and materials to the greatest extent possible in publishing our books.

Manufactured in the United States of America

10 9 8 7 6 5 4 3 2 1

Also available as an ebook

CONTENTS

Introduction

FREDERICK E. GREENSPAHN

The journalist Ari Shavit once observed that "Israel was a narrative before it became a state."[1] In truth, it has long been a narrative or, better, several narratives that are at odds with each other and even, sometimes, with reality. Although the Bible describes the land as flowing with milk and honey, the Judeans who returned there from Babylonian captivity saw it quite differently.[2] That experience was repeated in our own time, when the Zionists who sought to make the desert bloom expressed frustration at its being "the one spot in the Middle East that has no oil."[3]

Recent scholarship has exposed numerous instances of the gulf between contemporary Israel's image and reality. Examples extend from the 1948 War of Independence, where the prevailing narrative has proven far more simplistic than what actually took place, to the country's social life, politics, language, arts, and religion. Sadly, these insights have rarely reached beyond the academy, leaving the disjuncture between Israel's image and reality intact. Not only does that disconnect complicate efforts to resolve the nation's problems, but it also distracts from other issues, making it harder for both defenders and detractors to address the real Israel.

This book does not seek to rehash the nation's past or to resolve its struggle with the Arab world, both of which have received ample attention elsewhere.[4] Instead, it presents a look at what contemporary scholarship has learned about modern Israel, highlighting those areas where the reality differs from its prevailing image. Our goal is to shed light on the people who live there and the world they have created in order to provide a deeper grasp of the nation's culture and society that extends from its approaches to immigration and citizenship to the impact of religious fundamentalism and the women's movement.

As we will see, the real Israel is far more complex, in both these areas and many more, from what is widely thought. In part, that is due to changes that have taken place over the course of Israeli history. As Ilan Troen observes, Israel has evolved into something quite different from what its founders intended. No longer the pioneering, egalitarian society envisioned by eastern European socialist idealists—a reality dramatized by recent social protests[5]—it has become a collectivity of communities from diverse geographic and political backgrounds with a host of historical experiences. Even Israeli Judaism differs from what it is widely supposed to be, whether the secular socialism of its early years or the monolithic fundamentalism that was widely thought to prevail in recent decades. Although the chapters that follow provide only samples of the contemporary nation's reality, they illustrate the importance of recognizing the Israel that actually exists rather than the one in our imagination and the ways in which scholarly insights can enrich our understanding of the issues that confront it.

The complexity of this project is evident in Nehama Aschkenasy's description of the problems inherent in the ostensibly simple label "Israeli literature": Does it embrace *everything* Israelis write or only compositions in Hebrew? And what about literature by Israel's Arab citizens or accounts of Israeli Jews' experiences prior to their arrival in the Middle East? Further complicating matters, Calvin Goldscheider outlines the diversity of Israel's population and the internal struggles that heterogeneity has created. The state's founders envisioned Israel as a haven for Jews who were doomed to oppression and persecution elsewhere, but the very process of realizing that dream has led to social tension. Immigrants from the Middle East, World War II Europe, Ethiopia, and the former Soviet Union, with their diverse backgrounds and experiences, were not always treated well, leading to geographic separation, economic stratification, and divergent political expectations. The resulting strains are exacerbated by the fact that several of these groups did not experience the Holocaust, which has become central to Israel's self-understanding. Further questions about the nation's role as a sanctuary are raised by the growth of émigré communities, who leave Israel in search of a higher quality of life.[6] And then, of course, there are the Arabs, who constitute approximately one-fifth of Israel's population and, as Nadim Rouhana and Areej Sabbagh-Khoury explain, have struggled to find their place in a country that defines itself as Jewish. Over time, they have come to see themselves as part of the Palestinian people with national aspirations of their own. That perception, which is now shared by many Jews, has had important consequences for both Israel's self-definition and its relationship with its neighbors.[7]

The Hebrew language, which was revived as part of the effort to connect the nation with its ancient past,[8] is another facet of Israel that is not what it is widely thought to be. Modern Israeli usage is significantly different from the language of Moses, David, and Isaiah, leading one linguist to characterize it as "a European language in transparent Hebrew clothing."[9] Following the principle that "it is not single words that change the character of a language but rather its inner structure,"[10] Shmuel Bolozky points out how contemporary Hebrew has evolved in ways that are typical of living languages. While these changes may connect modern Hebrew to its predecessor forms, they have also raised questions about Israeli identity, as was dramatized by the public outcry that followed the government's mandate that Israeli schools use a translation of the Bible into modern Hebrew.[11]

The kibbutz movement, in which men and women were supposed to work side by side without the hierarchical structures that are characteristic of most societies, is yet another feature of Israel that differs from its prevailing image. Despite their hold on the popular imagination, kibbutzim never constituted more than a small percentage of the population, albeit one that played a disproportionate role in Israeli society. However, Raymond Russell explains how economic pressures have forced them to adopt a more capitalistic structure, far different from their original model.

Of course, societies constantly change, even if their reputations sometimes lag. Israel's military may never have been either the melting pot or the bastion of egalitarianism it is sometimes still thought to be. The relaxation of mandatory conscription, which resulted in a growing proportion of Mizrachi, Russian, and Ethiopian soldiers as well as increasing numbers of modern Orthodox Jews, has magnified that complexity. While the military is often thought of as one of Israel's key strengths, this demographic shift has led to concern as to its reliability for carrying out political policies, especially those that may be unpopular within segments of the Israeli population.[12]

The post-1967 rise of Jewish Orthodoxy, which parallels the growth of conservative religious movements around the world, has had significant political consequences, creating another area in which the Israeli reality is more complex than is often recognized. This process has taken place in two arenas: (1) so-called ultra-Orthodoxy, which seeks to isolate itself from the rest of society in order to accommodate its demanding lifestyle and forms of observance, and (2) nationalistic ideologies that provoke conflict with the Arab world. Both of these have created problems within Israel, the first by trying to impose its religious views on the entire country and the second by seeking to carry out its militant political agendas. Yet Michael Feige suggests that focusing on religiosity can obscure other dynamics, specifically the possibility that some of the more dramatic incidents emanating from the latter faction may owe more to social and ethnic tensions than to religious belief.

Israeli Orthodoxy has also been challenged from within, particularly with regard to its gender hierarchies, as demonstrated by Paula Birnbaum. Israel had already had a female prime minister by the early 1970s, and women have long served alongside men in its military, leading some people to think that Israeli women have greater access to power than their peers elsewhere do. But true gender equality has proven difficult to achieve. Nonetheless, Patricia Woods shows how Israel's feminist movement has resisted pressure to subordinate its goals to the interests of the state, even if its activities are not always visible. Most remarkably, some of its approaches have been borrowed from various Arab societies.

The fact that several feminist and militant Orthodox activities have been instigated by American immigrants demonstrates the dynamic nature of Israel's relationship with the Jewish diaspora, notwithstanding widespread laments about the country's fraying ties with American Jewry. As noted earlier, large numbers of Israelis have emigrated to the United States. Meanwhile, programs such as Taglit-Birthright send diaspora adolescents to visit Israel in order to strengthen their Jewish identity, leading one observer to note that "for many young American Jews, Israel has become an identity theme park. One goes there to have her 'Jewishness' recharged, [and] identity affirmed, and then returns to her diasporic life largely unchanged."[13] Diaspora Jewry also provides political and financial support to Israeli social movements on both the right and the left. Two of Israel's most recent ambassadors to the United States were born and raised in America, as were leaders of the liberal Women of the Wall and Rabbis for Human Rights. Israel's largest circulation newspaper is owned by an American Jew, and approximately one thousand American Jews serve in the Israeli army. From facts such as these, Theodore Sasson concludes that the relationship between the world's two largest Jewish communities is not dissipating but changing. Indeed, Israel has become a focal point in the American Jewish community, albeit one that is increasingly divisive.

Although it is impossible to cover all that could be said about contemporary Israel in the pages of one book, the topics included here, taken together, illustrate the importance of understanding the reality of contemporary Israel rather than romanticized images, whether positive or negative. As Arieh Saposnik warns, scholarship is not always free from ideological agendas. Nor can it resolve either the country's internal debates or its struggle with the Arab world. But it can inject facts into the emotionally laden and often unrealistic images that so often infect treatments of this subject.

The real Israel is a multifaceted society that, like all countries, encompasses numerous competing points of view—Arab and Jewish, Ashkenazi and Mizrachi, left and right, classical and modern, religious and secular. By exposing reality, scholarship makes it possible to approach issues of concern with facts rather than fears. Disciplines as diverse as art, linguistics, history, and sociology have something to contribute to this project. Collectively, they paint the portrait of a society that is far more complicated than the prevailing narratives—one that was created to be a center for world Jewry but struggles to define itself, including its relationship to the Jewish past, to other Jewish communities, and to its non-Jewish population.

Like the series as a whole, this volume has benefited from the contributions of more people than those listed in the table of contents. Herbert and Elaine Gimelstob's generosity provided the impetus for the larger project of which it is a part. Howard Adelman, Judith Baskin, Lisa Eisen, Miriam Elman, Reuven Firestone, Alan Levenson, Ella Levy, Kristen Lindbeck, Susan Marks, Heather McKay, Joel Migdal, Gilead Morahg, Derek Penslar, Robert Rabil, Joel Rosenberg, Marianne Sanua, Seth Ward, Yael Warshel, and David Wright all assisted in the formulation and execution of this particular volume. Inbal Mazar's dedication, hard work, and generous suggestions helped in both the conception and the implementation of an often difficult undertaking. Jennifer Hammer's encouragement and guidance, along with that of the NYU Press readers and staff, helped turn the idea into a reality. And finally, as always, Barbara Pearl provided not only support in every way needed but also insights and insistence that elevated the final results beyond what could have otherwise been achieved.

NOTES

1. Serge Schmemann, "Ari Shavit: An Insider's Guide to Zionism," *Moment* 39:3 (May–June 2014): 78.
2. Neh. 1:1–3 and 2:3, 11–17; cf. Exod. 3:8, 17, 13:5, 33:3; Lev. 20:24, Num. 13:27, 14:8; Deut. 6:3, 11:9, 26:9, 15, 27:3, 31:20; Js. 5:6; Jer. 11:5, 32:22; Ezek. 20:6, 15.
3. Golda Meir, as quoted in the *New York Times*, June 10, 1973, 3.
4. E.g., Howard Sachar, *A History of Israel from the Rise of Zionism to Our Own Time*, 3rd ed. (New York: Knopf, 2007); Barry Rubin, *Israel: An Introduction* (New Haven, CT: Yale University Press, 2012); Anita Shapira, *Israel: A History* (Waltham, MA: Brandeis University Press, 2012); and Colin Shindler, *A History of Modern Israel* (Cambridge: Cambridge University Press, 2013).
5. Cf. Paul Krugman, "Israel's Golden Age," *New York Times*, March 16, 2015, A19.
6. Cf. Steven J. Gold, *The Israeli Diaspora* (Seattle: University of Washington Press, 2002).
7. Yitzhak Reiter, *National Minority, Regional Majority: Palestinian Arabs versus Jews in Israel* (Syracuse, NY: Syracuse University Press, 2009), esp. 148.
8. Cf. Jack Fellman, *The Revival of a Classical Tongue: Eliezer Ben Yehuda and the Modern Hebrew Language* (The Hague, Netherlands: Mouton, 1973).
9. Gotthelf Bergsträsser, *Introduction to the Semitic Languages: Text Specimens and Grammatical Sketches*, trans. Peter T. Daniels (Winona Lake, IN: Eisenbrauns, 1983), 64, from *Einführung die semitischen Sprache: Sprachenproben und grammatische Skizzen* (Munich: Max Hueber Verlag, 1928), 47.
10. Joshua Blau, *The Renaissance of Modern Hebrew and Modern Standard Arabic: Parallels and Differences in the Revival of Two Semitic Languages* (Berkeley: University of California Press, 1981), 140.
11. Tamar Rotem, "Education Ministry to Ban 'Bible Lite' Study Booklet," *Haaretz*, September 5, 2008. In fact, a translation of the book of Amos into modern Hebrew had been produced over sixty years earlier. Joseph Klausner, *Sefer Amos im Parshegen [Paraphraza Ivrit] be-Tseruf Meḥqar Meforat al Ishiuto shel Amos HaNavi, Zemano U-Nevuotav* (Tel Aviv: Sreberk, 1942).
12. Cf. Yagil Levy, "Military-Society Relations: The Demise of the 'People's' Army," in *Israel since 1980*, ed. Guy Ben-Porat, Yagil Levy, Shlomo Mizrahi, Arye Naor, and Erez Tzfadia (New York: Cambridge University Press, 2008), 117–45.

13. Shaul Magid, in "Affinities and Israel: A Roundtable," *Sh'ma* 38:647 (January 2008): 5. Cf. Shaul Kelner, *Tours That Bind: Diaspora, Pilgrimage, and Israeli Birthright Tourism* (New York: NYU Press, 2010); and Leonard Saxe and Barry Chazen, *Ten Days of Birthright Israel: A Journey in Young Adult Identity* (Waltham, MA: Brandeis University Press, 2008).

PART I

History

1

Contesting Israel

Narratives in Scholarship and Beyond

ARIEH SAPOSNIK

No study of Israel is without contestation. The very terminology one uses in discussing Israel is virtually never value neutral. There are many reasons for the contentious and contested character of the field of Israel studies—some substantive, others less so. First is simply the cantankerous nature of academics and academic work. Scholarship is, in fact, nourished by argument and debate in which ideas confront and challenge one another and in the process—at least when this works best—enrich and enliven the thinking that is the business of academics. And if disputation tends to be the rule in both the best and the worst of academic discourse, this is the case even more pronouncedly in those fields broadly labeled "area" or "ethnic" studies. In many of these—and in this sense Israel studies is far from unique—even the best academic work often finds itself contending with multiple points of contact with issues that arise out of identity politics (political activism in which a sense of collective identity is the paramount factor) and the academic theorizing that is often entangled in it.[1]

We live in an era that, some people have suggested, is lacking in historical memory and perspective. What might arguably be termed the "postmodern condition" and, more importantly, the postmodern critique of the very notion of historical truth has led, in academic and popular circles alike, to profound doubts regarding the nature, viability, and legitimacy of the historical pursuit itself. Indeed, acceptance of the core postmodern critiques of the historian's craft and of the very possibility of knowledge about the past, at least in their most radical forms, would lead to the conclusion that "meaningful historical writing would be impossible."[2] And yet, perhaps paradoxically, the rise of ethnic and identity politics with their often attendant politics of victimhood, is but one factor that has, at the same time, made history once again a particularly critical form of knowledge. Battles over history have become central in many contemporary political struggles and to the identity making that is often a part of it.

The 1990s saw an increased interest in culture as a pivotal historical force in academic circles, and with it came an emphasis on identity as a major focus of interest in a wide range of fields in the humanities and social sciences. In this setting, history and historical consciousness have regained a place of prominence both as a matter for study and as sites of polemics and political debate (although the word "history" may itself, of course, mean very different things in these different contexts). "It is easy," as Peter Charles Hoffer has written, "to demolish the very *idea* of historical knowing but impossible to demolish the *importance* of historical knowing. For who can know the past, forever gone, and who can ignore the past, always with us?"[3] This confluence of the politics of the age and the renewed centrality of some kind of historical thinking and image making has helped to charge the work of the historian with a marked political relevance and hence a particularly high wattage of prickliness and combativeness.

The Academics and Identity Politics of Israel Studies

If the foregoing assessment is an all but universal phenomenon of many "area studies," other factors specific to Israel studies help make it particularly thorny. Indeed, it is precisely the near universality of the struggles over history, memory, and identity that bring to light the distinctiveness of the Israel studies case. In Belgium there have been recent struggles over museum representations and historical memories of Belgian history in Congo.[4] New Zealand has grappled with the issue of Maori territorial claims, which have taken the form of repeated court trials and an attempt at resolution through the 1975 establishment of a government commission of inquiry charged with researching the history of government-Maori agreements.[5] A quick survey of two recent issues of the journal *History and Memory* shows articles with such titles as "Narrating Genoa: Documentaries of the Italian G8 Protests of 2001 and the Persistence and Politics of Memory"; "Sofia Was Bombed? Bulgaria's

Forgotten War with the Allies"; "'A Lasting Gift to His Descendants': Family Memory and the Great War in Australia"; and "The Yasukuni Shrine and the Competing Patriotic Pasts of East Asia."[6] These cases show the contested nature of memory in a vast array of places. Some refer to episodes that might resonate to some of us; others are obscure to all who are neither specialists in the field nor participants in the relevant events.

In the Israeli case, such questions of memory and identity have a resonance that goes well beyond Israel and the would-be ivory-tower confines of a small coterie of specialists who study it to a far broader public and seemingly pressing contemporary political matters that are often of worldwide concern. Indeed, if academics at times wonder about the impact of their work beyond the "ivory tower," that is not the case for Israel studies, whether that is pleasing or displeasing to the scholars themselves. Over the past three decades or so, academic work on Israel has had a profound and unmistakable impact on shaping the discourse about Israel well beyond the confines of the campus.

Many of the heated academic arguments about Israel and its past have taken up residence in movies, television programs, and popular history and literature. Both scholarly and popular understandings of the 1948 war and the birth of the Palestinian refugee problem have undergone thorough revision, particularly since the publication of Benny Morris's *The Birth of the Palestinian Refugee Problem* in 1988 and much of his subsequent work (along with that of others who followed in his footsteps).[7] Morris's early work sought to undermine the traditional narratives of Israelis and Palestinians alike regarding the war, although the almost traumatic impact on Israeli popular memory seems to have been far more marked. Generations of Israelis—and in many cases their supporters abroad—had been raised with the notion that Israelis sought to welcome their Arab neighbors into their new state but that the Arabs fled in the hope of returning after the projected destruction of the Jewish state. While the histories differ, sometimes dramatically, in the relative weights and stresses they attribute to various factors, it is fair to say that this traditional perception has been largely replaced with a now prevalent sense that the refugee problem was the result, at least, of a far more complicated combination of flight, expulsion by Israeli forces (whether as a matter of policy or more spontaneous practice—a matter for continuing debate), occasional atrocities, and a spreading fear of potential atrocities on the part of the Arab population. Conditions in neighboring Arab countries and policies adopted by the new Israeli government seem also to have proven critical factors.[8]

The ethnic divide in Israel, between Jews of European origin and those whose families originated in the Muslim world, is a continuing—at times festering—social issue. It is not surprising that the history of the relations between these groups—and in particular the story of the mass immigration of Jews from Middle Eastern countries, largely in the 1950s and '60s—is a matter of sometimes bitter debate among scholars and in the Israeli popular media. At stake are such matters as the nature of the encounter itself as either welcoming or jaundiced, the foundational perceptions of the Middle Eastern newcomers by the usually European veterans, and the complicated interconnections between ethnic differences and class disparities.[9]

As these controversies indicate, much of the heat in Israeli historiographical debates centers on questions related to some of the more painful moments and challenges of Israel's early years. In line with this trend, another focal point for debate both among scholars and in the public arena has been Holocaust survivors' encounter with Israeli society and the shaping of Holocaust memory. Did Zionists do what they could for the Jews in Nazi-occupied Europe, or did they abandon their brethren to their fate? Did survivors arrive in Palestine, and later Israel, out of choice and commitment to Zionism, or were they manipulated by Zionist emissaries in Europe? Once in Israel, were they greeted as traumatized brethren or silenced, ridiculed, shamed, and even accused of having been collaborators or for the mere fact of having survived?[10] These, too, are questions that exercise not only specialists but public discourse and popular culture in Israel.

As a result of changes in fundamental academic paradigms regarding Israel, then, the imagery of Israel in the media and in public discourse has been profoundly impacted by what might otherwise have seemed obscure debates among historians, sociologists, and political scientists. As a result, the field of Israel studies finds itself, virtually by nature, looking with one eye to the world of scholarship while at the same time inevitably embroiled in current political and social debates in the public sphere. This situation is gratifying to some scholars and perturbing to others; but whatever one's view, there is no doubt that the fusion of academic and popular discourses makes Israel studies a field that is both exciting and filled with challenge.

This excitement helps to explain the substantial growth in Israel studies over the past decade. This process began in the United States, where there are now roughly three dozen academic centers, programs, and chairs. More recently, the trend has been echoed in Israeli universities, which have given new streams of funding and curricular restructuring to Israel studies. Although slower on this front, Europe too has seen increasing numbers of centers and professorships dedicated to the study of Israel.

In the US, one important piece of the backdrop to the establishment of such programs has been donors' interest with the image of Israel on university campuses, a concern that intensified after the demise of the Oslo peace process and the outbreak of the second Palestinian intifada in 2000. But donor interest alone does not, of course, explain growing student enrollment, increased class offerings (supported by centers generally and by such programs as the Brandeis Summer Institute, which trains faculty members to incorporate Israel into their classroom teaching), and an array of faculty study trips to Israel and the Palestinian territories. Beyond the influx of funding, in other words, Israel simply appears to be of interest.

This may not be terribly surprising to those who study Israel. Its presence (indeed, its arguably disproportionate ubiquity and role) in world affairs and in the headlines that address them is one obvious (and good) reason for students and academics to take an interest in the country. But this is not the only reason. As the title of one book exploring the complexity of Jewish attitudes indicates, the Land of Israel/Palestine/the Holy Land is the "impossible land"[11] (the multiplicity of names and the impossibility of neutral naming are indications of the complex issues involved), and the State of Israel, one might add, may similarly be deemed at least "improbable." And yet there they both are—and this, of course, is a source of some fascination.

What such descriptions point to is that studying Israel affords opportunities to examine multiple topics that are of interest to scholars in many fields, from the study of nationalism (postcolonial and otherwise) to religion and politics, secularization and sacralization, immigration, migration and immigrant labor markets, postwar reconstruction projects, linguistic evolution, and more. Placed in comparative and international perspectives, Israel seems to share much with certain other cases but to stand out as offering unique vistas in many other respects.

This multiplicity of academic areas to which Israel studies might contribute points to another reason why this is an interesting time in Israel studies: the ongoing expansion that has been taking place in the horizons of the field itself. Not long ago, Israel studies was all but limited to sociology and political science—questions pertaining to a very contemporary scene—with the occasional contribution of a historian. Today, as the programs of recent meetings of the Association for Israel Studies indicate, one finds law and legal theory, film and theater, literature, gender studies, environmental sciences, cultural studies, history, music and dance, museology, migration, art history, and much more.[12] In other words, the field has not just grown quantitatively but has expanded and enriched itself qualitatively.

Given the multiple contexts in which Israel studies takes place and the manifold developments and challenges that characterize it today, I would like to survey and analyze some of what I think are central trends in scholarship on Israel as it has been taking shape in recent years and to try to understand how that scholarship has been influenced by, and has in turn influenced, the changing environments in which it is being produced. From this survey, I will attempt to assess the methodological standing of the field, particularly where my own discipline—history and historiography—is concerned.

Israel Studies from Then to Now

It is fair to say that Israel studies emerged as a discrete field of academic research and teaching in the 1980s. It was then, in 1985, that the Association for Israel Studies was established. It is not a coincidence, moreover, that it was right around that time that questions pertaining to Israeli society, politics, and history were becoming increasingly and more vociferously disputed and contentious in both academic settings and public discourse. Israel itself was changing in palpable ways: less than a decade had elapsed since the political earthquake that ended nearly thirty years of Labor Party rule and brought Menachem Begin and the Likud party to power—a political manifestation of multiple changes that were taking place (and that were further catalyzed by the political change) in ethnic relations, the religious-secular divide, attitudes to the land itself and in particular the 1967 territories, and understandings of the very meaning of Israel, Israeliness, and the Israeli past.

One illustrative example of this latter point is the reshaping of public spaces and thus the identity of the state that was wrought through changes in street names, so that Jabotinsky (the leader of Revisionist Zionism, the ideological progenitor of the Likud) and Etzel and Lehi (the pre-1948 Revisionist underground groups) became far more visible than ever before. Another indication of the efforts to reshape historical memory was the attempt by Begin's government to redress what Revisionists and former Revisionists had long deemed a historical injustice by establishing a governmental commission of inquiry to investigate the 1933 assassination of the Labor Zionist leader Chaim Arlosoroff, which had long been a lightning rod for often bitter tensions, with accusations from the Labor camp that Revisionists were both directly and indirectly responsible for the murder (a question that, in spite of the commission's efforts, remains unsolved to this day).

Israeli historiography, and with it the historiography of Israel, began to come into its own as a distinct and professionalized field of study in the 1970s, a short time prior to the emergence of Israel studies as an interdisciplinary field. Critical here was the work of a group of scholars such as Anita Shapira, Yosef Gorny, and Israel Kolatt, who came of age in those years. To be sure, histories of Israel were being written virtually beginning on May 15, 1948 (and histories of Zionism from almost the moment of Zionism's birth); but we may use the 1970s as our starting point, given the fact that it is the work of these scholars that became the principal point of reference in the 1980s, with the emergence of the critical, revisionist, or as some people would call it, the post-Zionist school of Israeli history and sociology. Derek Penslar has characterized the earlier generation of scholars as "in-house critics" of the Labor Zionist establishment that was, at the time, still the dominant political, cultural, and ideological force in Israeli life.[13] To the generation that began to come of age in the mid- to late 1980s—prominent among them are Benny Morris, Gershon Shafir, Avi Shlaim, and Ilan Pappé—it was the "in-house" component of this group that seemed far more prominent than the critical, and they directed their own critical arrows primarily at this cohort and their scholarship.

The dramatic changes that took place in Israeli society in the 1980s, then, had a powerful reflection in Israeli academia. Under the impact of the Likud's rise to power in 1977, Israel's first Lebanon war in 1982 and the unprecedented levels of civil dissatisfaction and opposition to that war (particularly in the wake of the massacre at Sabra and Shatila), and the overall decline of what had been the society's ideological charge and galvanizing ideology, a new, challenging historiography began to appear. Beginning with such books as Simcha Flapan's *The Birth of Israel*, Benny Morris's *The Birth of the Palestinian Refugee Problem*, Gershon Shafir's *Land, Labor, and the Origins of the Israeli-Palestinian Conflict*, and Avi Shlaim's *Collusion across the Jordan*, Israeli historians (and historians of Israel) began to present what was seen as a radically different picture from that of the preceding generation, one that placed Israeli conduct in 1948 in a far more complicated and, at times, difficult light than had previously been familiar.[14]

The revisionist thrust of this generation began with examinations of Jewish-Arab relations (often with a particular stress on the 1948 war). By the 1990s, other scholars began to tackle additional matters in Israeli history, such as the encounter between the young state and the survivors of the Holocaust and the absorption of the mass immigration of Jews, primarily from Arab lands, in the 1950s and early 1960s. The often highly critical thrust of many of these works led to the sometimes inaccurate association between them and the notion of "post-Zionism," whether as an ideological stance (itself often not clearly distinguished from "anti-Zionism") or as one possible description of the social and cultural reality of Israel in the 1990s: a "normalized" society no longer held together by ideological fervor and concomitant efforts at social engineering—the creation of a "new Jew" that was the corollary of that ideology.

In the background to all of these works—and stimulated further by them—were tectonic shifts that were taking place in a wide range of Israeli self-perceptions: the memory of the Holocaust, the meanings attributed to Zionism itself, the still raw scars of the history of immigrant absorption, and most obviously (certainly outside Israel itself) a changing perception of the relationship between Israel and the Palestinians. These shifts were hastened and intensified by the Lebanon war and Menachem Begin's famous speech in the Knesset in which he termed it a "war of choice," a phrase quickly adopted (with a reversal of meaning) by the opposition. The Sabra and Shatila massacre, in which Israel Defense Forces provided lighting and background support to Christian Fallangist forces while they massacred hundreds of Palestinian civilians in these two refugee camps on the outskirts of Beirut, was surely the most traumatic event of the war and seemed to connect the question of Israeli-Palestinian relations to profound changes in many Israelis' perceptions of the history of their country's resort to military force. The profound questions and the identity crisis that these events aroused were then further exacerbated toward the end of the decade with the outbreak of the first Palestinian intifada in December 1987.

The reshaping of memory and identity, and the often bitter debates that were a part of this process both within academic circles and beyond, continued into the 1990s. The dramatic unfolding of the Oslo peace process by 1993 created a sense that indeed the conditions in which Israel was living were undergoing radical change. As Israelis and Palestinians seemed to be moving closer together during the heady early days of Oslo, when peace and reconciliation seemed to be within reach, with Israelis flocking to the casino in Jericho and to nightclubs in Ramallah, a sense emerged in many Israeli academic circles that perhaps the bitterly opposing narratives that had animated the two societies for decades, shaping the ways in which the two nations understood who they were, might themselves find some mode of reconciliation as well. Perhaps some degree of de-Zionization of Israeli historical memory would be necessary, the message seemed to be, in order to allow for a meeting of the two pasts.

The Demise of the Peace Process and the Post-Oslo Era

The exhilaration of those early Oslo years, as we know all too well, did not last long. As early as November 1995, a massive rally in support of that process in Tel Aviv was clearly motivated by a perceived need to give it a new injection of life. Bitter opposition had grown within Israeli society, and the difficulties and tensions that were built into Oslo began to be acutely felt. That was also the famous Tel Aviv rally at which Prime

Minister Yitzhak Rabin was gunned down; and with his death, as was already becoming evident, particularly with the wave of suicide bombings that came in the subsequent months of early 1996, the promise of peace seemed to be unraveling. And unravel it did, rather definitively, with the outbreak of the second Palestinian intifada in the late summer of 2000.

The outbreak of the second intifada, which seemed to lay the hopes of the 1990s to rest, was coupled with a certain fatigue with the historiographical debates and struggles over memory that had been raging for more than a decade. As Derek Penslar has pointed out, two things happened: On the one hand, many of the once radical arguments of some of the revisionist works—in particular, Benny Morris's work on the Palestinian refugee problem—had been more or less absorbed into the mainstream of Israeli academic work and public discourse. On the other hand, some of the more extreme claims, arguments, and attempts at ideological modification were rejected and to some degree marginalized.[15] This is an important point to which I return later, given that this would-be dismissal seems to me to have spelled not the end of these positions but rather their reemergence in new forms. Since their reemergence was in response to the new currents in Israeli historiography, we would do well to survey the postrevisionist trends before addressing their twenty-first-century forms.

"Post-Post-Zionism"

In the past decade or so, a new body of literature has emerged. While the works that have been identified as belonging to this "postrevisionist" or "post-post-Zionist" trend in Israeli historiography vary considerably from one another, two salient characteristics have provided a basis for grouping them together. First, if the revisionist trend tended to focus on political and military history, many of the works of the past decade reflect a shift to cultural and social historical questions. Works such as Anat Helman's on the social history of Tel Aviv and Orit Rozin's on the austerity regime of the 1950s and the role of ordinary housewives in shaping a changing Israeli society represent a move to a cultural focus and a history of mentalities characterized by a growing interest in history from below.[16]

The second shared characteristic of much of this work is its tendency to be less self-consciously revisionist and less charged with an ideological and polemical tone. Although, as Assaf Likhovsky has pointed out, there is in fact a wide range of ideological commitment and outlook among the scholars who can be grouped as part of this new trend, those ideological commitments tend to be less central to their academic endeavors.[17] A central premise among the "revisionist" generation had been that the history of Israel and Zionism had previously been written in the service of national ideology. Their writings were, consequently, often quite explicit and deliberate efforts to challenge those ostensible ideological underpinnings.

There were at least two different types of critique playing central roles in the work of the revisionists. Some ostensibly targeted the ideological motivation of the earlier work. For others, the target was the *Zionist* orientation to which the earlier work had ostensibly been tethered and that needed to be dismantled in favor—obliquely in some cases and quite explicitly in others—of a different ideology that was deemed preferable. In either case, ideology played an important role as an underlying motivation in these works.

Although some people—Ilan Pappé, for example—have characterized the latest trend as "neo-Zionist,"[18] it seems more accurate to say that it is mostly characterized by a relaxation of ideological charge. Much (if by no means all) of this work evinces a less critical approach to Zionism and Israel than did much of the work of the previous generation of scholars. The ideologies to which many of these works are committed are primarily academic ideologies, matters of theory and methodology.

Complicating the picture, of course, is the fact that questions of fundamental theoretical framework are never entirely distinct from what might more commonly be seen as ideology. It was not an accident that the designation "post-Zionist" for the critical schools of the 1980s and '90s paralleled the designation "postmodern" for challenges to prevailing paradigms that had pointed particularly acerbic barbs at the very possibility of historical knowledge and truth.[19] Some of the proponents of the "post-Zionist" school base their works on the terminology, theoretical frameworks, and epistemological premises taken from the thought of such postmodern figures as Michel Foucault and Edward Said, who posed powerful and lasting challenges to the very foundations of historical work.[20] For example, postmodernist underpinnings proved crucial for many of the arguments that suggested that academics serve in essence as part of the mechanisms of power by generating "truths" that uphold ideological infrastructures designed to justify the power of the powerful. This was often a good part of the intellectual footing for arguments showing the complicity of Israeli academic work with the power structures that maintain the imbalances of power and lingering injustices to Palestinians, Mizrachi Jews, Holocaust survivors, and others. Such arguments, of course, formed the basis for calls for a paradigm shift—a new or "revisionist" approach to that history, thereby intertwining epistemological and ethical-moral concerns.

Sources of the New Currents

How should one make sense of these new approaches to the study of Israel? Assaf Likhovsky has suggested that the adoption of a different methodological framework may help explain them. He points in particular to many historians' move to an anthropological model rooted in global trends, which tends to stress empathy with the subjects of one's research.[21] While this seems an important part of the story, deeper social-cultural shifts, some specifically Israeli, appear also to lie at the base of the changing historiographical tone.

Inherent in the work of at least many of the postrevisionists is a casting off of an earlier rejection. One might, in fact, make a case for a long trajectory of rejections and counterrejections as a central underlying theme of the history of Zionism from its earliest days, when much of Zionist thought and culture production was aimed at the construction of a new "usable past" and a reshaping of Jewish historical memory, often on the basis of a rejection of traditional Jewish understandings of the past. In this scheme, the revisionist work of the 1980s and 1990s and the current postrevisionist trend are links in a much longer chain of what the author Micha Yosef Berdiczewsky, in the early days of Zionism, called "destruction and creation"—indeed, destruction at times as the handmaiden of creation.[22]

The eruption of a grassroots social and economic protest movement in Israel in the summer of 2011 bore many of the marks of new tectonic shifts in Israeli culture and identity. In some manifestations of that protest movement, one could identify once again the fundamental role of a changing and shifting historical consciousness. In one speech, the Jerusalem City Council member Rachel Azaria pointed to the history of the state not as a shameful or reprehensible chapter from which Israeli society ought to liberate itself but rather as a model for a new structuring of Israel's economic structure and social relations. She spoke about her own discovery, after becoming involved in the protest movement, of the fact that one of the first pieces of legislation passed by the very first Knesset—as early as 1949—was the law for mandatory free education. Why, she asked, could a young, cash-strapped Israel pass this law at a time when it was still reeling from its War of Independence and grappling with immigration that would double its population within its first three years, while an Israel that boasts of its economic successes could not spare the funding necessary to bolster the long-crumbling educational system?[23] This historical recollection was, for her, one of the foundations of the demand for a different kind of distribution of the benefits of what some people have called Israel's economic miracle. Indeed, over the past two decades, Israel's economy has grown and blossomed in seemingly impossible ways. One price for that growth has been a rapidly growing gap between rich and poor and a heavy burden of taxation and an insuperable cost of living on much of the middle class.

What is interesting about this historical reference in the present context is its mass-mobilized demand for change that is rooted in a return to history and an almost nostalgic longing for aspects of an Israel that is no more. The summer protests of 2011 seem to have grown out of currents that had been simmering below the surface of Israeli life for some time. These stemmed from a dissatisfaction with—indeed, a rejection of—the atomized and privatized identities that had been central to the discourse of the 1980s and particularly the 1990s. (Although there is now much talk of the protest movement's dissipation, its fundamental call for reorienting Israel's social and economic priorities seems very much alive.) In a series of important articles, Daniel Gutwein has drawn a compelling link between the privatization of the Israeli economy and the privatization and atomization of Israeli identity that has come along with it.[24] If the era of "post-Zionism" was in large measure an outgrowth of a decline of Israel's collectivist ideology and galvanizing pioneering/Zionist/*mamlachti* vision, then the new era—both socioculturally and academically—is the product of the next decline: the decline of the privatization project. Israelis have discovered that privatization's liberation and many benefits (and anybody who can remember trying to get a telephone in Israel in the 1970s is familiar with those benefits) came with some hefty price tags. As much of Baruch Kimmerling's sociological work indicated, by the 1990s Israelis had become hyphenated at best, divided into divergent camps at odds with one another at worst.[25] If there were those who evinced some dissatisfaction with this trend all along, its encounter with the post-second-intifada reality sharpened and disseminated the displeasure, coupled now with a sense of alarm: if indeed there was no more Israeliness, then any purpose for remaining in Israel and being committed to it seemed to have been lost at precisely a time when a sense of existential threat was being reawakened. To be sure, not everybody went so far as Gutwein, who concluded that the privatization of identity was not the progressive, multicultural boon it was made out to be but rather an ideological buttress to inequality in Israeli life. But some sense that perhaps the outright rejection of all that had been the collectivist Israel of the 1950s through the 1970s may have been overly rash seemed to take root—even if in amorphous form—among a broad swath of Israeli society. As one example, this sentiment could be seen in the enormous market that has emerged in Israel in recent years for musical nostalgia (the tens of thousands who attended the reunion concerts of Kaveret, or Pugi, in the summer of 2013 are a clear manifestation of it, worthy of an analysis of its own) or in the thirst for new ways to rediscover and reclaim the traditional Jewish sources—a repair to what is once again an older rejection than that of the 1990s (classical Zionism's dismissal of traditional Judaism). The summer protests and tent cities were merely a peak outburst of these currents, which had been simmering for some time.

This rediscovery and reclamation taking place in Israeli social and cultural discourse over the course of the past decade or so has had its reflection in scholarship on Israel. There, the bankruptcy of what has seemed to some people an amoral postmodernism fused with a general fatigue with debates over the past that were cast as black-and-white. With a sense that the debates of the preceding decade were no longer novel[26] or methodologically interesting and that they were substantively unsatisfying, scholarship began to turn elsewhere. It seems, in other words, that Israeli society and scholarship about it have outgrown an adolescence of sorts and entered a new phase. They are now able to digest some of the critiques that became pivotal in the 1980s and 1990s without feeling a need to reject the entire package out of hand.

A particularly heartening aspect of this change is the return to history. In a recent review of Shlomo Sand's book *The Invention of the Jewish People*, Derek Penslar has argued that the setting for works such as Sand's is an Israeli society that has become jaundiced in its view of its own history. Indeed, Penslar argues, there is "a general crisis of historical consciousness in contemporary Israel."[27] To be sure, Penslar seems to have identified a very real phenomenon in Israeli historical consciousness; however, it is one that is very much at odds with this other, very different approach to the past, which seeks to reengage it and rehistoricize the Israeli present. One aspect of what the 2011 summer protest movement represented is that the new historiographical school is rooted in significant social and cultural changes and a return to history that is, in turn, rooted in attempts to recapture an Israel that was one of ideals and shared goals—however much those might come in for serious scrutiny. It seems to me that there is a very real search for a mature and thoughtful relationship with the Israeli past, and this search, this new sculpting of the past, is a cultural force to be reckoned with.

Academic Work on Israel and Academic Integrity

Arguably, it is precisely this normalization in the academic field of Israel studies—and its corollary institutional success as the field finds increasing placement in universities around the world—that has led to a new reentrenchment on the part of those previously marginalized "extreme" and ideologically driven positions of the previous period. Two characteristic current manifestations illustrate this trend: a rhetoric of victimhood and what might be termed an extreme postmodernist framework of discourse.

A number of recent publications have been marked—and marketed—in part through representation of their authors as academic victims. More than a mere marketing ploy, this is a trope that has become an integral component of these works, their substantive theses, and, it seems, the scholarly and ideological current that they represent. Obvious examples are Ilan Pappé's *The Ethnic Cleansing of Palestine*, the cover of which carries an endorsement by the filmmaker John Pilger, who attests to Pappé's being Israel's "bravest, most principled, most incisive historian."[28] This characterization echoes Pappé's own presentation of himself as an academic victim in his memoiristic survey *Out of the Frame*.[29] Similarly, in the preface to *The Invention of the Jewish People*, Shlomo Sand presents himself as a lone, courageous warrior for truth (notwithstanding his self-proclaimed epistemological relativism) facing a coterie of colleagues, few of whom "feel it their duty to undertake the dangerous pedagogical mission of exposing conventional lies about the past" the way he does.[30]

The rhetorical claim to the status of academic victim is tremendously effective, particularly for a nonacademic audience, because it undermines any academic critique of a given work and serves to realign relations of power through knowledge: if one is the victim of a persecuting academy, that academy loses its validity and its claim to be the holder of certain keys to knowledge and (more importantly) to certain tools for gaining knowledge. Knowledge—and the power to determine what it is—is democratized, so to speak. Time spent in archives, empirical documentation as a basis for an argument, the experience and skill employed in constructing a framework within which to put the empirical pieces together on the basis of familiarity with contexts—in short, careful and rigorous research—are all made irrelevant as criteria for determining truth and the validity of historical narratives. The archival evidence, for example, is no longer a source of authority, because the authority of academe over knowledge is questioned through an often flippant use of the Foucauldian notion of "regimes of truth."

If the postmodern challenge to historiography has generally proven formidable, it appears that in the case of Israel some historians are willing to make concessions that they seem far less likely to make in most other contexts. In a review of Sand's book, the eminent New York University historian of modern Europe Tony Judt concedes that "from a purely scholarly perspective," he has "no quarrel with" the critics who suggested that the book's would-be contribution was at best redundant. Nevertheless, he praises the book as being of great importance for its potential to lead Jews in Europe and the United States to take "their distance from Israel" so that ultimately policy makers in Washington "might come to see the futility of attaching American foreign policy to the delusions of one small Middle Eastern state."[31] It is difficult to imagine a similar kind of argument—acknowledgment of scholarly mediocrity coupled with profuse praise for ideological reasons—issuing from so eminent a historian on just about any other subject.

It is not surprising that the trope of academic victimhood is most evident in the case of the most strident arguments, which also tend to be the weakest from the point of view of scholarly criteria. It is a tool that serves to bolster claims that might otherwise be weakened through scholarly scrutiny. As in the case of Sand, it transforms virtually all academic scrutiny into an indication of hostility, a loyalty to the oppressive academic "ancien régime," and therefore illegitimate in its very origin and essence, in which case there is no need, and indeed no real possibility, for actual argumentation.

If the fundamental argument is that Israel is a powerful (indeed, at times, almost all-powerful), oppressive state and if the morality play of these works is a simple and straightforward black-and-white perpetrator-victim model, then the scholar who can show himself to be a victim casts himself as clearly being on the side of good. When the authors are themselves Israeli (as in the case of Pappé and Sand), such formulations become a virtual necessity, lest the fused epistemological and ethical implications make them suspect for having something to do with the oppressor. The claim of victimhood, then, becomes not just an adornment for an audience with an automatic inclination to support the apparent underdog but a central component of the structure and evidence of the argument itself and of the author's ethical placement (a matter that is deemed of equal significance in this fusion of the epistemological and the ethical).

Postmodernist Epistemology and the Task of the Historian

There is a chic associated with the philosophies on which these arguments are seemingly made that gives their narrative of the past a position so prominent in center stage as to all but preclude the role of evidence and proof. This rejection of an outside reality in favor of language as a symbol that does not refer to any objective reality but rather only to itself, whatever its claims to speak in the name of the oppressed and to offer a new and better ethical stance, is based on the same philosophical foundations that serve a might-makes-right moral philosophy. If history is mere narration with little substantive difference from fiction and no reality with which historical narratives interact more or less faithfully, then the moral claim of the ostensible underdog is merely another amoral jockeying for position, a bid to be the one in power.

"The limitation of relativism," writes Carlo Ginzburg, "is that it misses the distinction between judgment of fact and value judgment."[32] Intellectual sophistry and ethical poverty, in other words, are of a piece, making this a concern that goes beyond the interest of historians, philosophers of history, sociologists, and other academics. The implications run deep. "The historian's craft," Ginzburg adds elsewhere, "involves something that is part of everyone's life: untangling the strands of the true, the false, and the fictional which are the substance of our being in the world."[33]

In the past few decades, multiple social and economic changes and political upheavals have transformed the self-image of Israelis and the image of Israel abroad. These have been reflected in, and at times catalyzed by, understandings of Israel, Zionism, and their histories, as well as the intellectual paradigms within which they are understood. This is neither surprising nor menacing. But where academic discourse about Israel has been about occluding knowledge or obscuring the distinction between intellectual discernment and facile moral judgment, this is an abdication of academic responsibility and an assault on academic integrity. In this sense, what goes on in the academy is very much of interest not only to academics but to the broader public as well. Israel has become a cultural code of sorts in a great deal of contemporary intellectual and public conversation. For this reason, the discourse about Israel as it takes shape in the academy ought to be of concern to all who have an interest in maintaining thought that is not Orwellian and in intellectual discourse that remains in actual fact free.

NOTES

1. See, e.g., the discussions on the place and politicization of ethnic and area studies in William G. Moseley, "Area Studies in a Global Context," *Chronicle of Higher Education*, November 29, 2009; Kenneth P. Monteiro, "Who Gets to Define Ethnic Studies?," *Chronicle of Higher Education*, July 4, 2010; Gary Y. Okihiro, "The Future of Ethnic Studies," *Chronicle of Higher Education*, July 4, 2010.

2. Georg G. Iggers, *Historiography in the Twentieth Century: From Scientific Objectivity to the Postmodern Challenge* (Hanover, NH: Wesleyan University Press, 1997), 11.
3. Peter Charles Hoffer, *The Historians' Paradox* (New York: NYU Press, 2008), ix.
4. See in particular Adam Hochschield, "In the Heart of Darkness," *New York Review of Books* 52 (October 6, 2005): 15.
5. See, e.g., Hannah Blumhardt, "Multi-textualism, Treaty Hegemony and the Waitangi Tribunal: Making Sense of 19th Century Crown-Maori Negotiations in Te Urewera," *Victoria University of Wellington Law Review* 43:2 (2012): 263–88; Jessica Orsman, "The Treaty of Waitangi as an Exercise of Māori Constituent Power," *Victoria University of Wellington Law Review* 43:2 (2012): 345–71.
6. Melody Niwot, "Narrating Genoa: Documentaries of the Italian G8 Protests of 2001 and the Persistence and Politics of Memory," *History and Memory* 23 (2011): 66–89; Irina Gigova, "Sofia Was Bombed? Bulgaria's Forgotten War with the Allies," *History and Memory* 23 (2011): 132–71; Bart Zino, "'A Lasting Gift to His Descendants': Family Memory and the Great War in Australia," *History and Memory* 22 (2010): 125–46; and Shaun O'Dwyer, "The Yasukuni Shrine and the Competing Patriotic Pasts of East Asia," *History and Memory* 22 (2010): 147–77.
7. Benny Morris, *The Birth of the Palestinian Refugee Problem, 1947–1949* (New York: Cambridge University Press, 1988).
8. The literature on this subject is vast. Among the leading works of the "new historians" (in additional to Benny Morris's extensive body of work), see Avi Shlaim, *The Iron Wall: Israel and the Arab World* (New York: Norton, 2000); and Ilan Pappé, *The Ethnic Cleansing of Palestine* (Oxford, UK: Oneworld, 2006). Attempts at direct rebuttals include Efraim Karsh, *Fabricating Israeli History: The "New Historians"* (London: Frank Cass, 1997); and Yoav Gelber, "The Israeli-Arab War of 1948: History versus Narratives," in *Never Ending Conflict—Israeli Military History*, ed. Mordechai Bar-On (Mechanicsburg, PA: Stackpole Books, 2006), 43–68.
9. Here, too, there is a vast literature on multiple aspects of the history and social dynamics of this division. One of the most pointed critiques is without a doubt Ella Shohat, "Sephardim in Israel: Zionism from the Standpoint of Its Jewish Victims," *Social Text* 19/20 (1988): 1–35. See also Yehouda Shenhav, *The Arab Jews: A Postcolonial Reading of Nationalism, Religion, and Ethnicity* (Stanford, CA: Stanford University Press, 2006); Aziza Khazzoom, "The Great Chain of Orientalism: Jewish Identity, Stigma Management, and Ethnic Exclusion in Israel," *American Sociological Review* 68 (2003): 481–510; Amnon Raz-Krakotzkin, "The Zionist Return to the West and the Mizrahi Jewish Perspective," in *Orientalism and the Jews*, ed. Ivan Kalmar and Derek Penslar (Waltham, MA: Brandeis University Press, 2005), 162–81; Yaron Tsur, "Israeli Historiography and the Ethnic Problem," in *Making Israel*, ed. Benny Morris (Ann Arbor: University of Michigan Press, 2007), 231–77.
10. On these questions, see, e.g., Tom Segev, *The Seventh Million: The Israelis and the Holocaust* (New York: Hill and Wang, 1993); Idith Zertal, *From Catastrophe to Power: The Holocaust Survivors and the Emergence of Israel* (Berkeley: University of California Press, 1998); idem, *Israel's Holocaust and the Politics of Nationhood*

(New York: Cambridge University Press, 2010); Dina Porat, *The Blue and the Yellow Stars of David: The Zionist Leadership in Palestine and the Holocaust, 1939–1945* (Cambridge, MA: Harvard University Press, 1990); Tuvia Friling, *Arrows in the Dark: David Ben-Gurion, the Yishuv Leadership, and Rescue Attempts during the Holocaust* (Madison: University of Wisconsin Press, 2003).

11. Jean-Christophe Attias and Esther Benbassa, *Israel: The Impossible Land* (Stanford, CA: Stanford University Press, 2003).
12. As an illustration of this diversity of perspectives, see selected past programs of the annual meetings of the Association for Israel Studies at http://www.aisisraelstudies.org/ais/papers.ehtml. Unfortunately, only a few, mostly recent, past programs are available.
13. Derek J. Penslar, *Israel in History: The Jewish State in Comparative Perspective* (New York: Routledge, 2007), 15. On this genealogy and evolution of Israeli historiography, see also D. Penslar, "Innovation and Revisionism in Israeli Historiography," *History and Memory* 7 (1995): 125–46; David Nathan Myers, "Bein Yisra'el le-Amim: Hirhurim al Matzav Limudei ha-Historia ha-Yehudit be-Yisra'el," *Zion* 74 (2008–9): 339–52; Michael Feige, "Introduction: Rethinking Israeli Memory and Identity," *Israel Studies* 7:2 (2002): v–xiv; and Assaf Likhovsky, "Post-Post-Zionist Historiography," *Israel Studies* 15:2 (2010): 1–23.
14. Simcha Flapan, *The Birth of Israel: Myths and Realities* (New York: Pantheon Books, 1987); Morris, *Birth of the Palestinian Refugee Problem*; Gershon Shafir, *Land, Labor, and the Origins of the Israeli-Palestinian Conflict, 1882–1914* (New York: Cambridge University Press, 1989); and Avi Shlaim, *Collusion across the Jordan: King Abdullah, the Zionist Movement, and the Partition of Palestine* (New York: Columbia University Press, 1988).
15. See Penslar, *Israel in History*. Ilan Pappé's departure from Haifa University to take up a position at the University of Exeter in Great Britain is, perhaps, a symbolic manifestation of this rejection and marginalization.
16. Anat Helman, *Young Tel Aviv: A Tale of Two Cities* (Waltham, MA: Brandeis University Press, 2010); Orit Rozin, *The Rise of the Individual in 1950s Israel: A Challenge to Collectivism* (Waltham, MA: Brandeis University Press, 2011). This argument is elaborated more fully in Assaf Likhovsky, "Post-Post-Zionist Historiography," *Israel Studies* 15:2 (2010): 1–23.
17. Likhovsky, "Post-Post Zionism."
18. Ilan Pappé, "The Vicissitudes of the 1948 Historiography of Israel," *Journal of Palestine Studies* 39:1 (2010): 6–23.
19. For useful discussions of these critiques and responses to them, see, e.g., Joyce Appleby, Lynn Hunt, and Margaret Jacob, *Telling the Truth about History* (New York: Norton, 1994); and Richard J. Evans, *In Defense of History* (New York: Norton, 2000).
20. See, e.g., Uri Ram, *Israeli Nationalism: Social Conflicts and the Politics of Knowledge* (New York: Routledge, 2011), 28, 118–21. In a study of post-Zionism, Laurence Silberstein both challenges the idea of a direct link between post-Zionism and

postmodernism and explores it in such a way that seems to make a case for such links. Laurence Silberstein, *The Postzionism Debates: Knowledge and Power in Israeli Culture* (New York: Routledge, 1999).

21. See Likhovsky, "Post-Post Zionism."
22. A good English-language sampling of some the Berdiczewky's writings—some of those that were most influential in Zionist circles—is in Arthur Hertzberg, *The Zionist Idea: A Historical Analysis and Reader* (Philadelphia: Jewish Publication Society, 1997), 290–302.
23. The text of Azaria's speech (in Hebrew) is available at http://rachelazaria.blogspot.co.il/2011/08/blog-post.html.
24. Daniel Gutwein, "From Melting Pot to Multiculturalism; or, The Privatization of Israeli Identity," in *Israeli Identity in Transition*, ed. Anita Shapira (Westport, CT: Praeger, 2004), 215–31; idem, "Left and Right Post-Zionism and the Privatization of Israeli Collective Memory," *Journal of Israeli History* 20:2–3 (2001): 9–42.
25. See, e.g., Baruch Kimmerling, *The Invention and Decline of Israeliness: State, Society, and the Military* (Berkeley: University of California Press, 2005).
26. One of the terms by which the critical historical school came to be known was "the *new* historians," a term coined by Benny Morris. But one might borrow Peter Burke's remark regarding "the new cultural history": "Novelty," Burke wrote, "is a rapidly diminishing asset," and hence "it might be wiser to describe the new style in another way." Peter Burke, *Varieties of Cultural History* (Ithaca, NY: Cornell University Press, 1997), 192. A similar sense regarding the erstwhile novelty of the new history (and new sociology) seems to be an animating force behind some of the new work being produced on Israel and Zionism.
27. Derek Penslar, "Shlomo Sand's *The Invention of the Jewish People* and the End of the New History," *Israel Studies* 17:2 (2012): 156.
28. Pappé, *Ethnic Cleansing of Palestine.*
29. Ilan Pappé, *Out of the Frame: The Struggle for Academic Freedom in Israel* (New York: Pluto, 2010). For a trenchant critique, see Yossi Ben-Artzi, "Out of (Academic) Focus: On Ilan Pappé, *Out of the Frame: The Struggle for Academic Freedom in Israel*," *Israel Studies* 16:2 (2011): 165–83.
30. Shlomo Sand, *The Invention of the Jewish People* (New York: Verso, 2009), xi.
31. Tony Judt, "Israel Must Unpick Its Ethnic Myth," *Financial Times*, December 7, 2009, http://www.ft.com/cms/s/0/7f8fafee-e366-11de-8d36-00144feab49a.html#axzz2f4BCTxsC.
32. Carlo Ginzburg, *History, Rhetoric, and Proof* (Hanover, NH: University Press of New England, 1999), 20.
33. Carlo Ginzburg, *Threads and Traces: True False Fictive* (Berkeley: University of California Press, 2012), 6.

2

Palestinian Citizenship in Israel

A Settler Colonial Perspective

NADIM N. ROUHANA AND AREEJ SABBAGH-KHOURY

This chapter examines how Palestinian citizens in Israel have understood their collective status as a national group, their collective history, and, primarily, the nature of their political relationship with Israel.[1] We trace the various phases of their political experiences and perceptions of their political status since the establishment of Israel in 1948. For Palestinians, 1948 marks the year in which the Zionist movement established a foreign state in their homeland, resulting in the dispossession and destruction of their society.

The chapter conceptualizes the relationship between Israel and its Palestinian citizens as a distinct and complex case of settler colonial control. In order to trace the specificities of the collective political position of the Palestinians in Israel, we consider the conflict between the Zionist movement, a settler colonial movement with national claims, and the Palestinian national movement. All Palestinians, including those who would become Israeli citizens, encountered the threat and presence of the Zionist project on their homeland several decades before Israel's establishment. Palestinians actively resisted—to varying degrees—what they understood as a settler colonial effort to take over their homeland. The Palestinians who became Israeli citizens understood their particular circumstances to be a result of a chaotic process of ethnic cleansing in which the majority of their people were expelled from their homeland, mostly to neighboring states.

After the 1948 war and the cease-fire agreements between Israel and the neighboring Arab countries, approximately 156,000 Palestinians stayed in the postwar borders of the Jewish state, representing 18% of its total population.[2] Small communities, many of which were internally displaced, remained in historically Palestinian cities, including Jaffa, Ramle, Lydda, Acre, and Haifa.[3] In other Palestinian cities, such as Safad, Tiberias, and Bisan, the Israeli army completely expelled the Arab residents.[4]

In order to fulfill the United Nations' stipulations for the partition of Palestine, Israel granted citizenship to the Arabs who remained in the newly established state. Most Zionist groups did not oppose offering citizenship to these Palestinians because they saw them as a small and unorganized community that would not threaten the state's hegemony. However, the national interests of the state still governed the rights and duties of the Arabs' citizenship. Israel's future depended on settling millions of Jewish immigrants in order to fulfill the Zionist vision of a strong Jewish state; the Palestinians who remained were not included in the state's vision of itself. Therefore, in 1948, the Israeli government immediately placed Palestinian citizens under a strict military regime and enacted emergency regulations.[5] While government officials claimed that military rule was necessary for the state's security, it is clear that the regime served other purposes. Military rule facilitated the state's control of Palestinian land, economy, and demographics while enforcing daily authority and total surveillance over the minority Arab population.[6] Similar dynamics of control and limited citizenship can be found in other settler colonial cases, such as apartheid South Africa and French Algeria. In this way, the military-rule system during Israel's early years created the foundation for a new type of citizenship, what we call "settler colonial citizenship."

Starting with the period of military rule (1948–66), this chapter traces the evolution of settler colonial citizenship over four historical phases. After the end of the military regime, dominant political forces within the Palestinian community began to promote an "equality paradigm" (1970s–1990s), which sought to achieve equality in the state without challenging its Jewish Zionist identity. The next phase arose in the aftermath of the 1993 Oslo Accords and called for Israel's transformation from an ethnic Jewish state to a democratic state for all its citizens. Finally, a new phase emerged after the Israeli police shot and killed thirteen Palestinian citizens in the Galilee in October 2000, during a demonstration against Israeli violence toward Palestinian protesters in Jerusalem and other parts of the West Bank at the beginning of the second intifada. After these events, Arab political elites and professionals began to gradually shift their conceptualization of the relationship between the state and the Palestinian community. Arab citizens in Israel started to demand collective rights while also recognizing the settler colonial structure of the conflict. We term this most recent phase "the return of history," which emerged parallel to the gradual decline of the two-state paradigm.

Although we trace separate historical periods, we do not assume a linear development of political consciousness. The diverse Arab community in Israel has held numerous discourses and perspectives in all historical periods. We are primarily concerned with the prominence and resonance of some perspectives over others. Additionally, systemic interactions among complex social and political forces, including internal developments within the Palestinian community, regional developments, and interactions with Israel's ideology and policies, affected each phase. We do not claim to offer an analysis of these interactions but instead identify and describe the defining characteristics and historical context of each phase.

The Foundations of Colonial Citizenship: The Military Government Period

The period of military rule was a critical time in which the Israeli government set the parameters of the relationship between the state and its Arab citizens. For the majority of the Arab residents in Palestine, Israel's establishment signified a foreign occupation in which settlers, mostly from Europe, took ownership of their homeland.[7] Many Palestinians originally believed this invasion was only temporary. The Jewish state, on the other hand, perceived the Arabs who remained in Israel as an obstacle to achieving the Zionist vision of creating a state for the Jewish people. In order to overcome this obstacle, Israel constructed the legal, political, and cultural foundations necessary to eliminate any political influence of this national group within the Jewish state in order to further dispossess Palestinian society and achieve its settler colonial goals. But granting Arabs Israeli citizenship complicated efforts to openly implement settler colonial policies of dispossession and displacement. Indeed, the decision to grant citizenship to the indigenous population critically impacted the dynamics of relations between Israel and its Palestinian citizens and between Israel and the Palestinians in general, in addition to affecting Israel's own place and legitimacy in the international community.

While Israel granted Palestinian citizens the right to vote and be elected, the state also enacted policies that prevented meaningful citizenship. In the early years of Israeli statehood, government leaders opened the country's gates to Jewish immigrants only (while denying Palestinian refugees the right to return and killing thousands who attempted to return);[8] established an exclusive Jewish political sovereignty tied to a privileged citizenship for the Jewish majority; and promoted exclusive Jewish control over land and space. Through these policies and practices, the Israeli government institutionalized and constitutionalized the state as Jewish despite the fact that approximately 18% of its citizens were Arabs.

Military rule fragmented the Palestinian population in Israel, while allowing the state to transfer Palestinian property and land to Jewish hands and to erase the traces of Palestinian society. For almost a whole generation, Arab communities in Israel were isolated from each other, from the Arab world, and from the Jewish population.

Control of Land and Elimination of Space

Perhaps the most prominent aspect of the settler colonial project for its native Palestinian inhabitants was the continuous elimination of their space.[9] The Israeli state from its early years sought to control the spoils of war and transfer them to Jewish ownership—including Arab lands, as well as property that Palestinians had left behind, including real estate, factories, stores, and banks.

The government publicly and openly implemented this process, calling it "Judaization": the transformation of Palestinian space into Jewish space. Over the years, the Israeli government has used different programs to "Judaize" Palestinian space.[10] Through well-documented legal maneuvering, the state transferred the majority of Palestinian land to the Jewish National Fund (JNF). JNF land is held exclusively for "the Jewish people," which includes Jews who are not citizens of Israel but excludes citizens of Israel who are not Jewish.[11] For example, the state used Article 125 of Israel's emergency regulations (which allowed the military governor to declare a place "closed" due to unspecified security reasons) to forbid Arab residents to reach their lands. Once Arabs had not cultivated the land for a specified number of years, it was then "legally" confiscated by the state.[12] In the first three years after Israel was established, 305 Jewish localities were constructed, many of them on land expropriated from Palestinians.[13] However, to this day, not one single Arab town has been established (other than the Bedouin townships, which the state constructed in order to evict the Bedouin from their ancestral land).[14]

Israel erased Palestinian space both physically and symbolically. The state completely demolished hundreds of towns that had been inhabited by Palestinians before the 1948 ethnic cleansing.[15] This process continued vigorously after 1967. Even Palestinian spaces that were not physically destroyed were symbolically erased. For example, Ein Houd was one of the very few Palestinian villages that Israel did not physically eliminate, but its Palestinian inhabitants were expelled and became either internally displaced (many camping just outside their town)[16] or refugees in Arab countries.[17] However, the village's houses and landscape were almost completely preserved and transformed into an "artists' town." The town was given a Hebraized name: Ein Hod. This renaming and appropriation severed the town's Palestinian features from their cultural, political, and national identity.[18] Thus, the Palestinian town, even if powerfully present, became a tangible example of the power of Zionist symbolic erasure.[19]

Similarly, Palestinian neighborhoods that were still standing after 1948 in cities whose Palestinian citizens were expelled were stripped of their Arab identity and used to settle the influx of Jewish immigrants.[20] While these neighborhoods, such as the Katamon neighborhood in Jerusalem or the artists' neighborhood in the old city in Jaffa, remained physically intact, they experienced a symbolic erasure in which their political identity and cultural history were erased, and they became disconnected from their national roots and transformed into Jewish neighborhoods.[21] Even many Palestinian houses and buildings that were built with unique Arab architecture became the homes of Jewish immigrants while maintaining their "authentic character" and thus higher market value. These buildings became known in the real estate market innocuously as "Arab houses."

This drive to eliminate Palestinian spaces was so powerful that it was even applied to many mosques, which the state transformed into spaces for public use, such as bars and restaurants.[22] The Israeli government also replaced Palestinian names of streets, mountains, streams, and valleys. The state performed this Judaization in a deliberate way in which a special committee negotiated the naming process in order to eliminate Palestinian history or disguise Palestinian origins.[23] Occasionally, the original Palestinian names were Hebraized in order to give the impression that the Palestinian places were historically Jewish and had been "reclaimed" by Israel.

The state even replaced the collective name of those Palestinians who remained, referring to them as "Israeli Arabs." The term reflects Israel's settler colonial policy: not recognizing Palestinians as a national group, denying their indigenous identity, weakening their Arab identity, while also asserting that they are not completely Israeli.

Israel's attempts to erase indigenous Palestinian space targeted the relationship between the Palestinians and their history and land. The destruction of Palestinian spaces hindered the refugees' dreams of returning to their homes while also hiding traces of the dispossession project from the Jewish public and the international community.

History and Culture

A comparable process has been applied to history and culture, eliminating Palestinian history and replacing it with Jewish history. The state implemented this process by using powerful institutions such as media, education, and military service. Jewish settlers needed an epistemological structure that justified establishing a Jewish state in Palestine. Thus, erasing physical traces of the Palestinian people and their history and culture became essential to the epistemological and psychological justificatory system. In addition to place names, time coordinates that defined the history of the country were radically reallocated to underscore biblical Jewish history and to deemphasize Arab history, in effect drawing a continuous connection between biblical history and modern Zionist history.[24]

The state-controlled education system that determined the curriculum for both Arabs and Jews placed the Arab educational system under the jurisdiction of the state security apparatus.[25] The Zionist narrative has prevailed ever since, silencing pre-1948 Palestinian history and veiling the violence of expulsion and displacements from both the Arab and Jewish curricula.[26] Silencing continued in the Israeli academic sphere until the mid-1980s with the appearance of what became known as post-Zionism and new sociology,[27] but it continues to this day in school curricula. In response, Palestinian citizens have used oral history and family stories to maintain the essence of their narrative in the face of the official Zionist narrative.[28]

Israel employed the settler colonial eliminatory impulse against Palestinian culture, particularly those aspects that required institutional support, such as cultural associations and cultural production like theater and literary work. Like Palestinian history, Palestinian culture that was rooted in identity and narrative became all but taboo. The name "Palestine" was erased not only from maps, the media, and educational material but also from public discourse. The "Palestinian people" as a whole were made invisible in the eyes of the Jewish public and replaced euphemistically with "Arab refugees," "Arabs of the Land of Israel," "locals," and other similar names. This elimination included the naming of the Palestinian citizens themselves, who were given various names so as to eliminate their historical roots and connection to their homeland and to deny their national identity. They have been referred to as "Israeli Arabs," the "Arabs of Israel," and "minorities." For decades, the Israel Statistical Bureau referred to them as "non-Jews." Sometimes they are called, lightly, "our Arabs." Today, the Israeli media refers to Palestinian citizens commonly as *Arviyeh Yisrael* (the Arabs of Israel).

One of the most far-reaching and devastating goals of this colonial project was its attempt to eliminate the very relationship of the Palestinians with their homeland. Palestinians, particularly in the context of land and demography, were described as "foreigners," "invaders," "infiltrators," and other terms that deny their relationship with their homeland. Thus, the settler immigrants were recast as natives, replacing the actual natives, who had been eliminated through both physical expulsion and symbolic erasure.

Palestinians preserved their culture and narratives in the private sphere through poetry, folk songs, literature, and fine arts. Arab society nourished these media, even under the military government, in unofficial spaces that were uncensored by the military government. In addition, the Israeli Communist Party (ICP) promoted Palestinian culture in its literary periodicals, publications, and public meetings, as long as the cultural content—which represented unmediated Palestinian narrative—remained isolated from the political spheres.[29] This is why cultural modes became the main vehicle for expressing the Palestinian narrative and a central force in promoting the Palestinian identity that reemerged among the Arab citizens in the early 1970s.[30]

Demographic Elimination (Riddance)

Many Zionists, particularly the leadership of the mainstream and dominant Labor Party, acknowledged that in order to create a Jewish state in Palestine, the movement would have to get rid of as many Palestinian inhabitants as possible.[31] This seems to have also become clear to Zionist groups identified as the "radical left."[32] Throughout the extensive deliberations about the future of the Arabs (what was known as the "Arab Question" in the Zionist vernacular until 1948)[33] and in particular the issue of their expulsion,[34] physical elimination was not considered an option, as it was for other settler colonial projects. Even so, the Zionist forces committed many massacres against Palestinians in 1948,[35] some of which are recognized in the Zionist narrative. But Zionist fighters used massacres strategically to terrorize Palestinians into leaving their towns. This tactic followed the settler state's goal of "demographic elimination," as opposed to "physical elimination." Following Patrick Wolfe, we argue that the logic of demographic elimination is an inherent part of Zionist ideology, although it has manifested itself in different forms across the history of the Zionist movement.[36]

Once Jewish forces evacuated most of the Palestinian inhabitants from the territory that was to become Israel, the newly established Israeli state sought to maintain that "achievement" by settling Jewish immigrants in the places belonging to Palestinians. The Law of Return and the Citizenship Law together constitute the bases for acquiring citizenship in Israel. According to the 1950 Law of Return, immigration to Israel is an almost absolute right for Jews and their family members. On the other hand, Palestinians who were expelled or who left under the duress of war were prohibited from returning to their homes or to any other place in the country (except for a few thousand cases of family reunification under strict conditions).[37] Israel considered those who tried to return from across the borders after the cease-fire "infiltrators," and in thousands of cases, they were killed while en route.[38] These policies guaranteed that the reversal of the demographic composition of the country by force of law was completed early in the military-rule period.

Israel continues to attempt to control its demographic composition by restricting Arab repatriation. Recently, the Knesset passed laws preventing certain spouses of Arab citizens from becoming Israeli citizens. In 2003, the Knesset enacted the Citizenship and Entry to Israel Law (Temporary Order 2003), which imposed prohibitions on family reunification in cases in which a Palestinian citizen of Israel is married to a Palestinian residing in Palestinian territories that were occupied in 1967, making it impossible for these families to live together legally in Israel. Since the law's enactment, despite the fact that its name indicates its temporality, the Knesset has consistently extended its validity, making it a permanent feature of the Israeli legal framework on immigration.[39]

Despite the massive demographic elimination that took place in 1948, Israel is still possessed with the same settler colonial mind-set—what is known in Israeli Zionist parlance as the "demographic ghost," referring to the increase in the number of Palestinian citizens, an increase that is essentially limited to natural growth.[40] Israeli politicians have over the years offered various policy ideas to deal with this "ghost," all of which include a common element: further demographic elimination by various means to alter the demographic balance in the country in their favor.[41]

The Political Organization Laws and the Tyranny of the Majority

In order for the Israeli government to implement its colonial policies, it has applied Emergency Regulations to stifle meaningful national political organization by its Arab citizens. These regulations have been used to prohibit collective and national political organization and to limit the rights and liberties of the Palestinians.[42] At the same time, Israel has attempted to colonize the politics, culture, and consciousness of its

Arab citizens. For example, the dominant political parties at the time the Emergency Regulations were imposed, mainly Mapai (the predecessor of the Labor Party) and Mapam, tried to establish subservient Arab satellite parties while not accepting them as regular members in the overall party, in order to recruit Arab votes and serve the party's agenda.[43]

At the same time, the state outlawed independent Arab political organization. In 1965, a group of Arab activists associated as Al-Ard (the land), forming a "Socialist List" in order to run for office in the parliamentary elections.[44] The movement had been declared an "illegal association" months earlier because of its political activities and attempts to organize the Palestinians in Israel as part of a larger Palestinian collective and Arab nation. Al-Ard's effort to participate in Israeli elections was the first organized attempt by Palestinians to participate in the elections as an Arab party, as opposed to a Jewish-Arab party (like the Communist Party). However, the Supreme Court outlawed the list, invoking "defensive democracy" arguments.[45]

After this failure to access political representation, Arab activists in Israel made no similar attempt until 1984. In that year, the Progressive List for Peace (PLP), a joint Arab-Jewish list headed by the former Al-Ard activist Mohammad Mi'ari, sought to participate in elections. The Central Election Committee banned the list from participating. The list appealed to the Supreme Court, which accepted the appeal and allowed the list to participate in the elections. As a result, the Knesset enacted section 7A of Basic Law: The Knesset in 1985. This section gave the Central Election Committee the authority to ban the participation of any list if its goals and actions, explicitly or by implication, included "the negation of the existence of the State of Israel as the state of the Jewish people," the negation of its democratic character, or incitement to racism. This section was amended in 2002, combining the two components into one, changing the language of the law to read "the negation of the existence of Israel as a Jewish and democratic state," while adding another reason to ban a party: support of armed conflict by an enemy state or terror organization.[46] This provision severely limits Arab political participation.

On the one hand, existing demographic laws (mainly citizenship laws) guarantee an overwhelming Jewish majority for the foreseeable future. This majority advances laws to maintain settler colonial privileges[47] and to ensure that it is illegal to challenge the sources of these privileges: the principle that Israel is the state of the Jewish people and not all its citizens. At the same time, the state has continued to instill a sense of fear in the Arab population[48] through a sophisticated system of surveillance.[49] Details of how community members were recruited to spy on each other in return for basic rights are still being revealed.[50]

The Equality Paradigm and the Seeds of Challenge to the Jewish State

After Israel ended the military government in 1966, Palestinian citizens could move freely without needing a pass or military permission. But when they traveled throughout their homeland, they found that Israel's establishment had transformed their geographical and cultural landscape. During and following the 1948 Nakba (catastrophe), the Israeli army demolished most of the Palestinian villages, and the state Judaized the major Palestinian cities.

The Palestinians' ability to move freely created new opportunities for employment, education, and political reorganizing. Direct surveillance under the military regime was gradually transformed to a new, nondirect system of control.[51] Almost two decades of explicit colonial subjugation deeply affected the Palestinian citizens' political discourse and cultural organization.[52] Amid these new realities, the 1967 war erupted, resulting in Israel occupying Gaza and the West Bank, including East Jerusalem (in addition to Sinai and the Golan Heights). This expansion of power put the entirety of Mandatory Palestine under Israeli control, making contact between Palestinians all over historic Palestine possible for the first time in a generation.

Israel's occupation of the West Bank and Gaza in 1967 has had contradictory effects. On the one hand, it made possible communication between the isolated Palestinians in Israel and other Palestinians, revived the dormant nationalism among Palestinians in Israel, and ended the hermetic isolation of the Arab community within Israel, providing a window—albeit narrow—to the Arab world through the West Bank and Gaza. On the other hand, it revealed the salient privileges Palestinians in Israel had acquired as Israeli citizens in comparison to the situation of Palestinians in the 1967 occupied territories. The uniqueness of Palestinians in Israel as "citizens," albeit with settler colonial citizenship, was underscored by the dominant Arab political leadership inside Israel, which sought to distinguish their political status from that of the Palestinians under occupation.

The "equality paradigm" emerged from this context. The Israeli Community Party (ICP) promoted this paradigm post-1967, and it dominated the discourse from the 1970s through the early 1990s. The paradigm endorsed full equality for Arab citizens in Israel, an end to the military occupation of the West Bank and Gaza, and the creation of a Palestinian state in these territories. In this way, it underscored the different status and different future of the Palestinians in Israel from Palestinians under Israeli military occupation. The popular slogan during this phase became "equality and no less than equality."

The ICP's equality paradigm emphasized broadly defined human rights and focused on discrimination in resource distribution in education, local-government budgets, state services, and economic opportunities. The party took up the cause of the expropriation of Arab land, which had accelerated under the military government and continued well into the 1970s. For historical reasons, the ICP constituted the dominant political force among the Arab population.[53] Being the only non-Zionist political party with significant Palestinian leadership that Israel allowed among Arab citizens, it became home for many Arabs who opposed Israel and its policies but who did not necessarily adhere to the party's ideology. Some Arab ICP supporters did not agree with the party's emphasis on the importance of class struggle in the Israeli-Palestinian case or its acceptance of the UN partition plan. Thus, in 1977, the Democratic Front for Peace and Equality (DFPE), a coalition that included Arab groups and prominent community leaders as well as some marginal Jewish left-wing groups, was established with the ICP as its spinal column.[54]

As the name indicates, the DFPE focused on two central issues: peace with the Palestinians in the framework of a two-state solution according to the 1967 borders—making it one of the first political parties in the whole Middle East to champion the slogan "two states for two peoples"—and equality for the Palestinian citizens in Israel. Both of these became the central elements of a broad political consensus within the Palestinian community in Israel for many years.

The dominant discourse among Palestinians, led by the ICP and later the DFPE, conformed to the equality paradigm without challenging the existing political framework, that is, the concept of a Jewish state. Indeed, by focusing on a limited meaning of citizenship, which related to distribution of resources and human rights, this paradigm did not explain the implications of equality for the state's identity and structure and how the Arab community would be integrated into this structure. This effectively meant accepting the UN partition plan and seeking equality within the framework of the emergent state that expanded beyond that plan; however, the state itself did not recognize Palestinians as part of its own project. It excluded them, even if citizens, from the collective that defined the "we" that the state sought to encompass[55] and continued to deprive them of their own resources, the most prominent of which was land. Thus, the struggle for equality within the equality paradigm could not stop the settler colonial project's ambitions to control as much land as possible, turning land, in the eyes of the colonized as well as the colonizer, into the potent symbol of the conflict.

On Land Day (March 30, 1976), the National Committee for the Defense of Arab Lands, the first organization to claim representation of the entire Palestinian community in Israel, called for a national strike in response to the continued confiscation of Palestinian land[56] as part of the planned "Judaization of the Galilee." As a result of the strike and various local demonstrations, Israeli police killed five Palestinian men and one woman; many others were wounded, and both police and army forces arrested hundreds. Land Day has since become a national day commemorated by the whole Palestinian people, both those on their land and those in exile. The significant historical events of Land Day exemplified the protracted struggle between a state representing a settler colonial project and the native population. But like other settler colonial struggles, its colonial nature was obscured by the discourse of equality, which was made fleetingly credible by the citizenship that Israel had granted the Arabs in 1948.

The equality paradigm defined Palestinian discourse in various areas, including resources allocated to education (but less related to the question of the right to define the group's educational policies), employment, and municipal budgets. In the early 1980s, the Arab Higher

Follow-Up Committee (composed of Arab mayors, Arab members of the Knesset, secretaries and chairpersons of the political parties, and leaders of nongovernmental organizations) established subcommittees on health, education, social welfare, and so forth to investigate inequalities and to provide information for advocacy groups.[57] On June 24, 1987, "Equality Day" was declared as a national strike day to protest discrimination and promote equality. This approach continued even after the paradigm was challenged in the 1990s. Thus, a number of active nongovernmental organizations (NGOs) seeking equality were established, most prominently Mossawa (equality) Center, the Advocacy Center for Arab Citizens in Israel, which advocates for equality in various areas, and Adalah (justice), the Legal Center for Arab Minority Rights in Israel, which uses legal means to work toward the advancement of equal rights. These organizations became two of the most well-funded (by international donors) and most active NGOs in the Arab community; similarly Sikkuy (a chance), an Arab-Jewish NGO funded by many American Jewish family foundations, zeroed in on manifestations of discrimination without contesting their ideological and structural foundations.

While the equality paradigm dominated the discourse and defined the directions of internal Arab policy advocacy after the Oslo Accords and well into the 1990s, different factions in the Arab community in Israel began to criticize its limitations and legitimacy. Many argued that the ICP had deemphasized the national (and later the settler colonial) dimension of the conflict between Zionism and the Palestinian national movements in favor of class struggle. Although the ICP fought against national discrimination, it focused much attention on the interests of the working class—Jews and Arabs—and the struggle for class equality. Nationalist groups that emerged at the beginning as local associations stressed the national component and the privileges that Jews have regardless of their class status within the structure of the Jewish state. Academics and intellectuals started to underscore the contradiction between the idea of a Jewish state and the principle of equality.

Although the equality paradigm enabled significant political work on both the micro and macro levels, its scope was limited by the ideological constraints of its leading proponent, the ICP. In particular, its platform was confined to a forward-looking approach to fighting discrimination at the expense of a historical approach, which would instead emphasize compensatory justice and address the ideological structure that underpins inequality. Thus, the struggle over land confiscation concentrated on preventing further confiscation rather than advocating for a compensatory justice framework that would return previously confiscated land.

Finally, by focusing on resources, services, and opportunities, the equality paradigm avoided fundamental issues of importance to the Arab population. These issues emanated from the very essence of the Palestinians' relationship with Israel as a settler colonial project: privileges granted to Jewish citizens and noncitizens over Arab citizens because of the state's structure and identity as Jewish, the legitimacy of Israel as a Jewish state, and the right of return for expelled Palestinians.

Arab scholars, activists, and politicians organized political challenge to the equality paradigm on various fronts. First, the Abnaa al-Balad (sons of the country) Movement offered a different conceptual framework for understanding the conflict between Zionism and the Palestinian national movement. Abnaa al-Balad held its first national conference in 1972.[58] The group, which saw itself as an extension of the Palestinian national movement in exile, did not recognize the legitimacy of the UN partition plan in Palestine or the legitimacy of the Jewish state. It considered Zionism a settler colonial movement and adopted a political plan that was originally presented by the Palestine Liberation Organization (PLO) for resolving the Israeli-Palestinian conflict by establishing a secular democratic state in all of Palestine with full equality among the three religious groups: Christians, Jews, and Muslims. In contrast to the ICP, which it considered an Israeli party that accepted the rules and legitimacy of the Jewish state, the Abnaa al-Balad Movement emphasized the historical aspects of the relationship between Israel and the Palestinians. This movement attracted some support among elites and Arab students in Israeli universities but failed to achieve broad popular support; its main influence was in propagating political ideas and discourse in the public sphere rather than broad-based political activism. Yet it was strong enough to provoke, at various points in time, severe attacks from the adherents of the equality paradigm as well as persecution by the state security apparatus. Its main influence was in challenging the dominant political framework championed by the ICP and constantly reminding the community and the political elites of the fundamental issues of Israeli-Palestinian conflict. In the 1990s, factions of this movement joined a new political party that competed for leadership among the Arab citizens, while others who refused to recognize the legitimacy of the Jewish state continued to boycott the parliamentary elections.

Since the mid-1980s, challenges to the equality paradigm have increased. In 1982, the Progressive List for Peace (PLP) emerged on the political scene.[59] Despite opposition from the state's security apparatus, the Supreme Court ruled the PLP a legal list that could run in Knesset elections. Despite a fierce ICP campaign questioning the new party's credibility, the PLP was the first "legal" political party outside the DFPE to declare full solidarity with the Palestinian cause. The PLP emphasized the national Palestinian identity of Arabs in Israel as well as the conflict's nationalist dimension (as opposed to the DFPE's class analysis). Although operating within the boundaries of Israeli citizenship, it foregrounded the Palestinian belonging of the Arab citizens, deemphasized their Israeli belonging, and made clear that its first loyalty was to the Palestinian cause.[60] As such, it was considered a strong opponent of the ICP and its equality paradigm. The PLP was made up of local Arab nationalist organizations joined by left-wing Jews, and it maintained Knesset seats from 1984 to 1992, after which it failed to achieve sufficient support.[61]

From the 1980s on, the Islamic Movement gained increasing support,[62] becoming a significant political actor in the Arab community with two factions, one that participates in parliamentary elections and another that boycotts them.[63] The Movement focuses on providing local services, supporting basic human needs of Palestinians in the West Bank and Gaza, and protecting Islamic holy places. Ideologically, the Movement's goal is to achieve an Islamic state in Palestine, making the question of equality just a pragmatic concern.

Thus, during this phase, the dominant political forces among Palestinian citizens sought to achieve full equality without challenging the Zionist discourse. However, they failed to solicit any state commitment to equality. The case of the ICP and its total failure in light of the state's increasing emphasis on its Jewish identity inadvertently confirmed the settler colonial structure of the Israeli state to many Palestinians.

A "State for All Its Citizens" and Collective Rights

The Oslo Accords in 1993 brought what turned out to be the false hope that a two-state solution could be achieved. The first few years after Oslo had an enormous impact on the political thought and organization of the Palestinian citizens, with often contradictory effects. The agreement provided significant validation for the equality paradigm by supporting two central elements of the Palestinian consensus: Israeli peace with the Palestinians in the occupied territories and their legitimate leadership, the Palestine Liberation Organization, and equality for the Palestinian citizens within Israel. Yitzhak Rabin's government started speaking openly about existing discrimination (which had previously been denied) and reducing state discrimination against Arab citizens in various spheres.[64] As it became clear that the future of Arab citizens would be inside the Israeli state as Israeli citizens, this development opened the door for more fundamental questions about their destiny. The sense of temporariness that had hitherto permeated much of the political consciousness regarding their collective future started to fade away. This realization, therefore, brought to the fore the question of their political status and their own relationship with the state concerning three issues: the meaning of equality and its political implications; collective status and collective rights of the Arab citizens within the State of Israel; and state identity.

The challenge to the Palestinian elites was to present a democratic vision that could give substantive political and constitutional meaning to equality and at the same time deal with one of the most fundamental concerns lingering below the surface: the legitimacy of the Jewish state, which by and large Palestinians did not accept.[65] A new political party, the National Democratic Alliance (NDA), responded to this challenge by advocating for Israel to become a "state for all its citizens."[66] The NDA was an alliance of leading political activists who left the ICP during the late 1980s, factions of the Abnaa al-Balad Movement, cadres of the National Progressive Movement, and a number of members of other nationalist organizations. The party attracted Arab elites and intellectuals and posed a serious challenge to the concept of a Jewish state. In addition to its political program, which centered on the demand for democratic citizenship in a state for all of its citizens and not just one group, and in contrast to the ICP, the party argued that the Arab community should be empowered through organization on a national basis in the public space: NGOs, cultural and political organizations, and elected national leadership in the existing, but unelected, Higher Follow-Up Committee for Arab Affairs.

The basic democratic idea of a state for all its citizens presented fundamental challenges to Zionism and to the concept of a Jewish state. The NDA's platform finally introduced this contradiction to the Israeli political discourse. Many Israeli academics had pointed to a "tension," but not a contradiction, between being Jewish and being democratic;[67] however, other, mainly Arab, academics had argued that this contradiction cannot be reconciled.[68] Israeli academics had offered theories to reconcile and perhaps justify the contradiction, such as the concept of "ethnic democracy," which was presented by Sammy Smooha[69] and broadly endorsed by other Israeli scholars. Many Arab scholars and some Israelis dismissed the theory as a politically motivated and futile academic exercise attempting to mask a profound and irreconcilable contradiction.[70]

The vigorous political debates that involved Arab and Jewish academics marked Israeli public discourse. The Arab public, by and large, endorsed the discourse proposed by the NDA party and accepted the meaning of equality that the party had offered without necessarily adhering to its line on other issues. Thus, even the strongest adherents of the "equality paradigm" incorporated into their political discourse the concept of "a state for all its citizens," the substantive questions about equality, and the sharp contradiction in the Israeli state between being Jewish and democratic. Within the Jewish community, reactions to this new paradigm were diverse, ranging from considering the slogan "a state for all its citizens" to be a fatal threat to the Jewish state to seeking to reconcile it with what is in our view a self-contradictory definition of Israel as "Jewish and democratic." The result of this debate was that most Arab citizens became conscious of the contradiction between the interests of a Jewish state and the possibility of equal citizenship.

The slogan "a state for all its citizens," while bringing the question of the Jewish state to the forefront of the political and intellectual discussion in both communities, never went so far as openly adopting a settler colonial discourse. While the manifestations of Israel's policies as a settler colonial project was rather explicit in the NDA's literature, settler colonialism was not central to its political discourse. A settler colonial framework started to gradually appear out of demands for collective rights. The NDA's emphasis on national organization, cultural autonomy, and the right to national empowerment resonated with Palestinian academic and cultural elites. Three separate groups gathered around the same time (2005–7) in the form of expansive think tanks to examine the collective status of the Palestinian citizens within a potential two-state solution. After extensive discussion, they issued three separate documents, collectively referred to as "The Future Vision Documents," which asserted that Palestinians in Israel seek collective rights, mainly by claiming national rights within Israel in the form of a binational or multicultural state.[71] The Jewish public's reaction to these documents—texts that referred to Israel as a settler colonial project—was intense and in some cases resulted in veiled threats to the Arab community.[72] The documents elicited such severe responses because all three texts made it clear that a Jewish state cannot also be democratic.

In our view, these documents contributed to reviving and heightening the settler colonial discourse among some Palestinian elites. The "Haifa Declaration," in particular, endorsed by hundreds of community leaders, academics, and intellectuals, offered a paradigm of reconciliation between Israelis (not Zionism) and Palestinians that echoes anticolonial discourse in other settler colonial settings. Yet it should be noted that this debate about the nature of collective rights and settler colonialism remained within limited elite Palestinian circles without permeating broader public awareness, even if many in the Palestinian community implicitly understood Israel as a settler colonial project.

The Return of History and the Consciousness of Settler Colonial Citizenship

The past fifteen years or so have witnessed a new phase in the history of the Palestinians in Israel, a phase that we refer to as the "return of history." This phase contrasts previous periods characterized by competing paradigms, such as the equality paradigm or "a state for all its citizens."[73] In essence, there is a growing awareness among all Palestinian parties across the partisan divide that their citizenship is rooted in the historical events of the Nakba.

In 1998, on the fiftieth anniversary of the Nakba, some Palestinian organizations in Israel started to coordinate a "Nakba March" along with Palestinians in the territories that Israel occupied in 1967. The first march took place on May 15, Israel's Independence Day. In the following years, an organizing committee established the tradition of a "Return March," choosing a different destroyed Palestinian village for each year's destination. The marches, which sought to bring to the forefront the displacement of the Palestinians from their towns, took place on Israeli Independence Day in order to remind Israelis, "Your day of independence is our Nakba." These marches were the first collective articulation of Nakba-related Palestinian history in the "official public sphere."

While Palestinians' emphasis is, in general, on Nakba commemoration in both the 1967-occupied territories and across their places of dispersion, Palestinian discourse in Israel additionally emphasizes the issue of return, as powerfully symbolized by the massive "return" to one displaced town for one day. Yet access to the destroyed villages is a "privilege" made possible by Israeli citizenship, a privilege that other Palestinians do not have. The collective action that this accessibility allows is instrumental to the return of history. The Arab citizens' mourning when the state celebrates; their massive, organized marches surrounded by police forces; their speeches about homeland and return—all tell the story of a different kind of citizenship caused by the Nakba they commemorate. Unlike Palestinian commemorations in other places, Arab citizens commemorate the Nakba within the framework of citizenship: what the state did to us. What is highlighted by the Return March, in addition to the question of refugees and Palestinian return, is the settler colonial essence of their citizenship—"their" state's actions of displacing them, refusing to let them return, and giving their towns to Jewish citizens.

The fact that the march is organized inside Israel on the actual day of independence poses a serious challenge to the narrative of the Jewish state and its history. During the first five decades of the state's independence, Israeli Jews celebrated Independence Day without challenge. The Return Marches have become a living reminder of the settler colonial actuality that, in our view, underlies Israel's "Nakba Law," enacted in 2011. This law "calls on the government to deny funding to any organization, institution, or municipality that commemorates the founding of the Israeli state as a day of mourning."[74]

The Return March turned out to be one of the most important collective activities initiated by the Palestinians in Israel. For several years prior, it was Land Day, commemorated annually since 1976, often by national strikes, that galvanized the collective popular action of the Palestinian citizens. But the emergence of the Return March a whole generation later and its rise to prominence signifies the return of history and marks a change in the popular understanding of the meaning of citizenship.

We argue that Palestinians' rising preoccupation with their history stands behind the reemergence of a different phase in their understanding of citizenship, a citizenship acquired within a settler colonial framework. This phase, in fact, closes the circle, which started with the same view. We do not claim that average Palestinians articulate their citizenship status in settler colonial terminology, but that they perceive the State of Israel as having taken over their homeland by force in the name of the Jewish people and understand that genuine citizenship status is reserved for Jews only, while their own citizenship, despite the rights it does provide, is empty in theory and practice. Although this sense of empty citizenship is descriptive rather than analytical, we argue that it is precisely the consequence of the settler colonial policies we have described and that there is a rising awareness among Palestinians of the settler colonial relationship.

Three factors contributed to the emergence of this awareness of settler colonial realities and their relationship to the Nakba. The first is the spectacular failure of the earlier paradigms and, in effect, their impossibility within a Zionist state. The adherents of the equality paradigm seemed to support their paradigm because of their ideological consciousness as Communists who accepted the partition plan and the legitimacy of Israel. They believed that equality was possible if Israel changed its policies. But the continued settler colonial processes, particularly as described earlier in relation to land, space, culture, and demography but also the policies that maintained disparities in resources, services, and employment opportunities, brought this paradigm to an end. The recent plans to expropriate more lands from Arab Bedouin citizens in the southern part of the country and transfer them to Jewish citizens[75] have highlighted the fact that maintaining a Jewish state entails continued settler colonial policies that relentlessly transfer resources from the colonized to the colonizer.

Palestinian citizens presented the "state for all its citizens" paradigm, unlike the equality paradigm, in order to contest Zionism and show that it is incompatible with the basic democratic principle of a state for all its citizens. The intense public reaction in Jewish society to the "Future Vision Documents" only highlighted what was already clear: that a Jewish state and equality are fundamentally incompatible.

Second, the increasing public conviction among both Palestinians and Israelis that the Oslo Accords failed and that the two-state solution is an illusion gave rise to considering alternatives to partition, including one state with equality for Arabs and Jews in the entire area of historic Palestine. Understanding history is an essential element to envisioning such alternatives, and the validity and legitimacy of partition and its aftermath in terms of Palestinian dispossession and Jewish privileges sharpens awareness about the settler colonial characteristics of the Jewish state.

Third, while the Arabs behaved as citizens, the state treated them as colonial subjects and in critical moments even as enemies. In October 2000, after the failure of the Camp David negotiations in July, Palestinians in the West Bank and Gaza started demonstrations that developed into what became known as the second intifada. When Israeli forces killed tens of Palestinians in the Al-Aqsa area in Jerusalem and elsewhere, Palestinians in Israel demonstrated in solidarity with the Palestinians in the West Bank and Gaza. They demonstrated *as citizens* to protest the killing of other Palestinians and to support the cause of a Palestinian state in the West Bank and Gaza. However, Israel treated them no differently than the other Palestinians: thirteen were killed, tens wounded, and hundreds arrested. Even then, these Palestinians reacted as citizens, demanding an official commission to investigate the killings of the thirteen citizens but not the hundreds who were killed in the 1967 occupied Palestinian territories during the same period.

The Or Commission that was established to investigate the events that led to the killing of the citizens occupied a central place through public hearings until its report was published in 2003.[76] But instead of taking advantage of the proceedings and the report as a historic occasion to deal with the deep feelings of injustice, the state demonstrated that citizenship provides no protection. One major demand of the Arab public was that those who had shot Arab demonstrators be prosecuted. But in 2008, after lengthy legal deliberations, the government chose to close the investigation file because of lack of evidence in what human rights organizations believed contradicted the commission's report.[77] This decision convinced Palestinians that the state does not view their citizenship as seriously as they do. The demonstration against this decision has been described as one of the Palestinian citizens' biggest demonstrations since the state's inception.

This incident demonstrated not only that equality was not possible but also that, in moments of crisis, the state would treat Palestinians as colonial subjects rather than as citizens. Such moments, which are frequent in both personal (airport and crossing points) and collective (with police, land, immigration laws, etc.) experiences, have been critical in cementing Palestinians' awareness that their relationship with the state is, in fact, a settler colonial one.

In summary, in this chapter we have argued that the relationship between Palestinians who became Israeli citizens and the State of Israel is best characterized as settler colonial citizenship. We have also argued that the foundations of this citizenship were established during the first two decades after the Nakba through the imposition of a military government from 1948 to 1966. We traced Palestinians' perceptions of their relationship to and understanding of the Israeli state, focusing on their political discourse and collective organization. We claimed that although consciousness and activism have gone through different phases, the awareness of Palestinians in Israel now seems to be returning to its point of departure: they increasingly recognize their citizenship status as settler colonial citizenship.

Under the military government, Palestinians tried to live in dignity and maintain their roots after the traumatic experience of losing their nation and homeland, despite lacking the power to resist the settler colonial policies. Israeli military rule symbolized foreign rule, but citizenship was granted to Palestinians by the state that, in their language at the time, "occupied them."[78] This citizenship, together with other regional developments such as the rise of the two-state-solution paradigm in the international discourse about the conflict, obscured the settler colonial essence of their relationship with Israel. Thus, these Palestinians vainly attempted to grapple with different frameworks in order to become equal citizens. In the first phase after the military rule, they advanced the discourse of equality without examining its implications for the state's identity and structure. However, since the mid-1990s, a different political framework emerged that demanded a "state for all its citizens," stressing both full citizenship and historical justice while emphasizing that their settler colonial citizenship was a result of the Nakba. During this era, various Palestinian political parties in Israel accepted the discourse of "a state for all its citizens."

We have also argued that a new phase emerged after the failure of the "equality paradigm" and the realization that a state for all its citizens is incompatible with a Zionist Jewish state, alongside the dissipating hopes of achieving a two-state agreement. In this phase, characterized by the "return of history," many Palestinians take as their point of departure understanding their relationship with Israel, the Nakba, and its consequences for them and for the Palestinian people. If this process continues, it will foreground the awareness of their settler colonial citizenship, thus closing a circle in their historical relationship with Israel.

NOTES

1. In this chapter, we use the terms "Arab" and "Palestinian" interchangeably to refer to the Palestinian Arabs who became citizens of Israel in the aftermath of the Palestinian Nakba.
2. N. N. Rouhana, *Palestinian Citizens in an Ethnic Jewish State: Identities in Conflict* (New Haven, CT: Yale University Press, 1997), 30.
3. For more information about the Palestinians in these cities, see A. Sabbagh-Khoury, "Palestinians in Palestinian Cities in Israel: A Settler Colonial Reality," in *The Palestinians in Israel: Readings in History, Politics and Society*, 2nd ed., ed. N. N. Rouhana and A. Sabbagh-Khoury (Haifa, Israel: Mada al-Carmel—Arab Center for Applied Social Research, in press); and D. Monterescu and D. Rabinowitz, ed., *Mixed Towns, Trapped Communities: Historical Narratives, Spatial Dynamics, Gender Relations and Cultural Encounters in Palestine-Israeli Towns* (Aldershot, UK: Ashgate, 2007), 1–34.
4. For historical accounts of the ethnic cleansing of the vast majority of the Palestinians in the part of Palestine on which Israel was established, see I. Pappé, *The Ethnic Cleansing of Palestine* (Oxford, UK: Oneworld, 2006); W. Khalidi, *All That Remains: The Palestinian Villages Occupied and Depopulated by Israel in 1948* (Washington, DC: Institute for Palestine Studies, 1992); N. Masalha, *Expulsion of the Palestinians: The Concept of "Transfer" in Zionist Political Thought, 1882–1948* (Beirut, Lebanon: Institute for Palestine Studies, 1992); and N. Masalha, *Maxi-*

mum Land, Minimum Arabs: Israel, Transfer and the Palestinians, 1949–1996 (Beirut, Lebanon: Institute for Palestine Studies, 1997) (Arabic).

5. For more information on the military government and emergency regulations, see Y. Bäuml, "The Military Government," in *The Palestinians in Israel: Readings in History, Politics and Society*, ed. N. N. Rouhana and A. Sabbagh-Khoury (Haifa, Israel: Mada al-Carmel—Arab Center for Applied Social Research, 2011), 47–57, available at http://mada-research.org/en/files/2011/09/ebook-english-book.pdf; S. Jiryis *The Arabs in Israel* (New York: Monthly Review Press, 1976).
6. For the debate on the security justification of the military rule, see Y. Bäuml, "The Discrimination Policy towards the Arabs in Israel, 1948–1968" [in Hebrew], *Iyunim Bitkumat Yisrael: Studies in Zionism, the Yishuv, and the State of Israel* 16 (2006): 391–413; and Y. Bäuml, *A Blue and White Shadow: The Israeli Establishment's Policy and Actions among its Arab Citizens: The Formative Years: 1958–1968* [in Hebrew] (Haifa, Israel: Pardes, 2007).
7. It is possible that some Palestinians who operated within the Israeli Communist Party accepted the legitimacy of the Jewish state, on the basis of the party's public support for UN Resolution 181.
8. Benny Morris puts the number at about five thousand. Benny Morris, *Righteous Victims: A History of the Zionist-Arab Conflict, 1881–2001* (New York: Vintage Books, 2001), 272–74.
9. L. Veracini, "Introducing Settler Colonial Studies," *Settler Colonial Studies* 1:1 (2011): 1–12; and P. Wolfe, "Settler Colonialism and the Elimination of the Native," *Journal of Genocide Research* 8:4 (2006): 387–409.
10. R. Khamaisi, "Territorial Dispossession and Population Control of the Palestinians," in *Surveillance and Control in Israel/Palestine: Population, Territory and Power*, ed. E. Zureik, D. Lyon, and Y. Abu-Laban (New York: Routledge, 2011), 335–52; N. Bashir, *Judaizing the Place: Misgav Regional Council in the Galilee* (Haifa, Israel: Mada al-Carmel—Arab Center for Applied Social Research, 2004) (Arabic); and G. Falah, "The Facts and Fictions of Judaization Policy and Its Impact on the Majority Arab Population in the Galilee," *Political Geography Quarterly* 10:3 (1991): 297–316. Many Palestinian citizens saw "Judaization" policies as racist; some Israelis also complained about the explicitly racist implications of the term. Thus, the terms "Galilee Development" or "Development" of the Naqab are often euphemistically used to describe the project. Y. Jabareen, "National Planning Policy in Israel," in Rouhana and Sabbagh-Khoury, *Palestinians in Israel*, 2nd ed., 75–85.
11. A. Kedar, "The Legal Transformation of Ethnic Geography: Israeli Law and Palestinian Landholder 1948–1967," *New York University Journal of International Law and Politics* 33:4 (2000): 923–1000; W. Lehn and U. Davis, *The Jewish National Fund* (London: Kegan Paul, 1988).
12. Bäuml, *Blue and White Shadow*; Jiryis, *Arabs in Israel*.
13. Jabareen, "National Planning Policy in Israel."

14. I. Abu-Saad, "The Indigenous Palestinian Bedouin of the Naqab: Forced Urbanization and Denied Recognition," in Rouhana and Sabbagh-Khoury, *Palestinians in Israel* (2011), 120–27.
15. A. Golan, *Changing the Space-War's Results: Previous Arab Spaces in the State of Israel (1948–1950)* [in Hebrew] (Beersheba, Israel: Ben Gurion Heritage Institute, 2001).
16. D. Grossman, *Sleeping on a Wire: Conversations with Palestinians in Israel*, trans. H. Watzman (New York: Farrar, Straus and Giroux, 1993).
17. For more information on the internally displaced persons (IDPs), see A. Sabbagh-Khoury, "The Internally Displaced Palestinians in Israel," in Rouhana and Sabbagh-Khoury, *Palestinians in Israel* (2011), 26–45; H. Cohen, *The Present Absentee: Palestinian Refugees in Israel since 1948* [in Hebrew] (Jerusalem: Van Leer Jerusalem Institute, 2000).
18. Similar processes of symbolic erasure took place in other Palestinian spaces, such as Jaffa and Jerusalem.
19. For more information on the story of Ein Houd, see A. Slyomovics, *The Objects of Memory: Arab and Jew Narrate the Palestinian Village* (Philadelphia: University of Pennsylvania Press, 1998); and Grossman, *Sleeping on a Wire*. To complete the ironic story of Ein Houd, it should be mentioned that some of its original Arab population who gathered on part of the town's land outside the town itself built a small community that became one of the unrecognized Arab villages. The state recognized the town in 1996 after a long legal struggle, and it became known as Ein Hawd, with the emphasis on the classical Arabic pronunciation and transliteration of the original town's name in order to distinguish it from the now Judaized town Ein Hod.
20. H. Yacobi, "The Architecture of Ethnic Logic: Exploring the Meaning of the Built Environment in the 'Mixed' City of Lod–Israel," *Geografiska Annaler, Series B, Human Geography* 84:3–4 (2002): 171–87.
21. M. LeVine, "Planning to Conquer: Modernity and Its Antinomies in the 'New-Old Jaffa,'" in *Constructing a Sense of Place: Architecture and the Zionist Discourse*, ed. Haim Yacobi (Burlington, VT: Ashgate, 2004), 92–224; M. LeVine, *Overthrowing Geography: Jaffa, Tel-Aviv, and the Struggle for Palestine, 1880–1948* (Berkeley: University of California Press, 2005); and D. Monterescu, "The Bridled Bride of Palestine: Orientalism, Zionism and the Troubled Urban Imagination," *Identities: Global Studies in Culture and Power* 16:6 (2009): 643–77.
22. J. Cook, "Israeli Eradication of History: Disappearing Mosques," *Al-Akhbar*, July 9, 2012, http://english.al-akhbar.com/node/9554.
23. M. Benvenisti, *Sacred Landscape: The Buried History of the Holy Land* (Berkeley: University of California Press, 2000).
24. Ibid.
25. M. Al-Haj, *Education, Empowerment, and Control: The Case of the Arabs in Israel* (Albany: SUNY Press, 1995).

26. We describe silencing of the Arab community within the climate of fear under military government and try to explain this silence in the face of traumatic events as the way the community dealt with the fear it felt regarding its own fate, in "The Return of History, and the Future," in *Ethnic Privileges in the Jewish State: Israel and its Palestinian Citizens*, ed. N. N. Rouhana (Cambridge: Cambridge University Press, forthcoming).
27. See, for example, L. Silberstein, *The Postzionism Debates: Knowledge and Power in Israeli Culture* (New York: Routledge, 1999).
28. N. N. Rouhana and A. Sabbagh-Khoury, "Collective Memory," in Rouhana, *Ethnic Privileges in the Jewish State*; F. Kassem, *Palestinian Women: Narrative Histories and Gendered Memory* (London: Zed Books, 2011); and I. Nusair, "Gendering the Narrative of Three Generations of the Palestinian Women in Israel," in *Displaced at Home: Ethnicity and Gender among Palestinians in Israel*, ed. R. Kanaaneh and I. Nusair (Albany: SUNY Press, 2010).
29. Rouhana and Sabbagh-Khoury, *Palestinians in Israel* (2nd ed.).
30. Rouhana, *Palestinian Citizens in an Ethnic Jewish State.*
31. A. Sabbagh-Khoury, "Constructing Settler-Colonial Sovereignty: Archive, Political Economy and Collective Memory among the Kibbutzim of Hashomer Hatzair in the Jezreel Valley: 1936–1956" (PhD diss., Tel-Aviv University, forthcoming).
32. Sabbagh-Khoury, "Palestinians in Palestinian Cities in Israel."
33. See, for example, Y. Gorni, *Zionism and the Arabs, 1882–1948: A Study of Ideology* (Oxford, UK: Clarendon, 1987).
34. See, for example, Masalha, *Expulsion of the Palestinians*; Masalha, *Maximum Land, Minimum Arabs*; and Pappé, *Ethnic Cleansing of Palestine.*
35. S. Jawad, "Zionist Massacres: The Creation of the Palestinian Refugee Problem in the 1948 War," in *Israel and the Palestinian Refugees*, ed. E. Benvenisti, C. Gans, and S. Hanafi (New York: Springer, 2007), 59–127.
36. Wolfe, "Settler Colonialism and the Elimination of the Native."
37. See D. Peretz, *Israel and the Palestine Arabs* (Washington, DC: Middle East Institute, 1958).
38. B. Morris, *Israel's Border Wars, 1949–1956: Arab Infiltration, Israeli Retaliation and the Countdown to the Suez War* (Oxford, UK: Clarendon, 1993).
39. M. Masri, "Family Reunification Legislation in Israel," in Rouhana and Sabbagh-Khoury, *Palestinians in Israel* (2nd ed.).
40. R. Kanaaneh, *Birthing the Nation: Strategies of Palestinian Women in Israel* (Berkeley: University of California Press, 2002).
41. Over the years, Israel has considered various plans to reduce the number of Arab citizens. Recently, many politicians have advanced plans promoting the idea of a land exchange with the Palestinian Authority, including, for example, a "population exchange" that involves annexing land with Jewish settlements in return for land with Arab citizens. D. Newman, "The Geopolitics of Peacemaking in Israel-Palestine," *Political Geography* 21:5 (2002): 629–46; C. Kaufmann, "When All

Else Fails: Ethnic Population Transfers and Partitions in the Twentieth Century," *International Security* 23:2 (1998): 120–56.

42. Jiryis, *Arabs in Israel.*
43. I. Lustick, *Arabs in the Jewish State: Israel's Control of a National Minority* (Austin: University of Texas Press, 1980); N. N. Rouhana, "Collective Identity and Arab Voting Patterns," in *Elections in Israel, 1984,* ed. A. Arian and M. Shamir (New Brunswick NJ: Transaction, 1986), 121–49.
44. L. Dallasheh, "The Al-Ard Movement," in Rouhana and Sabbagh-Khoury, *Palestinians in Israel* (2nd ed.).
45. Rouhana, *Palestinian Citizens in an Ethnic Jewish State.*
46. Masri, "Family Reunification Legislation in Israel."
47. N. N. Rouhana and A. Sabbagh-Khoury, "Dominance, Tolerance, Space and the Privileged Situation" [in Hebrew], in *Knowledge and Silence: On Mechanisms of Denial and Repression in Israeli Society,* ed. H. Herzog and L. Kinneret (Jerusalem: Van Leer Jerusalem Institute and Hakibbutz Hameuchad, 2004), 62–74.
48. Cf. the Panopticon effect that influenced the political discourse and organization for years, as described by A. Sabbagh-Khoury, "Palestinian Predicaments: Jewish Immigration and Refugee Repatriation," in Kanaaneh and Nusair, *Displaced at Home,* 171–88.
49. N. Shalhoub-Kevorkian, "Settler Colonialism, Surveillance, and Fear," in Rouhana, *Ethnic Privileges in the Jewish State.*
50. H. Cohen, *Army of Shadows: Palestinian Collaboration with Zionism, 1917–1948* (Berkeley: University of California Press, 2008).
51. Y. Bäuml, "The Military Government and the Process of Its Abolishment, 1958–1968" [in Hebrew], *New East* 23 (2002): 133–56.
52. A. Sabbagh-Khoury, "Between the Right of Return and the 'Law of Return': Contemplation on Palestinian Discourse in Israel" (master's thesis, Tel-Aviv University, 2006); Sabbagh-Khoury, "Palestinian Predicaments."
53. As mentioned earlier, Israel did not permit the emergence of Arab national parties or political (or even cultural) organizations during the military-government period and much beyond. The ICP was allowed to operate for multiple reasons: it was an Arab-Jewish party with dominant Jewish leadership; it accepted the UN partition plan and supported the creation of a Jewish state in Palestine according to that plan; and it kept open channels to the Soviet Union, which supported the partition plan. Yet it was (and still is) considered to be outside the Israeli-Zionist consensus and as such has been under the watchful eyes of the state apparatus. For detailed discussion of the relationship between the ICP and the Israeli state, see E. Rekhess, *The Arab Minority in Israel: Between Communism and Arab Nationalism, 1965–1991* [in Hebrew] (Tel Aviv: University of Tel Aviv, 1993).
54. A. Adiv, "Israel's Communist Party: At the Crossroads, 1948–2012," in Rouhana and Sabbagh-Khoury, *Palestinians in Israel,* 2nd ed.; and Rekhess, *Arab Minority in Israel.*

55. In a critically important deliberation of section 7A of the Basic Law: The Knesset, the Israeli Knesset considered the various possibilities of what Israel should be: a state for the Jewish people (in Israel and outside Israel), a state for its citizens, or a state for the Jewish people and its citizens; it voted overwhelmingly for being the state of the Jewish people. See Rouhana, *Palestinian Citizens in an Ethnic Jewish State*, for a discussion of the Knesset debate and decision and its implications for the Palestinians.
56. K. Nakhleh, "*Yawm al-Ard* (Land Day)," in Rouhana and Sabbagh-Khoury, *Palestinians in Israel* (2011), 83–89; and Bashir, *Judaizing the Place*.
57. M. Amara, "The Higher Follow-Up Committee for the Arab Citizens in Israel," in Rouhana and Sabbagh-Khoury, *Palestinians in Israel* (2011), 90–99.
58. A. Haidar, "The Nationalist Progressive Movement," in Rouhana and Sabbagh-Khoury, *Palestinians in Israel*, 2nd ed.
59. Ibid.
60. Rouhana, *Palestinian Citizens in an Ethnic Jewish State*.
61. I. Pappé, *The Forgotten Palestinians: A History of the Palestinians in Israel* (New Haven, CT: Yale University Press, 2011); and Rouhana, *Palestinian Citizens in an Ethnic Jewish State*.
62. A. Ghanem, "State and Minority in Israel: The Case of Ethnic State and the Predicament of Its Minority," *Ethnic and Racial Studies* 21:3 (1998): 428–48.
63. N. Ali, "The Islamic Movement in Israel: Historical and Ideological Development," in Rouhana and Sabbagh-Khoury, *Palestinians in Israel*, 2nd ed.
64. T. Sorek, "Public Silence and Latent Memories: Yitzhak Rabin and the Arab-Palestinian Citizens of Israel," *Israel Studies Review* 26:1 (2013): 78–97.
65. N. N. Rouhana and A. Saabneh, *Attitudes of Palestinians in Israel on Key Political and Social Issues: Survey Research Results* (Haifa, Israel: Mada al-Carmel—Arab Center for Applied Social Research, 2007), available at http://mada-research.org/en/2007/10/30/attitudes-of-palestinians-in-israel-on-key-political-and-social-issues-survey-research-results-english-2007/.
66. The party did not openly state that it sought the transformation of Israel from a Jewish state to a democratic state for all its citizens. It simply emphasized the latter part, "the state for all its citizens," in order to avoid being outlawed according to Israeli laws that do not allow a party to run for the Knesset if it rejects Israel as a Jewish state. Indeed, the Elections Committee banned the party, but the decision was later reversed by the Supreme Court. Masri, "Family Reunification Legislation in Israel"; N. Sultany and A. Sabbagh-Khoury, *Resisting Hegemony: The Trial of Azmi Bishara* (Haifa, Israel: Mada al-Carmel—Arab Center for Applied Social Research, 2003).
67. R. Gavison, "Jewish and Democratic? A Rejoinder to the 'Ethnic Democracy' Debate," *Israel Studies* 4:1 (1999): 44–72; S. Smooha, "Types of Democracy and Modes of Conflict-Management in Ethnically Divided Societies," *Nations and Nationalism* 8 (2002): 423–31.

68. A. Bishara, "Reflections on October 2000: A Landmark in Jewish-Arab Relations in Israel," *Journal of Palestine Studies* 30:3 (2001): 54–67; A. Bishara, *From the Jewish State to Sharon: A Study in the Contradictions of Israeli Democracy* (Ramallah, Palestine: MUWATIN—Palestinian Institute for the Study of Democracy, 2005) (Arabic); Rouhana, *Palestinian Citizens in an Ethnic Jewish State.*
69. S. Smooha, "Ethnic Democracy: Israel as an Archetype," *Israel Studies* 2 (1997): 198–241.
70. A. Bishara, "Two Kinds of Citizenship in the Jewish State: The Essential and the Incidental," in Rouhana, *Ethnic Privileges in the Jewish State*; A. Jamal, "Beyond 'Ethnic Democracy': State Structure, Multi-cultural Conflict and Differentiated Citizenship in Israel," *New Political Science* 24:3 (2002): 411–31; Rouhana, *Palestinian Citizens in an Ethnic Jewish State*; N. N. Rouhana, "Jewish and Democratic? The Price of a National Self-Deception," *Journal of Palestine Studies* 35:2 (2006): 64–74; A. Ghanem, N. N. Rouhana, and O. Yiftachel, "Questioning 'Ethnic Democracy': A Response to Sammy Smooha," *Israel Studies* 3:2 (1998): 253–67; O. Yiftachel, "'Ethnocracy': The Politics of Judaizing Israel/Palestine," *Constellations* 6:3 (1999): 364–90; O. Yiftachel, *Ethnocracy: Land and Identity Politics in Israel/Palestine* (Philadelphia: University of Pennsylvania Press, 2006).
71. The documents are "The Future Vision" by the National Committee for the Heads of the Arab Local Authorities in Israel (available at http://www.bitterlemons.net/docs/future-vision-english.pdf); "The Democratic Constitution" by Adalah: The Legal Center for Arab Minority Rights in Israel (available at http://adalah.org/Public/files/democratic_constitution-english.pdf); the "Haifa Declaration" by Mada al-Carmel—Arab Center for Applied Social Research (available at http://mada-research.org/en/files/2007/09/haifaenglish.pdf).
72. E. Rekhess, *The Arab Minority in Israel: An Analysis of the "Future Visions" Documents* (New York: American Jewish Committee, 2008).
73. Rouhana and Sabbagh-Khoury, *Palestinians in Israel* (2nd ed.).
74. See J. Kestler D'Amour, "Israel Criminalizes Commemoration of the Nakba," *Electronic Intifada*, March 29, 2011, http://electronicintifada.net/content/israel-criminalizes-commemoration-nakba/9289.
75. Amara, "Higher Follow-Up Committee."
76. *Report of the State Commission of Inquiry into the Clashes between Security Forces and Israeli Citizens* (August 2003), http://elyon1.court.gov.il/heb/veadot/or/inside_index.htm.
77. International Center for Transitional Justice, "Israel: Time to Heed Victims' Call for Justice," October 4, 2010, http://ictj.org/news/israel-time-heed-victims-call-justice.
78. Perhaps the best description of their collective experience at the time can be seen in the scant literary work produced about that period; see, in particular, E. Habibi, *The Secret Life of Saeed the Pessoptimist*, trans. S. K. Jayyusi and T. LeGassick (New York: Vantage, 1982).

PART II

Society

3

Immigration

Social Strains and the Challenge of Diversity

CALVIN GOLDSCHEIDER

Israeli society has been shaped by immigration more than most countries. Unique in comparative context is the large number of immigrants relative to the native-born population, the diverse national origins of the immigrant streams, and the powerful ideological underpinnings of Israel's immigration policies. As a result, Israel's population is now different from what it once was and what it is still sometimes thought to be. Building on and reinforcing family-Jewish-Zionist values, population changes have been critical in nation building and have had profound implications for the emergence of Israeli society: from the demographic impact of numbers to the complexities of politics; from internal ethnic-group formation to the Palestinian-Israeli conflict; from regional developments to social inequalities; from cultural diversity and pluralism to Westernization and capitalistic economic development. As for the United States at an earlier point in time, immigration *is* Israeli history.

Since 1948, when the State of Israel was established, and into the twenty-first century, over three million immigrants arrived in Israel from diverse countries of origin. They were added to a base population in 1948 of 650,000, in large part with the economic, political, and ideological support of the government. Immigration has been a major strategy of nation building in the State of Israel. The Zionist movement since the nineteenth century and the state from its establishment have sought to gather together in one country those around the world who consider themselves Jewish by religion or ancestry. The processes, patterns, and policies of immigration to Israel have been unique. The conditions preceding and following the Holocaust and World War II in Europe, the emerging nationalism among Jews around the world, the conditions of

Jews in Arab-Muslim countries, the radical changes beginning in the 1990s in eastern Europe with the breakup of the Soviet Union, and the reemergence of anti-Semitism in a number of countries in Europe and Latin America have been among the most obvious external circumstances influencing the immigration of Jews from a wide range of countries to Israel. The emergence of a large and integrated American Jewish community that has not immigrated in substantial numbers to Israel is another factor in understanding the selectivity of immigration to Israel.

There are of course specific internal contexts that reflect particular developments in Israel that have influenced the pace and selectivity of immigration over time. The growth of the Jewish population and the changing territories encompassed by the state, the expansion and attractions of economic opportunities and Jewish political control, and Israel's cultural developments and religious activities have been important factors in the decisions of many Jews to immigrate (and the decisions of many more not to immigrate). War and military conflicts and general internal conflicts have often generated national commitments and euphoria (as in the post-1948 period and the post-1967 war periods), but they have as well caused fear and anxiety about living in dangerous and uncertain circumstances.

Many who have immigrated to Israel are likely to come under some broad definition of refugee movement, in the sense of having been stateless, having been forced to move out of some country, or having been on the move with few other destination options. Throughout most of Israel's short history, the absence of alternatives for those with reduced options to stay where they were living has been a major force encouraging periodic large-scale immigration. A glance at immigration trends over time is marked by two peaks: the period of mass immigration immediately following the establishment of the state (1948–51) and more recent immigration from the former Soviet Union (1990s). Both of these immigration streams can be understood only in the context of major pushes out of places of origin with limited options to immigrate elsewhere. Those strong pushes out of places combined with the ideological and policy commitments of encouraging and subsidizing Jewish immigration explain much of the history of immigration to Israel.

Immigration to Israel symbolizes the renewal of Jewish control over national development, an important value shared by Jewish communities around the world. At the same time, immigration is, and has been, one of the core arenas of conflicts between Jews and Arabs in the Middle East. Even before the establishment of the state, Jewish immigration has been perceived in radically different terms by Jewish and Arab populations. Despite some conflict between immigration streams, the overwhelming majority of Israeli Jews are committed to the continuation of immigration as an implementation of the Zionist agenda and a justification of their own national commitments. The Israeli Arab population (and more broadly the Palestinians) view further Jewish immigration to Israel as part of the asymmetry between Jews and Palestinians in the state, as a further diminution of Arab political power, and as a dilution of national economic resources. In short, past and future immigration is viewed as a national raison d'être among Jews, a basis of strength, national renewal, and unity—that is, the building blocks of national identity and the cement of nationalism. Among Arabs, immigration is viewed as a perpetuation of their political subjugation in a "foreign" regional state, a basis for continued discrimination and inequality, a source of political-economic deprivation and second-class citizenship, and the basis for the continuation of the distorted allocation of limited national resources. As in the past, the powerful symbol of Jewish nationalism in its most conspicuous form is at one and the same time a source of tension and conflict with the Palestinian people and Arab nationalism.

Despite the unique features of immigration to Israel, it shares many common features with other countries. The strategy of nation building through immigration has been used by many countries. Third-world countries and industrialized nations have used immigration incentives to reinstate residents of other countries who share their identity. Many have courted their former country-persons to return home, particularly those with special skills, and have invested resources to lure back those living elsewhere who have obtained higher levels of education and commercial success. But perhaps in no other country is immigration so central a policy and an ideological doctrine. For no other country has immigration been of overwhelming importance in the composition and diversity of its population. And the "return" of Jews to their homeland from every corner of the globe has occurred after a two-thousand-year hiatus.

Looking Backward and Assessing Immigration

After over six decades of statehood, it is important to cast a brief glance backward in time to reconstruct the contours of immigration and its selectivity to Israel and outline some of the major consequences for economic and demographic growth, ethnic compositional changes, and political developments within Israel. (For a statistical overview of immigration history to Palestine and Israel, see table 3.1).

About two-thirds of all immigrants to Israel during the period 1948–2010 have been of European or Western origins; the rest have been from Asian and African countries but mainly from the broad Middle East region. Just as the number of immigrants was not evenly spread over the past sixty years, so have the national origins of the immigrants shifted significantly over time. The proportion from Asian-African countries has shifted from 70 percent in the period 1952–1957 to less than 10 percent starting in the 1970s. While immigration in the first period after the establishment of the state was from a very wide range of countries, the recent movement to Israel beginning in the 1990s was dominated (over 90 percent) by those with eastern European origins and largely from the former Soviet Union. A smaller but significant immigration from Ethiopia occurred at around the same time.

The formal context of Israel's immigration policy is contained in the Declaration of Independence (passed on May 14, 1948), which states, "The State of Israel is open to Jewish immigration and the Ingathering of Exiles." This policy statement was combined with the first order enacted by the provisional government, which was to abolish the British-imposed restriction on immigration to Palestine and to retroactively define those who had entered illegally as legal residents of the newly recognized state. These two elements formed Israel's immigration policy during the first two years of statehood. The Law of Return, enacted July 5, 1950, granted to every Jew in the world the right to immigrate and settle in Israel, with minor exceptions related to health and security. These formal regulations do not convey the main thrust of immigration policy in Israel, which was to actively encourage and subsidize the major phases associated with Jewish immigration and to facilitate the early stages of the immigrant settlement processes.

TABLE 3.1. Immigrants to Palestine and Israel, by Continent of Origin and Period of Immigration, 1919–2010 (in thousands)

	Total	Asia	Africa	Europe	Americas	Other
1919–1948	482.9	40.9	4.0	377.4	7.8	52.8
1948–2010	3,075.2	434.9	505.6	1,895.0	258.0	31.6

	Total	Asia	Africa	Europe	Balkan	Other West mass immigration
1948	101.8	5	9	54	29	3
1949	239.6	31	17	28	22	3
1950	170.2	34	15	45	4	2
1951	175.1	39	12	26	2	1
North African immigration						
1952–1954	54.1	25	51	12	5	8
1955–1957	164.9	6	62	23	6	3
1958–1960	75.5	18	18	56	2	6
1961–1964	228.1	9	51	32	1	6
1965–1968	81.1	19	31	37	2	11
Post-Six-Day War						
1969–1971	116.5	17	10	41	2	29
1972–1974	142.8	4	5	71	1	19
1975–1979	124.8	10	5	60	1	24
1980–1984	83.6	8	19	43	1	30
1985–1989	70.2	12	13	42	1	33
New Russian immigrants						
1990–1994	609.3	1	5	91	0	3
1995–1999	347.0	11	4	79	0	6
2000–2005	202.7				75	
2000–2010	284.9				51	

Source: This chart is based on data from various issues of the *Statistical Abstract of Israel*; the 2000–2010 data are from the 2011 volume (number 62, table 4.4).

The Four Immigration Streams

Since the establishment of the state, there have been four major waves of immigration, each with its unique character, building on the experience of a previous wave and entering a society characterized by a changing political, economic, and cultural context.[1]

Mass Immigration, 1948–1951

The first and most dramatic immigrant stream occurred immediately after the establishment of the state and is referred to as the period of "mass" immigration. In the context of the 1948 War of Independence and in the transition to national control and integration, a very high volume and rate of Jewish immigration from diverse origins arrived in Israel. The high rate doubled the size of the Jewish population—350,000 immigrants arrived in the first eighteen months after statehood, and an additional 350,000 arrived during the following year and a half. It was a massive undertaking to provide basic housing, jobs, schooling, and health services, exacerbated by the fact that many of the immigrants were not able to use the national language and often arrived from the depths of deprivation in postwar Europe. The country was immersed in a war for its survival as a new nation, and its economic base was fragile and weak.

Europeans dominated the first stage of mass immigration when Jewish refugees from the Holocaust arrived in a predominantly European-origin society. In 1948, 85 percent of the Jewish population of Israel was of European origin, as were the immigrants. As Jewish immigrants from Middle East countries joined the stream of immigrants, the ethnic-origin composition changed. By 1951, over 70 percent of the immigrants were from Asian and North African countries, mainly Iraq, Iran, and Libya. In conjunction with immigration during this early period of statehood, Israeli society expanded and consolidated its political, economic, and cultural institutions and developed and extended its welfare entitlement system.

North African Immigration

The second major stream of immigration occurred in the mid-1950s, when over half of the immigrants were from North African countries, particularly Morocco, Tunisia, and Egypt. The occupational skills, educational background, and exposure to urban modern society of these immigrants differed significantly from the earlier European immigrants. Selective immigration quotas and regulations to control the negative impact of large-scale immigration were imposed in Israel during this period. Between 1955 and 1957, 165,000 immigrants arrived; between 1961 and 1964, an additional quarter of a million immigrants arrived, the majority of whom were from North African countries.

Post-1967: Soviet and Western Immigration

A fluctuating but relatively low volume of immigration in the next decade was followed by the third major wave of immigration after the 1967 war. Most of these immigrants came from eastern Europe (the Soviet Union and Romania) and from Western countries (mainly the United States). Between 1972 and 1979, over a quarter of a million immigrants arrived, half from the Soviet Union and 8 percent from the United States. Of the 150,000 immigrants during the 1980s, 65 percent were from eastern Europe or the United States, 11 percent were from Ethiopia, and 6 percent were from Iran. This immigration occurred at a time of economic growth, geographic expansion, and new national political and military self-confidence.

Higher standards of immigrant integration within the society emerged during this period with attention to housing, jobs, and provisions for university-level education. These government policies contrasted sharply with the elementary health care and minimum living accommodations provided to previous immigrant waves. Most conspicuous were subsidies offered the European and Western immigrants, which contrasted with those available to the immigrants from the Middle East of earlier periods. By the mid-1980s, half the Israeli Jewish population was from Middle East origins, largely reflecting their higher rates of natural increase.

Russians: The New Masses

Beginning in 1989, significant numbers of Jews emigrated from the former Soviet Union. About half a million entered Israel in the four years to

1993. The number of immigrants (but not the rate per native population) was the largest since the period of mass immigration forty years earlier. It was the largest volume from any single national origin during such a brief period of time. An estimated one hundred thousand Ethiopian Jews arrived between 1989 and 2010. These immigrants symbolize Israel's continuing commitment to be the political haven for Jews around the world. Most of the Ethiopian immigrants have had very different cultural, religious, and economic experiences compared to those of previous immigrant streams and the Israeli-born population. Educational level, occupational background, and exposure to modern health care are weaker among them and contrast sharply with the Soviet immigrants.

In the decade 2000–2010, most of the immigrants to Israel came from the former Soviet Union (including 144,000 from the European former Soviet Union and 25,000 from Asian republics of the former Soviet Union of Uzbekistan and Georgia). There were non-Ashkenazi Jews and non-Jews among these immigrants. Overall, there has been a noticeable decline of immigration to Israel during this period and especially in the period 2005–2010.

The major challenge of all the recent immigration is, as in the past, short-term integration with regard to housing, jobs, and education. Russian Jews are characterized by professional urban educations, high socioeconomic aspirations for their children, and low levels of exposure to Jewish education and Judaism. The experience of these immigrants with political democracy has been weak, and they formed an ethnic-based political party that was successful in the 1996 national elections and in the formation of the new coalition government. Most of the immigrants from the former Soviet Union are secular in their Judaic orientation.

Commitment to Jewish nationalism, Zionism, is involved in immigration to Israel, but ideological factors always operate in social, economic, and political contexts. Ideological changes do not account for the changes in the rates and sources of immigration over time. Similar to international migration elsewhere, economic factors have been critical in voluntary immigration to Israel, while political factors have been central in refugee and nonvoluntary movements. Changes in political conditions for Jews in countries outside Israel and the options available for migration to alternative destinations have shaped the fluctuating rates of migration to Israel and the changes in the national origins of immigrants. Zionist ideology is a necessary but not sufficient determinant of immigration to Israel. The political, social, and economic factors that have been critical in determining immigration to Israel are mostly beyond the control of the Jewish polity, either in or outside Israel. As such, immigration policies are not likely to have a major impact on the sources and rates of immigration to Israel, unless the policy was to limit and exclude immigrants. The ideological foundation of the society would have to be radically altered for that change to occur.

Some Conspicuous Immigration Consequences

The consequences of immigration patterns have reverberated throughout the society over the past sixty years. These have been most conspicuously linked to the fundamentals of demographic growth (and in turn its broader economic and sociopolitical implications) and to the changing ethnic mixture of the population (and in turn its implication for national integration and inequality).

The most direct effect of immigration has been the increase in the population size of the country. (See table 3.2 for a statistical overview of Jewish and Arab population changes in Israel.) The size of Israel's population doubled between 1948 and 1951, doubled again between 1951 and 1971, and increased to over five million in the subsequent two decades. The Jewish and Arab sectors have both increased at about the same rate over the sixty-year period, and the country has remained over 70 percent Jewish. This Jewish-Arab demographic balance is striking over this fifty-year period, since half of the total growth of the Jewish Israeli population after 1948 is *directly* attributable to immigration, while 98 percent of the Arab Israeli growth is due to natural increase. No reasonable assumption of future demographic dynamics would lead to an Arab Israeli demographic threat to the Jewish majority. Only the incorporation of the Arab/Palestinian populations that are currently not Israeli citizens (e.g., those living on the West Bank) or the mass emigration of Jewish Israelis from the country, both unlikely scenarios, would alter the minority demographic status of Arab Israelis.[2]

In addition to the impact of immigration on Jewish population growth, both directly and indirectly through the children of immigrants, immigration has resulted in significant ethnic compositional diversity

TABLE 3.2. Jewish and Arab Population Size and Percentage Jewish in Israel, 1948–2010

	Total number of Jews (thousands)	Total number of Arabs (thousands)	Percentage Jewish
1948	717	156	82.1
1950	1,203	167	87.8
1960	1,911	239	88.9
1970	2,582	440	85.4
1980	3,283	639	83.7
1990	3,947	875	81.9
2000	4,955	1,189	77.8
2010	5,803	1,574	75.4

Source: Estimates based on the *Statistical Abstract of Israel* 62, table 2.1. See notes there for variation of populations inclusions. The percentage Jewish is out of the total population including, after 1995, growing numbers of "non-Arabs" and "non-Jews." In 2010, there were 318,000 "others."
Note: After 1967, the Arab population of Israel includes the population living in East Jerusalem (about 66,000 in 1967).

within the Jewish population. Immigration has resulted in a shift away from total European dominance to a greater demographic balance between Jews from Western and eastern European origins and those from Middle Eastern origins. Given the overlap of ethnic origin with social and economic resources, political orientations, and culture, the ethnic compositional shifts have had and will continue to have major social, economic, and political implications.

Ethnic groups have been transformed over the generations. In some arenas, there have been major convergences or diminishing of differences between the various ethnic-origin groups in Israel (for example, in family and health patterns). There has also been continued ethnic distinctiveness in other areas (residential concentration, educational attainment and occupational concentration, political behavior, and cultural/religious styles). Although ethnic, social, and cultural differences remain salient and distance from the immigrant generation continues to be an important factor in understanding social change, some structural features of Israeli society have been critical in the retention of ethnic distinctiveness. This is particularly the case in local areas and in some regions of the country (e.g., development and border towns). Ethnic residential concentration is linked to access to educational institutions and job opportunities, to marriage markets and interethnic marriages, and to a reinforced sense of ethnic pride, connecting ethnic origins, families, and networks. Residential segregation is almost total between Jews and Arabs in Israel and characterizes significant segments of second- and third-generation Jews from European and Middle Eastern regions of the world.

Some of the ethnic differences in Israel are obvious carryovers from societies of origin and are most likely to be altered among the second and later generations. Other ethnic differences are deeply embedded in Israeli society, products of the emergence of ethnic communities in Israel amalgamated from specific countries, and reflect Israeli policies of settlement and integration. Ethnic differences tend to be reinforced by culture and politics and over time are discriminatory, with immigrants from Asian and African origins less advantaged economically than those from European origins. The generational transmission of ethnic inequality is reflected in disparities at the highest educational levels. Ethnicity has surely moved away from specific countries of origin toward an amalgamation of broader ethnic groups that represent new forms of ethnic differentiation. These new forms (such as "Asian-African" or "European-American") are specific to Israeli society and mark Jews off from one another.

The future of immigration is linked in part to the unknowable: the political and social conditions of Jewish populations outside the State of Israel. Given the major depletion of some of the Jewish communities through emigration to Israel and elsewhere (almost all of the Middle Eastern Jewish communities and a significant proportion of the eastern European communities), there is a limited potential for large-scale future immigration. At least in the next generation, there is no reasonable basis for assuming any significant movement of Jews to Israel out of the large Jewish communities in North America.

Ethnicity and Religion

One of the important consequences of the immigration patterns to Israel has been the shifting context of Israeli Judaism. On the one hand, as have many other states, Israel has undergone processes of secularization wherein religion, Judaism (ideologically, behaviorally, and institutionally), has diminished. On the other hand, new sources of religious expression, politically and socially, have emerged. The tensions between these two processes—secularization and religious transformation and change—have resulted in increasing bifurcation of the Jewish population in the State of Israel. A conspicuous feature of twenty-first-century Israeli society has been the open conflicts and segregation between segments of the ultra-Orthodox Israeli community (the Haredim) and most Israelis, who define themselves as either "traditional" or, increasingly, secular.

Thus, as diverse immigration streams have resulted in increasing economic inequalities, so the transformation of Judaism in Israel has resulted in increasing conflict between various forms of Judaism and Israeli culture. And there are important connections between religious and ethnic changes in Israel. Immigrants from diverse societies and cultures have brought to Israel a variety of forms of Judaism, cultivated and developed in their different places of origin. Some secular developments in Israeli society have militated against the retention of some forms of religious practices and customs. New features of religious expression have emerged in Israel, influenced by and influencing variants of Zionism.

Several aspects of Israeli Judaism are important to note. The first is the role of the ultra-Orthodox or Haredi groups in Israel and the singular power of the Orthodox rabbinate in issues of marriage, divorce, and Jewish identity in a secular society. The second is the development of a strong political and social base to the "Sephardic," mostly Middle Eastern, community in Israel, mainly reflecting the ethnic base of politics, the development of the Shas political party, and the increasing power and linkage of North African–origin Jews to new forms of Judaic expression. Third, is the role of religion among the Jewish settler population in the Administered Territories, known as Judea and Samaria. These themes connect ethnicity and religion in Israel, reinforcing the ethnic cultural features of Judaism, the political and social context of religious expression, and the ways that expressions of Judaism result in conflict among ethnic communities. Just as the overlap of ethnicity and social class reinforces the salience of ethnic communities, so the overlap of ethnic origin and Judaic/religious expressions reinforces the diversity of Israeli Judaisms and its anchor in ethnic origins. Each provides sources of tension and division among Israeli Jews. Some of these religious divisions show signs of erosion, and there is a reduction of power and control of the ultra-Orthodox. Nevertheless, as of the beginning of the twenty-first century, religious political conflict continues in the public sphere, religious control over critical life-course transitions (e.g., marriage, divorce, burials) persists, and cohesion within religious divisions has been sharpened.

Jews in and outside Israel have been moving in very different directions over the past several decades and are likely to become even more polarized in the future. The oneness in culture and ideology that had characterized these communities in the past is weakening. For example, Jews in the United States define themselves and are in large part comfortable both as Jews and as full citizens of the place where they live. They are part of legitimate and accepted ethnic-religious communities and consider themselves a significant part of their societies, but they distinctly identify as Jews. They have developed complex local, national, and international institutions, lifestyles, and cultural forms that enrich their ethnic and religious expressions. For while Jews have assimilated and become secular in some ways, their communities have become stronger and more viable in other ways. They have developed creative responses to their Jewishness and new expressions of Judaism in a secular context at the same time that they have experienced assimilation. The overwhelming majority of Jews around the world are committed to Israel and the continuity of the Jewish people, but their "home" is where they live, where they expect to continue living, and where they are raising the next generation to live.[3]

Jews outside Israel relate emotionally to the *ideals* of Israel, not to the reality of a changing Israeli society. In the past, there were major commonalities of background and experience between Israeli Jews and Jews around the world. Both were heavily influenced by their mostly European origins; many were raised in families where Yiddish was spoken and were rooted in Yiddish culture. Many struggled with second-generation status and shared the cultural and social disruptions of secularization and assimilation. Most importantly, they shared the struggles of economic depression, war and Holocaust in Europe, and the rebuilding of the lives of Jewish refugees. They shared in the most tangible and dramatic ways the establishment and building of the State of Israel. They also shared limited exposure to Jewish education. Traditional Jewish ritual observances were rejected as part of the past, while national Jewish rituals were developed as substitutes. In short, there was a shared sense of origin, experience, and objective, even while living and building two different societies.

New generations are emerging that are more distant from Europe, from the commonalities of language; the Holocaust has become history, and immigrant origins are far away, as are the struggles of pioneering in Israel and upward mobility in the United States. The different experiences of Jewish communities in and outside Israel have shaped the lifestyles and the values of these communities. Not only have the past commonalities declined, but new gaps have emerged. Three critical elements of social life illustrate this gap between Israeli and American Jews.

We start with women. American Jewish women have been in the forefront of social changes in the liberation from traditional sex roles and family relationships. Many American Jewish men have shared and adjusted to these changes in the workplace and in families. In contrast, Israeli men and women tend to have much more traditional family and social roles. Family relationships are more patriarchal, and work patterns for women are more part-time and driven by economic considerations. And it is not at all clear that egalitarian values shared by American Jewish men and women are shared in Israel.

A second related shift involves the shift in Israel's ethnic composition, as noted earlier, away from European to Asian/African and Russian origins at both the leadership and the population levels. Language and lifestyle barriers have increased and imply diverse cultural origins and limited communication between communities.

These gender and ethnic differences are tied to the growing educational and occupational discrepancies between American Jews and Jews in Israel. The increases in the levels of education of both Jewish men and women and their attainment of high levels of occupation and income have been among the best documented aspects of American Jewish life. But being a college-educated, white-collar professional is characteristic of a relatively smaller segment of the Israeli Jewish community. Add the gender and ethnic dimensions to these social-class gaps, and the basis emerges for polarization of the experiences and orientations of the two groups.

The most serious manifestation of the gap between the two communities is religion. Judaism plays an important role in the lives of American Jews. In its diverse forms, Judaism remains one of the major anchors of Jewish identity for American Jews, marking Jews off from others, personally and institutionally. Rabbis are among the most articulate and conspicuous of the leadership of the general American Jewish community. In contrast, the political and politicized nature of religion in Israel precludes serious communication between religious leaders of the two societies, since neither Conservative nor Reform rabbis have legitimacy as rabbis in Israel. Add in the increasing role of women in American Judaism, and there is a stark contrast between the legitimacy of Reform and Conservative rabbis in America, on the one hand, and American women rabbis viewed in Israel as American exotica (or worse). In America, religious pluralism is normative and accepted, and American Jews are committed to the view that the multiple expressions of Judaism are legitimate and important. These forms of Jewish religious expression and religious leadership are delegitimated in Israel.

The trajectories of Jews in America and in Israel are therefore moving in directions that are likely to strain the relationships between the communities. As each community moves through its own developments, each is moving further away from the other. Changes in gender roles, social class, ethnic origin, language, and religion are rending apart the bonds of commonality between Israeli and American Jews. Differences between Jews in and outside Israel are likely to become accentuated, despite the connecting and neutralizing power of television, electronic communication, and visits in both directions.

Arab Israelis

More important than the Jewish ethnic difference along social-class and cultural lines is the Jewish-Arab divide within the State of Israel. Despite significant changes toward the political and social integration of Arab Israelis and important improvements in their family and economic characteristics, the evidence on residential, family, occupational, political, and cultural dimensions point to continuing divisions between Arabs and Jews in the younger generation.[4]

Demographic issues have been in the forefront of the conflict between Arabs and Jews in Palestine from the end of the nineteenth century until the establishment of the state. Subsequently, these issues have continued to be central in Israeli society. In the prestate period, there were political conflicts over the number of Jews permitted to enter the country relative to economic opportunities and rates of Arab demographic growth. In Israel, the economic and political implications of the different sources of Arab and Jewish population growth (high fertility among Arabs and immigration among Jews) have been raised. The relative size and growth rates of Arab and Jewish populations and their geographic distributions have been the most conspicuous demographic concerns under several political regimes and within different territorial configurations.[5] The analysis of Arab demographic patterns has generally been placed in the context of the Arab-Jewish conflict rather than used as a basis for understanding Arab social structure.

The changing Arab-Jewish population ratio in Israel has been considered *the* demographic issue of the Arab-Israel conflict, with powerful political, economic, and ideological implications for the Jewish state. The relative size and the implied growth rates of Jewish and Arab populations had been considered a key problem, recognized by all three political actors before the establishment of the state (i.e., Jews, Arabs, and the British). It became a different, but no less critical, issue in the years following the mass Jewish immigration from 1948 to 1951 and in subsequent periods, when the volume and rates of Jewish immigration to Israel fluctuated. The problem of the Arab-Jewish population ratio emerged in more dramatic form after the 1967 war, with the inclusion of Arab areas and populations under Israeli administration and control.[6] Although the younger cohorts of Jewish Israelis have moved toward zero population growth, the Arab Israeli population remains in a higher population growth stage. It does not take much demographic orientation to imagine (and exaggerate) the sociopolitical consequences of a rapidly growing minority population and a relatively low-growth majority population.

However, the issue of the relative number and rate of growth of Israeli Jewish and Arab populations and the implied demographic threat of Israeli Arab population growth rates to the political control of the Jewish majority is a profound ideological construction but without a demographic basis. Since the establishment of Israel, the Arab proportion of the total population of the state has fluctuated around a narrow and low range, around 20 percent in the period from 1948 to 1990. In 2010, the Arab proportion had increased but still is about 25 percent of the total population. No reasonable assumption of future demographic dynamics would lead to an Arab Israeli demographic threat to the Jewish majority without the political incorporation of Arab populations that are currently not Israeli citizens—for example, Palestinians living in the West Bank—or the mass emigration of Jewish Israelis from the country. Focusing on Israeli Arabs, not on Palestinians living outside the state, and assuming that mass emigration of Jews from Israel or mass immigration of Arabs to Israel are very unlikely (and hence unpredictable) events reveals unambiguously that, at the national level, the Arab population is likely to remain a permanent demographic minority in both the short and long run.

The key to understanding the Arab Israeli situation in Israel is an examination of the community's residential segregation. As noted earlier, the segregation of Arabs and Jews is almost complete. Reflecting social and normative relationships as well as public policy, the residential segregation of Arab Israelis has powerful implications for access to economic and educational opportunities and for the continuing limited role of Arab women outside the family and the reinforcement of extended family control of women.[7] As for other ethnic and racial groups, segregation is a major limitation on movement toward equality for minorities. Such segregation lends itself to direct discrimination in the community's distribution of resources and reinforces more subtle discrimination in the absence of economic and occupational returns on education.

Thus, on family, political, education, economic, and perhaps cultural grounds, the residential segregation of Arab Israelis reinforces their minority status and prevents their full integration into Israeli society. While their citizen status seems to be well protected and the changes in social and demographic characteristics have indeed been substantial, the bottom line is that discrimination against Arab Israelis has been significant and has prevented their full integration in Israel. There are few indictors in the communal and personal spheres of Israeli society of processes of full Arab Israeli integration. Comparatively, Jewish immigrants from Asian and African countries have experienced greater and continuous integration.

Concluding Thoughts

This review of changes over time in immigration, ethnic composition, and religion in Israel and the continuing discrimination against Arab Israelis points to the following conclusions:

1. Immigration has shaped Israeli society but is largely of the past. In the first decade of the twenty-first century, there have been occasional increases in immigration from select countries, largely reflecting anti-Semitism and anti-Israel activities (e.g., from France) and the religious attraction of Israel among religious Jews (e.g., from the United States). Despite the symbolic and ideological importance of these recent migrations, they have tended to be relatively small in volume. The key consequences of immigration are longer term and continue to shape the changing demographic growth and ethnic composition of Israel.
2. Ethnic pluralism has emerged as a direct consequence of the diverse origins of the Jewish population and the timing and ethnic selectivity of immigration. Ethnic Jewish groups have assimilated in some ways but remain distinctive culturally, socially, and politically through the third generation.
3. The Arab minority in Israel is likely to remain an important but discriminated-against ethnic population in Israeli society. It has experienced significant social and economic changes but without full integration. Along with Palestinians outside the state, Arab Israelis are a critical factor in the social and political processes within Israel. The expanding Jewish settler population in the West Bank represents new expressions of Zionism and settlement but also reflects a serious challenge to political reconciliation between Israel and the Palestinian population.
4. There is an underlying importance to issues of family values that characterize Israel and its ethnic minorities. Family networks shape economic mobility and demographic changes among ethnic Jewish populations; extended family control of women among Arab Israelis reinforces patterns of gender segregation and delays critical social changes from unfolding; family values are conspicu-

ous religious and demographic features among the Haredim and among other religious Jewish Israelis.

It is important overall to note the complexities of changes over the past decades in Israel among its diverse populations, changes that have created a country that is no longer what it is still sometimes thought to be. Oversimplified national-level analyses often miss the heterogeneity and the rich variation that characterizes the society. Projections of future changes that do not take into account the balance of changes among Israel's diverse population are likely to distort planning and limit policies. The challenges are great; the stakes of peace are high; and the ideals of a Jewish state confront the realities of demography and social transformation.

NOTES

1. For details, see Calvin Goldscheider, *Israel's Changing Society: Population, Ethnicity and Development*, 2nd rev. ed. (Boulder, CO: Westview, 2002); and Dov Friedlander and Calvin Goldscheider, *The Population of Israel* (New York: Columbia University Press, 1979).
2. See a fuller discussion in Calvin Goldscheider, *Cultures in Conflict: The Arab-Israeli Conflict* (Westport, CT: Greenwood, 2002); and Goldscheider, *Israel's Changing Society*.
3. Calvin Goldscheider, *Studying the Jewish Future* (Seattle: University of Washington Press, 2004); and Calvin Goldscheider, "American and Israeli Jews: Oneness and Distancing," *Contemporary Jewry* 30 (2010): 205–11.
4. See the fuller discussion in Goldscheider, *Cultures in Conflict*; and Majid Al-Haj, *Education Empowerment and Control: The Case of the Arabs in Israel* (Albany: SUNY Press, 1995).
5. See table 3.2 for the changing relative proportions of Arabs and Jews in Israel. Details on the Arab-Israel conflict and its demographic dimensions are in Calvin Goldscheider, "The Demographic Embeddedness of the Jewish-Arab Conflict in Israeli Society," *Middle East Review* 21:3 (Spring 1989): 15–24; Calvin Goldscheider, "The Embeddedness of the Arab-Jewish Conflict in the State of Israel: Demographic and Sociological Perspectives," in *Israeli Politics in the 1990s*, ed. Bernard Reich and Gershon R. Kieval (Westport, CT: Greenwood, 1991), 111–32; Goldscheider, *Cultures in Conflict*; and Calvin Goldscheider, "The Arab Israeli Population: Demography, Development, and Distinctiveness," *Asian and African Studies* 27 (1993): 67–84.
6. See the extensive discussions and analyses in Friedlander and Goldscheider, *Population of Israel*; and Dov Friedlander and Calvin Goldscheider, "Israel's

Population: The Challenge of Pluralism," *Population Reference Bureau Bulletin* 39:2 (April 1984).

7. See Calvin Goldscheider, "Religious Values, Dependencies, and Fertility: Evidence and Implications from Israel," in *Dynamics of Values in Fertility Change*, ed. Richard Leete, (Oxford, UK: Clarendon, 1999), 310–30, on the impact of residential segregation on family values and gender roles among Arab Israelis.

4

Kibbutzim

The Challenge of Transformation

RAYMOND RUSSELL

For many decades, the collective settlements known as kibbutzim stood out as one of Israel's most unique and best known institutions. Kibbutz members managed and worked farms and factories together, rotating jobs among the members and making major decisions together at meetings of the general assembly. Members lived in kibbutz-owned apartments and ate their meals in a communal dining hall. Insofar as kibbutz members had needs for cash, they shared resources on the principle of "from each according to his or her ability, to each according to his or her need."

In the years before statehood, the kibbutzim served as an attractive way to settle Jews on the land of Israel and to help them organize for their own self-defense. In the first decades after independence, the kibbutzim continued to grow and to prosper as they added manufacturing and services to their traditional agricultural base. The story of kibbutz success became part of the greater story of Israel's success, and a visit to a kibbutz became part of every tourist's stay in Israel, even though they never accounted for more than 6 percent of the Israeli population.

Although that perception still persists in some quarters, the image of the kibbutzim changed radically, both in Israel and abroad, in the 1980s. Whereas Israel had been governed by socialist-led coalitions, with the 1977 political victory in Israel of the right-wing Likud and the rise of international leaders like Ronald Reagan and Margaret Thatcher shortly thereafter, the kibbutzim found themselves encircled by ideological enemies instead of allies. For a few years, the significance of these changes went unnoticed. In 1985, however, a sudden shift in government policy from expansion to contraction exposed the kibbutzim as both overextended and friendless. Because the kibbutzim served as guarantors of each other's debts, the economic troubles of many individual kibbutzim drove the entire kibbutz movement into bankruptcy.

As a condition of the emergence of the kibbutzim from bankruptcy in 1990, they promised to introduce reforms designed to reduce their costs and increase their incomes. Each kibbutz was left free to choose for itself which reforms it would introduce and which it would not. In the 1990s, most kibbutzim "privatized" the budgets of individual kibbutz households. Each household received a cash allowance based on its needs and was left free to spend its allocation as it saw fit. Members who continued to eat meals in the kibbutz dining hall now paid for each meal, while other members used their money to purchase groceries and cook meals in their private apartments. Most kibbutzim also gave their members permission to take jobs outside their kibbutz, but the income from this outside employment went to the kibbutz, not to the individual member.

Between 1995 and 2011, 188 kibbutzim went on to make a more radical change, one that completely transformed their organizational identities. They began to pay their members differential salaries based on the market value of their work. This was a major departure from past practices and conceptions of the kibbutzim and caused many observers to ask whether a kibbutz that paid differential salaries to its members still deserved to be called a kibbutz.

In 2003, a public committee led by the sociologist Eliezer Ben-Rafael of Tel Aviv University recommended that kibbutzim paying differential salaries should still be considered kibbutzim, but they should be recognized as constituting kibbutzim of a new type. A kibbutz that continued to share resources on the basis of need would henceforth be known as a "collective" kibbutz (*kibbutz shitufi*). A kibbutz that paid differential salaries to members or that transferred ownership of housing or shares of stock in kibbutz ventures to individual members would be called a "renewed" kibbutz[1] or a "renewing" kibbutz (*kibbutz mitḥadesh*).[2] The recommendations of the Public Committee were quickly accepted by the kibbutz movement and by the government and became law in 2005.

This chapter surveys the literature on the kibbutzim that emerged during this period of transformation. It begins with works that address the origins and early history of the kibbutzim. Whereas classic accounts emphasize the Zionist and socialist ideals of the *chalutzim* (pioneers) who created the first kibbutzim, more recent works point to ways in which kibbutzim satisfied practical needs of the Jewish settlers for jobs and mutual defense. Later sections describe the economic and demographic crisis that the kibbutzim fell into in the 1980s and the changes that the kibbutzim introduced in response to these problems.

The Emergence and Growth of the Kibbutzim

Traditional accounts of the origin of the kibbutzim emphasize the unique aspirations of Jewish immigrants to Palestine during the two waves known as the Second Aliyah (1904–14) and the Third Aliyah (1919–23).[3] Coming primarily from Russia in a time of revolution, these immigrants were inspired by a combination of "practical Zionism"[4] and revolutionary fervor. They wanted to put both the diaspora and capitalism behind them by working the land together in the land of Israel in a way that could serve as a model for the whole world. In Henry Near's words,

> As Russians, they were influenced by the revolutionary spirit of the period. Young Jews, seeking solutions to their own problems and to those of humanity as a whole, found themselves in an intellectual ambience in which the concept of revolution, or the building of a new society purged of the evils that they saw around them, was a generally accepted ideal. Many of these young intellectuals found their way to Zionism and to Palestine as a result of the failure of the 1905 revolution. In Palestine, they attempted to apply the social ideals acquired in their adolescence to the very different realities they now had to face.[5]

Although such ideals clearly shaped the institutions that the pioneers created, the first kibbutz, Degania, was created in an act of improvisation. In the words of Yoseph Tabenkin, "The kibbutz came prior to its idea. It had no preplan."[6] The founders of Degania were not self-consciously attempting to create a new form of organization. Until 1909, they had been working at the training farm at Kinneret, sponsored by the World Zionist Organization (WZO). They now told the WZO representative Arthur Ruppin that they found conditions there intolerable. The Russian agronomist whom the WZO had hired to run the farm was hiring Arab workers to do many tasks and was treating Jewish immigrants like hired hands. Degania's founders asked Ruppin for a chance to show that, working together as equals, they could compete successfully with Arab workers.

While Degania's founders waited for Ruppin to allocate land to them, they supported themselves by working as hired agricultural laborers near the coastal town of Hadera. It was there that they first organized themselves as a *kvutzah*, or "communal group," pooling their wages and living and eating together. When Jewish National Fund–owned land became available in 1910, the *kvutzah* moved to Degania's current location next to the Sea of Galilee. The experiment at Degania was quickly hailed as a success, both by Ruppin and by the many opinion makers among the Jewish immigrants who came to work there. By 1920, the number of *kvutzot* had grown to ten.

Beginning in 1921, influential voices began to call for the *kvutzah* to be replaced by a new form of communal settlement, the kibbutz. Whereas the *kvutzah* was small and elitist, the kibbutz would be large and inclusive. Whereas the *kvutzah* focused solely on farming, the kibbutz would engage in a wide range of agricultural and industrial pursuits. The kibbutzim quickly came to outnumber the *kvutzot* and eventually gave their name to the entire population of collective agricultural settlements.

More recent accounts of the origin of the kibbutzim pay less attention to the ideals of the Jewish immigrants who created the kibbutzim and give more attention to their practical needs. For Gershon Shafir, the kibbutz was created most of all as a way to provide Jewish immigrants to Palestine with jobs.[7] During the First Aliyah (1882–1903), Zionist philanthropists provided farms to Jewish immigrants, who hired local Arab laborers to work the land. The kibbutz, in contrast, would be a form of "self-labor," in which all labor would be performed by members of the commune, all of whom would be Jewish immigrants in need of work.

Another practical advantage of the kibbutzim during the prestate period is that as tightly organized communities, they were better equipped to defend themselves against raids by local Arabs who were becoming increasingly resentful of Jewish immigration.[8] To meet this new threat, a new kind of kibbutz began to be established in the 1930s and 1940s. Because these new "border kibbutzim" were half settlements, half military outposts, they had their own unique architecture, featuring heavy use of barbed wire and observation towers.[9]

During the 1948–49 War of Independence, fighting reached the gates of many kibbutzim, including some like Degania that had not initially conceived of themselves as border kibbutzim. Although the kibbutzim and their members emerged from the War of Independence as heroes, in the future the new State of Israel would take the lead in organizing both the defense of the nation and the absorption of new immigrants, leaving the kibbutzim to search for new roles to play.[10]

In the decades following independence, the kibbutzim continued to expand their operations by adding manufacturing and services to their traditional agricultural pursuits. By 1977, 75.2 percent of kibbutzim had at least one industrial enterprise, and 24.5 percent had two or more.[11] Adding industrial ventures to their economic activities allowed the kibbutzim to reach new highs in productivity, income, and population regularly for many decades. Kibbutz members also played leading roles during this period in many other portions of Israeli society, including both the government and the military. Former kibbutz members contributed disproportionately to the army's officer corps and elite units for many years.[12]

The Decline of the Kibbutzim

In the first two decades after independence, kibbutz members typically filled one-sixth or more of the seats in the Knesset and made up a quarter or more of many cabinets.[13] Although kibbutz members remained part of every Israeli government until the victory of Likud in 1977, Near writes that even before this sea change in Israeli politics, "the years between 1954 and 1977 saw a marked decline in the influence of the kibbutz movements [federations] in the Israeli political system."[14] Near attributes this political decline in part to a decline in the status of the kibbutz, as kibbutz members came to be perceived less as heroes and more as an interest group, and in part to changes in the ways in which political parties chose candidates for offices, with rural voters and party officials losing influence to urban voters.

While the kibbutzim had entered a period of political decline even before 1977, Eliezer Ben-Rafael writes that

> The rise to power of the right-wing Likud party in 1977 . . . amounted to no less than an earthquake for the kibbutz movement. It dislodged the

> federations from the longstanding positions—in the Ministries of Agriculture, Education, or Commerce and Industry, and even the Ministry of Defense—where their presence had been strong through representatives and institutionalized lobbying. Moreover, in Parliament itself, the representation of the kibbutzniks was drastically cut, while they were now totally absent from the government where they customarily had held one or two positions under the Labor rule.[15]

In the early 1980s, the Likud government's economic policies were expansionary, making credit available on easy terms. These policies fueled inflation, making it ever easier to pay off old loans and obtain new ones. The kibbutzim joined other Israelis in becoming heavy borrowers during this period. In 1985, the Israeli government suddenly shifted its economic policy from inflationary to deflationary in order to stabilize the declining value of the currency. As part of the government's emergency price-stabilization plan, all debt in Israel would henceforth be indexed to the rate of inflation. The kibbutzim, like other Israeli borrowers, saw their debts grow larger with each increase in the rate of inflation, just as their ability to repay those debts was declining because the national economy had gone into a recession.

Businesses throughout the Israeli economy found themselves caught between upwardly spiraling debts and downwardly spiraling incomes. Many became bankrupt, including the nation's largest banks. Increasing numbers of individual kibbutzim found themselves unable to pay their debts. Because the kibbutzim were guarantors of each other's debts, the kibbutz movement as a whole fell into bankruptcy.

The account given so far portrays the kibbutzim as passive victims of macroeconomic forces beyond their control. Defenders of kibbutz traditions remained loyal to such accounts well into the 1990s. But growing numbers of critics pointed to many ways in which the kibbutzim had brought their economic problems on themselves. Many investments made in the early 1980s appeared with hindsight to have been unwise. These include both risky economic ventures that later went bad and the high proportion of capital resources that went to build larger living quarters.

The first and loudest voice to blame the kibbutzim for their own problems was the Likud government. Within Israel, the Likud government that had held or shared power since 1977 represented the victory of probusiness parties over labor parties and of Israelis with roots in Asia or North Africa over those with roots in Europe. Although the Likud leaders were themselves of European origin, their electoral success was largely attributed to the support of Oriental Jews who lived in development towns and often worked as hired laborers in factories owned by nearby kibbutzim.[16] Internationally, the Likud leaders were ideological allies of Margaret Thatcher and Ronald Reagan and shared their agenda.[17] The Likud leaders were quick to label the economic difficulties of the kibbutzim as additional examples of the failure of socialism. Like their allies abroad, they prescribed "privatization" as the solution.

Critics outside the kibbutz movement were soon joined by voices within it. In kibbutz managerial training centers like the Ruppin Institute and in the Takam federation's archive and publications center at Yad Tabenkin, kibbutz researchers began to identify practices of the kibbutzim that might have contributed to the recent poor performance of their economic ventures. Critics like Reuven Shapira argued that the rotation of managers in kibbutz factories was depriving those enterprises of the services of their most skilled and successful leaders.[18] For Gideon Kressel, the problem was that the collective ownership and decision-making practices of the kibbutzim left managers insufficiently accountable for their errors.[19]

As kibbutz members asked each other who and what had caused their current problems and what they needed to do to solve them, many began to lose confidence that the kibbutz remained viable in the contemporary Israeli economy. Many kibbutz members and adult children of members left to pursue more attractive opportunities elsewhere. This led the economic crisis of the kibbutzim to be compounded by a demographic crisis.

In 1985, the total number of members, children of members, and other residents living on kibbutzim stood at 125,200.[20] Spread over 268 kibbutzim, this represented an average of 467 residents per kibbutz. Both figures were all-time highs. Over the five years from 1986 through 1990, however, more adults departed from kibbutzim every year than new members joined them. In these years, the average kibbutz lost from six to ten residents per year and from thirty to fifty over the five years. Only natural population increase (the excess of births over deaths) allowed the total population of the kibbutzim to remain as high in 1990 as it has been in 1985.[21]

Stanley Maron examined the impact of departures of members and children of members on the changing age structure of the kibbutzim during these years. Between 1983 and 1986, the kibbutzim were successfully attracting and retaining adults with young or teenage children. Between 1986 and 1989, the number of kibbutz residents aged twenty-five to thirty-four fell by 11.4 percent, and the number of children under five years of age fell by 6.6 percent. The number of kibbutz members sixty-five or more years of age, in the meantime, grew steadily in both periods.[22]

The perception that the kibbutzim were failing to appeal to the younger generation and that they were losing many of their most promising workers lent urgency to calls for reform. By the late 1980s, reforms were being urged by voices both outside and inside the movement. Discussions about which reforms the kibbutzim should or should not adopt quickly became ideologically charged and hotly contested, both within individual kibbutzim and in the kibbutz federations.

The Diffusion of Reforms among Kibbutzim, 1991–2001

In the face of these economic and demographic challenges, critics both outside and inside the kibbutzim soon began calling for the kibbutzim to introduce reforms that could increase their incomes and reduce their costs. If members could bring in more revenue by working outside the kibbutz economy than within it, it was now suggested that they should be encouraged to take those higher-paying jobs. If kibbutz economic ventures could increase their incomes by hiring more nonmembers to work in them, they were now encouraged to do so, even though the rising use of hired labor would be widely seen as a sign of the transformation of the kibbutzim from cooperative into capitalist firms. If kibbutz members now ate their meals in their individual apartments rather than collective dining halls, then those dining halls should be closed.

In 1990, the kibbutz federations formally committed their member kibbutzim to adopt measures of this sort as a condition of their emergence from bankruptcy, but they left each individual kibbutz free to decide which specific innovations it would or would not introduce. Many kibbutzim set up "innovation teams" to identify reforms that looked especially appropriate for their kibbutz.[23] In making decisions about which changes to adopt, many kibbutzim also sought advice from their federations or from professional consultants.

Despite all of these influences encouraging them to change, many kibbutzim found themselves deeply divided between reformers and traditionalists and uncertain about what to do next.[24] Reforms tended to be backed by "technocrats," who sought a freer hand in management, and by younger, kibbutz-born or Israeli-born members, who sought lifestyles more similar to those of Israelis who lived outside the kibbutzim.[25] Traditional kibbutz values and practices tended to be defended by older members and by members born outside Israel.[26]

As previously noted, the kibbutz federations promised their creditors in 1990 that the kibbutzim would introduce reforms. To document the compliance of the kibbutzim with this pledge, the federations requested the University of Haifa's Institute for Research of the Kibbutz and the Cooperative Idea to conduct annual surveys of the kibbutzim. Every year from 1990 through 2001, the Institute surveyed all kibbutzim about reforms that were under consideration at the time.[27] These studies document that for most of the 1990s the kibbutzim embraced a number of mostly modest reforms while avoiding changes that threatened to alter the identity of the kibbutz. Most kibbutzim transferred authority for governing their economic ventures from the general assembly to boards of directors, but they refused to abolish the principle of rotating managers at the end of fixed terms. Most kibbutzim gave their members the right to take jobs outside the kibbutz, but the income that kibbutz members earned on such outside employment continued to be paid to the kibbutz, not the member. A growing portion of consumption expenditures, such as the costs of electricity and travel, became private rather than public, but most members' budgets continued to be based not on work but on need.

As responsibility for a growing proportion of consumption expenses was shifted from the kibbutz as a whole to individual households, it became common among kibbutz members to refer to such reforms as instances of "privatization."[28] Amir Helman noted at the time that this was a "strange use of the fashionable concept of privatization."[29] Whereas in the Great Britain of Margaret Thatcher and the transitional economies of eastern Europe, "privatization" referred to the sale of state-owned enterprises to private owners, among the kibbutzim of the 1990s, it was being applied to "any decision to decrease the collective's expenditure in order to increase the personal budget."[30] Helman pointed to the way kibbutz members talked about the new arrangements to pay for electricity as an instance of this word usage: "For example, if the general assembly decides that each family should pay for its own consumption of electricity (instead of the typical kibbutz total payment for all its members), then the members would say that they have 'privatized' the electricity budget."[31]

By 2001, most kibbutzim responding to the institute's annual survey reported that they had also privatized expenditures for recreation (58.1 percent) and for travel (86.4 percent). In 70.6 percent of responding kibbutzim, members were now being charged for the meals that they ate in the communal dining hall. In 67.8 percent, members were now free to own or use private cars. Large and growing minorities of kibbutzim also had voted to privatize their health services (26.1 percent) or laundry (38.1 percent), and about half of them (48.8 percent) were letting members increase the size of their homes at their own expense.[32]

In light of the widespread use of the term "privatization" to refer to many such changes then taking place on the kibbutzim, Helman suggested that we "may prefer a broader definition of privatization" that has the scope to cover them. He recommended that we think of privatization not as "the simple formal transferal of ownership" but as "a system which transfers power from the center to the individual." "Using this broad definition for privatization," Helman concluded that "the kibbutz is now in the middle of a strong privatization process."[33]

The Transformation of the Kibbutzim, 1995–2011

In the early 1990s, Kibbutz Ein Zivan and Kibbutz Snir became the first kibbutzim to announce that they intended to pay differential salaries to their members, but they were slow to put these plans into practice. The kibbutz federations threatened to expel any kibbutz that followed through on such plans, making other kibbutzim even more reluctant to take this step.

Beginning around 1995, Kibbutz Gesher Haziv and Kibbutz Naot Mordecai found a way to make payment of differential salaries more palatable to kibbutz members. They created the so-called safety net budget, in which members receive differential, market-based salaries, but their incomes are taxed progressively to support a minimal standard of living and level of social services for all kibbutz members. The safety net budget sounded more like Scandinavian socialism than like capitalism, making it a less radical departure from the traditional political culture of the kibbutzim. Politically, by using taxes collected from healthy members of working age to meet the needs of older and weaker members, the safety net budgetary system had the potential to create alliances between the two.[34]

When individual kibbutzim first began to adopt differential compensation in the 1990s, leaders of the federations warned them that any kibbutz that made this change would no longer be considered a kibbutz. Israel's Registrar of Cooperative Societies issued similar threats. In the years following these transformations, however, neither the federations nor the Registrar took action.

In 1999, eight members of Kibbutz Beit Oren finally forced the Israeli government to take a stand on this question when they asked the High Court of Justice to instruct the Registrar of Cooperative Societies to abolish the classification of Beit Oren as a kibbutz. Beit Oren had introduced differential salaries, closed its communal dining hall, and privatized education and other services, making it in the eyes of the petitioners no longer a kibbutz. Cases such as this one led the government of Israel to decide in February 2002 to form a public committee to examine this question. The Public Committee on the Issue of Kibbutzim, chaired by the sociologist Eliezer Ben-Rafael of Tel Aviv University, issued its report in 2003.

When Ben-Rafael's Public Committee began its work, a kibbutz was defined in Israel's Cooperative Societies Regulations as "a cooperative society that is a separate settlement, organized on the basis of collective ownership of assets, self-employment, equality and cooperation in production, consumption and education." The Public Committee recommended that this wording be retained as the definition of a "collective" or "communal" kibbutz and that a second definition should be added for the "renewed kibbutz." A "renewed" kibbutz would be defined as

> a cooperative society that is a separate settlement, organized on the basis of collective partnership in assets, self-employment, equality and cooperation in production, consumption and education, that maintains mutual responsibility among its members, and whose articles of association include some or all of the following:
>
> (1) Relative wages according to individual contribution or seniority;
> (2) Allocation of apartments;
> (3) Allocation of means of production to its members, excluding land, water and production quotas, provided that the cooperative maintains control over the means of production and that its articles of association restrict the negotiability of allocated means of production.[35]

Both the kibbutz movement and the Israeli government quickly accepted the recommendations of the Public Committee, and they became law in October 2005. The "renewed" form had become the predominant type of kibbutz several years before it gained legal recognition as a kibbutz.

Varieties of Kibbutzim

As of 2011, 188 nonreligious kibbutzim had transformed themselves into "renewed" kibbutzim, and 53 nonreligious kibbutzim continued to adhere to the traditional "collective" type of kibbutz.[36] Another 7 kibbutzim in 2011 illustrated the rapidly disappearing "mixed" form of kibbutz. In addition to these types, kibbutzim in 2011 also took a number of alternative forms.

Religious Kibbutzim

While kibbutzim of the mixed type have proved to be a transitory phenomenon, the religious kibbutz endures as the most important alternative to the better-known varieties of kibbutzim. There are sixteen religious kibbutzim, of which nine were established between 1937 and 1952 and the other seven between 1966 and 1982. Whereas the secular kibbutzim derive many of their collective ideals from socialism, the religious kibbutzim root their communalism in the Torah.[37] The religious kibbutzim are generally more prosperous than are the secular kibbutzim. They did not suffer as much as other kibbutzim from the economic crisis of the 1980s and did not participate in the 1990 agreement between the government, the banks, and the kibbutzim that committed the kibbutzim to introduce reforms. By 2012, three of the nine older religious kibbutzim and four of the seven younger ones had transformed themselves into renewed kibbutzim.[38]

Ecological Kibbutzim

In recent years, growing numbers of kibbutzim have begun to identify themselves as ecological kibbutzim. For example, Kibbutz Lotan in the Negev desert has espoused a philosophy of "eco-Zionism" since the 1950s. It is part of the Global Ecological Network and has made the goal of living in harmony with its desert environment a part of its vision statement. Kibbutz Nir Oz, also in the Negev, committed itself to water-wise agriculture as early as 1962. It harvests rainwater for use in irrigation, desalinates sea water, and has identified or developed more than nine hundred species of plants that require no irrigation. Other kibbutzim that have taken up the cause of environmental protection and/or organic gardening include Kibbutz Ketura, Kibbutz Neot Smadar, and Kibbutz Sde Eliyahu.[39]

While members of ecological kibbutzim often speak with great pride about events and achievements on their own kibbutz, the ecological kibbutzim have not yet developed a common identity or clearly articulated ideology. To date, their efforts have remained uncoordinated, leaving other kibbutzim to increase their consciousness of the environment one kibbutz at a time.

Urban Kibbutzim and Communal Groups

While the religious kibbutzim trace their roots to the 1930s and 1940s, a more recent development associated with the kibbutz movement has been the emergence of kibbutzim and communes within Israel's cities. Members of these urban kibbutzim and communes spend their days working as teachers or social workers or in other helping professions but gather after work to pool their incomes and live together in communal households.

The kibbutz movement had tried to establish such urban kibbutzim several times in the past, but it was not until 1979 that it achieved its first success. As Yuval Dror reported in 2011, "The first urban kibbutz was established in Jerusalem in 1979. Today there are four urban kibbutzim in Israel: Reshit (Kiryat-Menahem, Jerusalem, founded in 1979); Tamuz (Beit Shemesh, founded in 1987); Migvan (Sderot, founded in 1987); Beit Israel (Gilo, Jerusalem, founded in 1992). Each numbers dozens of members, living on various levels communally, while additional families and single people participate in their educational and other community work without becoming members of the kibbutz."[40]

When Ben-Rafael's Public Committee issued its report on the legal definition of the kibbutzim, it recommended that the law be expanded to give recognition not only to the renewed kibbutz but also to the urban kibbutz, defined as "a community living a communal life in a town or a city."[41] In keeping with this recommendation, Israeli law now identifies the kibbutzim as coming in three types: the collective kibbutz, the renewed kibbutz, and the urban kibbutz.

The urban kibbutzim were initially established with the cooperation and encouragement of the kibbutz movement, and they were founded by young adults most of whom had grown up on kibbutzim. Since the 1980s, large numbers of small and amorphous communes have emerged in cities all over Israel that have no ties of any kind to the kibbutz movement. Many of these urban communes have been created by graduates of Zionist youth movements in Israel and the Diaspora. In past decades, these youth movements and associated institutions like the army's Naḥal prepared young people for futures in kibbutzim. Now, members of these movements perceive the kibbutzim as having abandoned their communal values. These movements now encourage their graduates to create new communal institutions with a new mission. Whereas the original kibbutzim aimed to settle Jews on the land of Israel, members of the urban kibbutzim and communes seek to deliver educational and social services to underprivileged populations in Israel's cities.

The growing disaffection between the kibbutz movement and the youth movements was not only ideological but also structural. Until the 1980s, the kibbutz federations recognized the youth movements as important sources of members for the kibbutzim, and they sent emissaries and material support to these movements in return. When the crisis of the 1980s caused the kibbutzim to run short of both money and ideological commitment, the support they gave to the youth movements sharply declined. In the words of Dror,

> The changing kibbutz, plagued by crises, ceased to attract urban youth in search of worthy goals, leading to a sharp drop in the number of youth movement members, graduates that served as "Naḥal" soldiers (branch of the Israeli army) that aimed to join the kibbutzim, and above all of those choosing kibbutz life. This reduced still further the number of kibbutz members active in the youth movements and the financial support they received, since the kibbutzim realized that they did not benefit from this expenditure and no longer felt committed to assist them, creating a vicious circle.[42]

In 2009, James Horrox estimated that "at the time of writing, there are upwards of 1,500 people living communally across Israel, entirely unconnected to the kibbutz movement. . . . Approximately three-quarters of these are members of the Tnuat Bogrim or graduate movement groups of the youth movement Noar ve'Lomed (Working & Student Youth Movement), otherwise known by its acronym NOAL."[43] Other youth movements encouraging their graduates to live together in urban communes are Maḥanot Ha-Olim and Ha-Shomer Ha-Tza'ir in Israel and Ha-Bonim Dror in the Diaspora.

Horrox suggests that Israel's contemporary urban kibbutzim and communal groups now benefit from the youthful idealism that in previous generations fed the development of the classic kibbutzim. In his words,

> As kibbutz life was supposedly the ultimate fulfillment of their ideology, the kibbutz's abandonment of its original values left graduates of the youth movement without a means of achieving *hagshama* (self-realisation) or any structure for bringing about change in Israeli society. Many NOAL graduates began to look for alternatives. In the creation of new, more intimate settlements, they saw a way of achieving *hagshama* by practicing the youth movement's ideology and values in their daily lives.[44]

While members of the urban communal groups are critical of the contemporary kibbutzim, many groups model themselves after the *kvutzot* from which the kibbutz movement emerged. Horrox notes, "The fact that these groups choose to describe themselves as *kvutzot* rather than kibbutzim is itself a deliberate and conscious alignment with the intimacy of the small anarchistic settlements of the early years."[45]

The Renewal of the Kibbutzim

By the year 2010, the kibbutzim had finally emerged from their long economic slump, and the total kibbutz population stood at an all-time high (table 4.1). But most of the recent growth of the kibbutzim had come in the form of residents who live on the kibbutzim as nonmembers in neighborhoods built especially for them. The kibbutzim are now struggling to develop new ways to incorporate nonmember residents into the governance of their communities and to provide opportunities for them to become members.[46]

TABLE 4.1. Number of Kibbutzim and Total Population of Kibbutzim, 1910–2010

Year	Number of kibbutzim	Total population of kibbutzim	Population per kibbutz
1910	1	11	11
1920	12	805	67
1930	29	3,900	134
1940	82	26,550	324
1950	214	67,550	316
1960	229	77,950	340
1970	229	85,100	372
1980	255	111,200	436
1990	270	125,100	463
2000	268	115,300	430
2010	265	140,900	532

Source: Raymond Russell, Robert Hanneman, and Shlomo Getz, *The Renewal of the Kibbutz: From Reform to Transformation* (New Brunswick, NJ: Rutgers University Press, 2013), 22.

By 2011, more than three-quarters of Israel's 248 nonreligious kibbutzim had voted to transform themselves into "renewed" kibbutzim. Whether this change has in fact given new life to the kibbutzim still remains to be seen. Eliezer Ben-Rafael and Menachem Topel argue that the Hebrew term *kibbutz mitḥadesh* is better translated not as a "renewed" kibbutz but as a "renewing" kibbutz.[47] This implies that the kibbutzim involved viewed this act not as the end of a process of transformation but as the beginning of one.

If we compare recent events in the history of the kibbutzim to their earliest decades, a few enduring themes persist. Despite the popular image, kibbutzim have always come in more than one type, beginning with the rivalry between the kibbutz and the *kvutzah*. Since the beginning, kibbutzim have always been subject to numerous forms and processes of change. Throughout all of these periods in the history of the kibbutzim, Tabenkin's observation, quoted earlier, that "the kibbutz came prior to its idea" has continued to apply. Kibbutz members are constantly creating new realities on the ground that our conceptualizations about the kibbutz struggle to keep up with.

NOTES

1. Ronen Manor, "The 'Renewed' Kibbutz," *Journal of Rural Cooperation* 32 (2004): 37–50.
2. Eliezer Ben-Rafael and Menachem Topel, "Redefining the Kibbutz," in *One Hundred Years of Kibbutz Life: A Century of Crises and Reinvention*, ed. Michal Palgi and Shulamit Reinharz (New Brunswick, NJ: Transaction Books, 2011), 249–58.
3. E.g., Henry Near, *The Kibbutz Movement: A History*, vol. 1, *Origins and Growth, 1909–1939* (New York: Oxford University Press, 1992), 7–41.
4. Ibid., 9.
5. Ibid., 13.
6. Quoted in Aharon Kellerman, *Society and Settlement: Jewish Land of Israel in the Twentieth Century* (Albany: SUNY Press, 1993), 50.
7. Gerhson Shafir, *Land, Labor and the Origins of the Israeli-Palestinian Conflict, 1882–1914* (Cambridge: Cambridge University Press, 1989), 45–90, 181–86.
8. Tal Simons and Paul Ingram, "Enemies of the State: The Interdependence of Institutional Forms and the Ecology of the Kibbutz, 1910–1997," *Administrative Science Quarterly* 48 (2003): 592–621; S. Ilan Troen, *Imagining Zion: Dreams, Designs, and Realities in a Century of Jewish Settlement* (New Haven, CT: Yale University Press, 2003), 62–81.
9. Paula Rayman, *The Kibbutz Community and Nation Building* (Princeton, NJ: Princeton University Press, 1981), 27–28.

10. Simons and Ingram, "Enemies of the State," 601–3, 614.
11. Henry Near, *The Kibbutz Movement: A History*, vol. 2, *Crisis and Achievement, 1939–1995* (London: Vallentine Mitchell, 1997), 239–40.
12. Yehuda Amir, "The Effectiveness of the Kibbutz-Born Soldier in the Israel Defense Forces," *Human Relations* 22 (1969): 333–44.
13. Near, *Kibbutz Movement*, vol. 2, 258–59.
14. Ibid., 256.
15. Eliezer Ben-Rafael, *Crisis and Transformation: The Kibbutz at Century's End* (Albany: SUNY Press, 1997), 38.
16. S. N. Eisenstadt, *The Transformation of Israeli Society: An Essay in Interpretation* (Boulder, CO: Westview, 1985), 421, 492, 498; Howard M. Sachar, *A History of Israel from the Rise of Zionism to Our Time*, 3rd ed., rev. and exp. (New York: Knopf, 2007), 835.
17. Michael Shalev, "Zionism and Liberalization: Change and Continuity in Israel's Political Economy," *Humboldt Journal of Social Relations* 23 (1997): 219–59.
18. Reuven Shapira, "Leadership, Rotation, and the Kibbutz Crisis," *Journal of Rural Cooperation* 18 (1990): 55–66.
19. Gideon M. Kressel, "Managerial Blunders in the Kibbutz Enterprise: The Problem of Accountability," *Journal of Rural Cooperation* 19 (1991): 91–107.
20. Stanley Maron, "Recent Developments in the Kibbutz: An Overview," *Journal of Rural Cooperation* 22 (1994): 10.
21. Ben-Rafael, *Crisis and Transformation*, 28–30.
22. Stanley Maron, "Social Changes in the Kibbutz 1983–1989," *Kibbutz Trends* 1 (1991): 39–43.
23. Near, *Kibbutz Movement*, vol. 2, 352.
24. Michal Palgi, "Attitudes toward Suggested Changes in the Kibbutz as Predicted by Perceived Economic and Ideological Crises," *Journal of Rural Cooperation* 22 (1994): 113–30; and Ben-Rafael, *Crisis and Transformation*, 155–77.
25. Menachem Topel, *The New Managers: The Kibbutz Changes Its Way* [in Hebrew] (Ramat Efal, Israel: Yad Tabenkin, 2005); Menachem Topel, "The Changing Composition of Kibbutz Elites," in Palgi and Reinharz, *One Hundred Years of Kibbutz Life*, 47–57.
26. Eliezer Ben-Rafael's *Crisis and Transformation* provides the best single-volume account of the origins of the kibbutz reforms of the 1990s. Additional insights into this period are provided by contributions to Uri Leviatan, Hugh Oliver, and Jack Quarter, eds., *Crisis in the Israeli Kibbutz* (Westport, CT: Praeger, 1998). Christopher Warhurst's case study, *Between Market, State and Kibbutz: The Management and Transformation of Socialist Industry* (London: Mansell, 1999), provides a vivid portrait of one kibbutz's effort to reconcile kibbutz ideals with market forces.
27. Shlomo Getz, "Implementation of Changes in the Kibbutz," *Journal of Rural Cooperation* 22 (1994): 79–92; and Shlomo Getz, "Winds of Change," in Leviatan, Quarter, and Oliver, *Crisis in the Israeli Kibbutz*, 13–25. Summaries and analyses

of responses to these surveys have been reported by Raymond Russell, Robert Hanneman, and Shlomo Getz, "Demographic and Environmental Influences on the Diffusion of Changes among Israeli Kibbutzim," *Research in the Sociology of Work* 16 (2006): 263–91; Raymond Russell, Robert Hanneman, and Shlomo Getz, *The Renewal of the Kibbutz: From Reform to Transformation* (New Brunswick, NJ: Rutgers University Press, 2013); and Zachary Sheaffer, Benson Honig, and Abraham Carmeli, "Ideology, Crisis Intensity, Organizational Demography, and Industrial Type as Determinants of Organizational Change in Kibbutzim," *Journal of Applied Behavioral Science* 46 (2010): 388–414.

28. E.g., Getz, "Implementation of Changes in the Kibbutz," 82–83, 89.
29. Amir Helman, "Privatization and the Kibbutz Experience," *Journal of Rural Cooperation* 22 (1994): 23.
30. Ibid.
31. Ibid.
32. Russell, Hanneman, and Getz, *Renewal of the Kibbutz*, 60–61.
33. Helman, "Privatization and the Kibbutz Experience," 24.
34. The earliest descriptions of the introduction of such changes in compensation in individual kibbutzim appear in Daniel Gavron, *The Kibbutz: Awakening from Utopia* (Lanham, MD: Rowman & Littlefield, 2000); and Jo-Ann Mort and Gary Brenner, *Our Hearts Invented a Place: Can Kibbutzim Survive in Today's Israel?* (Ithaca, NY: Cornell University Press, 2003). Quantitative analyses of the adoption of safety net budgets among larger numbers of kibbutzim appear in Ran Abramitzky, "The Limits of Equality: Insights from the Israeli Kibbutz," *Quarterly Journal of Economics* 123 (2008): 1111–59; and Raymond Russell, Robert Hanneman, and Shlomo Getz, "Antecedents and Consequences of the Adoption of Market-Based Compensation by Israeli Kibbutzim," *Advances in the Economic Analysis of Participatory and Labor-Managed Firms* 11 (2010): 233–54; and Russell, Hanneman, and Getz, *Renewal of the Kibbutz*, 82–95, 157–66.
35. Manor, "'Renewed' Kibbutz," 43.
36. Russell, Hanneman, and Getz, *Renewal of the Kibbutz*, 110.
37. Aryei Fishman, *Judaism and Modernization on the Religious Kibbutz* (Cambridge: Cambridge University Press, 1992), 69–80; Yossi Katz, *The Religious Kibbutz Movement in the Land of Israel* (Jerusalem: Hebrew University Magnes Press; Ramat-Gan, Israel: Bar-Ilan University Press, 2003), 16–17, 30, 52, 58–59.
38. Russell, Hanneman, and Getz, *Renewal of the Kibbutz*, 112–13.
39. Michael Livni, "Ecology, Eco-Zionism, and the Kibbutz," in *One Hundred Years of Kibbutz Life: A Century of Crises and Reinvention*, ed. Michal Palgi and Shulamit Reinharz (New Brunswick, NJ: Transaction Books, 2011), 303–13.
40. Yuval Dror, "The New Communal Groups in Israel: Urban Kibbutzim and Groups of Youth Movement Graduates," in Palgi and Reinharz, *One Hundred Years of Kibbutz Life*, 316.
41. Ibid., 318.
42. Ibid., 319.

43. James Horrox, *Living a Revolution: Anarchism in the Kibbutz Movement* (Edinburgh, UK: AK Press, 2009), 104.

44. Ibid.

45. Ibid., 105.

46. Zeev Greenberg, "Kibbutz Neighborhoods and New Communities: The Development of a Sense of Belonging among the Residents of New Community Neighborhoods on Kibbutzim," in Palgi and Reinharz, *One Hundred Years of Kibbutz Life*, 271–87; Russell, Hanneman, and Getz, *Renewal of the Kibbutz*, 120, 122.

47. Ben-Rafael and Topel, "Redefining the Kibbutz," 249–58.

5

The Women's Movement

Mobilization and the State

PATRICIA J. WOODS

Civil society, that political debate, mobilization, and discussion allowed without interference from or attempts at organization by the state,[1] is one of the major hallmarks of democratic regimes. The degree to which civil society is allowed by a regime is a fairly standard measure of democratization.[2] While Israel, like many democracies, has issues with its democratic performance in some areas—including gender—it allows a remarkably high degree of civil society for all citizen populations. This chapter examines the Israeli women's movement as a model for organizing social and political mobilization and discourse outside the state.

Israel has long been perceived as a model of egalitarianism, as exemplified in the kibbutz movement and the election of women such as Golda Meir and, more recently, Tzipi Livni, Stav Shaffir, and Ayelet Shaked to prominent positions. However, in reality, women have struggled to achieve equality within the kibbutz system, the military, politics, and society in general. None of these came as easily as the national narrative would suggest. The Israeli women's movement has taken several iterations from the prestate pioneering era, characterized by a focus on women's labor and right to live independently from family, religion, and other external sources of authority; the early-state era, characterized by state-sponsored women's organizations; and the second-wave (post-1970) era, characterized by a plethora of independent grassroots and bureaucratized nongovernmental organizations working both together and apart to achieve gender equality across ethnic, religious, and other lines of identification. The second-wave movement is part of a broad array of social movements in Israel, many of which actively divide labor in the context of scarce resources, sharing the issues they see as in need of work. Like other movements in Israel (civil rights, labor, religious pluralism, etc.), they have moved away from the U.S. civil rights model of mass mobilization as the primary means to sway legislators, justices, and administrators alike. They have turned instead to a model based assiduously on *smaller* numbers of volunteers and recruits, a *mentoring process* over significant stretches of time, and the hope that these mentees will remain active volunteers over decades. To these basic traits of civil society activism, the Israeli women's movement adds volunteerism.

The Israeli women's movement is a small social movement that has been highly engaged in and informed by debates that come from the academic world. This is true of domestic and international scholarship, particularly relating to feminist theory, ethnicity, and Palestinian rights. Awareness of academic theories in these areas is to be found among leaders and volunteers who come from educated, middle- and upper-middle-class sectors of society as well as those from Israel's working classes. The movement has chosen a general model of mobilization self-consciously described in the early 1990s as based on what Fatima Mernissi, a Moroccan sociologist and feminist theorist, calls "doing daily battle."[3] Rather than aiming at legitimation by and eventually joining with the state to achieve its goals, when the movement has faced internal tensions, particularly relating to ethnicity and power among Ashkenazi,[4] Mizrachi,[5] and Palestinian[6] women, it has turned to feminist theory to choose what it sees as appropriate mobilization strategies.

In my fieldwork within the women's movement (1993–94, 1995, 1997, 2000, 2006, 2009, and 2010), I observed movement leaders cite the works of feminist scholars such as Fatima Mernissi on doing daily battle to encourage and mobilize discouraged members in the context of daily grassroots mobilization. Among an educated leadership and often an educated volunteer membership, other works commonly discussed in the 1990s included those by bell hooks, Judith Butler, Robin Morgan, Nancy Hartsock, Sandra Harding, Jocelyne Cesari, and Patricia J. Williams. The leadership clearly read many feminist works internationally and frequently took Middle Eastern feminist examples into account in their own work and discussions with their members. The Algerian Revolution was a particular favorite for edification as a countermodel for feminist engagement. Women there were revered for being active combatants during the revolution; however, they were pushed out of formal politics in the aftermath of the revolution.[7] Mernissi's work on Morocco and works by regional feminists such as Bouthaina Shaaban on Syria, Huda Shaarawi and Nawal el-Saadawi on Egypt, and others were very much a part of daily discourse in the early 1990s.[8] In no small part as a result of these examples highlighted in feminist scholarship and feminist theory, the Israeli women's movement made the concerted decision *not* to join the state in order to avoid appropriation of its agenda, talents, and labor hours. It has, instead, focused on "doing daily battle" against those structures still in place that it has seen as hindering women's political and social freedoms.

In addition to drawing on international and particularly regional examples, the second wave of the Israeli women's movement (1970 to present) learned the lessons of the first wave of the Israeli women's movement (approximately 1910 through the 1950s) in its choice largely to avoid the state. Yael Yishai described the early state's demand that the movement choose the "flag" over the "banner"; that is, she argued, the state demanded that the movement put the goals of the state above those of the movement in order to become part of the former.[9] According to Yishai, the first wave of the Israeli women's movement largely fell prey to this Archimedean choice. In response, the second wave has assiduously chosen the banner and relative obscurity rather than the fanfare and backing of the state to achieve its goals.

This chapter addresses this general model of mobilization of "doing daily battle," which eschews the state, focusing on small member numbers rather than stridently entering the public world. It has translated into a form of microlevel mobilization in which volunteers work with local politicians, police, judges, and rabbis in a way that is neither directed by the state nor subject to the positive and negative benefits of publicity (notoriety and scrutiny, respectively). I first address the relationship between this mobilization strategy and academic theories informing the movement. Then the chapter turns to the specific issue of tensions within the movement relating to ethnic relations among Ashkenazi, Mizrachi, and Palestinian women and the extent to which that has been navigated through recourse to academic feminist theories.

The Israeli Women's Movement in National Context

The Israeli women's movement is, I have argued, an expressly *Israeli* movement.[10] That is, in 2000, the year of the first national survey of women's movement volunteers, most of the movement's volunteers were born in Israel (65.8 percent, compared with 64.4 percent of the wider Israeli population for the same year) with Hebrew as their first language (59.5 percent).[11] Languages reported as maternal language included Hebrew (59.5 percent), English (13 percent), Russian (9.5 percent), Arabic (7 percent), German (4 percent), French (1.5 percent), Polish (1.5 percent), Spanish (1.5 percent), "Algerian" (0.5 percent), and "Moroccan" (0.5 percent).[12] It is an educated movement (86 percent reporting Israel as their primary country of education), with 9 percent of volunteers holding a Ph.D. (of those, 44 percent identify Hebrew as their maternal language) and at least 10 percent of the volunteer population being lawyers (0.03 percent of the wider population were lawyers that year).[13] Its volunteers are typically working women, most coming from modest beginnings (32 percent lower-middle income and 21 percent middle income). The volunteer base is upwardly mobile, with 53.8 percent having monthly incomes between 10,000–20,000 shekels (approximately \$2,500–\$5,000; the national average monthly income that year was 6,306 shekels, or approximately \$1,576, and women's national monthly average was 4,661 shekels, or approximately \$1,165). Twenty percent of volunteers in 2000 had monthly incomes of 5,000–10,000 shekels (approximately \$1,250–\$2,500); and 0.5 percent had monthly incomes of 2,800–5,000 shekels (\$700–\$1,250).[14]

The suggestion that Israel has not only a thriving but a remarkable civil society and a notably robust set of left-wing social movements is not to understate the host of issues that Israel faces in its efforts to maintain a democratic regime in the context of military conflict and ethnic divisions. These include tensions between substantive and electoral democracy, that is to say, voting rights versus substantive equal participation in political institutions and discourse at multiple levels;[15] the balance between being a Jewish and a democratic state;[16] and the choice of whether to be an ethnic democracy,[17] a liberal or republican democracy,[18] or a democracy with citizenship regimes that are fundamentally different from membership in the national community.[19] Despite these issues, Israel can boast a truly remarkable swath of leftist, often grassroots social movements that reflect a vibrant civil society.

Scholars have noted the explosion of civil society that emerged in the years after the 1967 war, replacing the single-coalition-dominant, if not single-party-dominant, regime that had been in place since the establishment of the state in 1948.[20] That social democratic regime fostered strongly hegemonic (top-down, dominating) norms of consensus within the Israeli society and state,[21] which limited the ability or willingness of Israeli citizens to speak out against state policies in many areas. Political parties remained citizens' main avenue of communication with the state until the late 1960s,[22] when an explosion of civil society emerged, reflecting a significant shift in the structure of Israeli politics and society. Social movements on both the right and the left began making demands on the state and battling with one another in the sea of public opinion.

One of the movements that emerged at this time was the second wave of the Israeli women's movement. It was established in 1971 by four women in Haifa, who began a regular feminist discussion group. One of these was the American-born Marcia Freedman, who was soon to become a member of the Knesset. Her sister was another, and the remaining two were Israeli-born "Haifa-ites," both relatives of first-wave Israeli feminist Ada Maimon, with family ties in the Haifa community that predated the establishment of the state. Women's groups emerged quickly in Tel Aviv, Jerusalem, and then elsewhere. By 1977, the Haifa group had established Israel's first battered-women's shelter, and by 1983, there were shelters in Tel Aviv, Herzliya, Jerusalem, and Ashdod. They had for some time been working with local municipalities and police departments to get existing laws enforced, and they achieved changes in national laws regarding violence against women. Marcia Freedman was elected to the Knesset in 1973 and became a vocal advocate for women's rights. The extent to which she was controversial suggests that women's equality was not broadly supported, but it also indicates that her demands received a wide hearing (if only to be rejected by many people).

By the late 1980s, the Haifa group took the name Isha l'Isha (woman to woman). The Haifa Feminist Coalition was established to act as the umbrella organization connecting Isha l'Isha, the Haifa Battered Women's Shelter, and the Haifa Rape Crisis Center, although these organizations were located in different buildings. By the late 1990s, Isha l'Isha and the Rape Crisis Hotline were located in the same building under the auspices of the Haifa Feminist Center. At the same time, Isha l'Isha broke into five different organizations, supporting separate agenda-setting initiatives on the part of women of different ethnicities as well as sexual orientations. All of these organizations are housed in the same Haifa Feminist Center in downtown Haifa.

This first center of second-wave Israeli feminism was followed by equally vibrant sets of organizations in Jerusalem and Tel Aviv; notably, the Israel Women's Network (IWN) in Jerusalem became the umbrella organization to which many smaller, regional organizations turned for larger coalition projects. The IWN became the center of political activism aimed at the national government. By 1997, there were nearly two hundred women's organizations across the country, with memberships ranging from four to several hundred. Most of these engaged in very focused grassroots work either with local populations or with municipal governments, police, rabbinical authorities, and the like. This microlevel approach to political mobilization became, I argue, the hallmark of Israeli women's movement activism. Organizations and individual activists worked with local officials, police officers, and the like to raise awareness of existing laws, to get existing laws enforced, to develop strategies for changing laws at the national level, and to develop strategies to address other, larger gender issues, such as the problem of *agunot* ("chained" women) in Israel's divorce law. They also engaged in widespread "consciousness raising" at the local level with organized courses, workshops, and speaker series aimed at all ethnic groups within Israeli society. Rather than gaining leverage on these issues through mass mobilization or mass demonstrations, women's organizations across the country adopted a microlevel approach, making changes at the most minute local level. These changes have transformed Israeli society on gender issues in the past forty years.

Why should we care about a small, relatively marginalized social movement that is often incorrectly seen as a foreign import, reflecting the Americanization of Israel? With perhaps two thousand activists in the late 1990s, perhaps a few thousand today, what does a small movement with little direct social support for its agenda have to tell us about the ostensible "death of the left" in Israel? I suggest that the Israeli women's movement is but one of several examples of not only the continuing vibrant nature of leftist social movements in Israel but also the very remarkable nature of their ongoing social mobilization, which (if we care about civil society) is nothing short of astounding at both the empirical and the normative levels. It is not an overstatement to say that this particular form of grassroots social mobilization in Israel has become a model for social mobilization around the world. One of the most concrete examples of that is Women in Black, which was established during the First Intifada as a silent, nonviolent protest to call the Israeli occupation of the occupied territories an "occupation" out loud in the public square. The women who volunteered to stand at the busiest intersections of all the country's major cities every Friday at rush hour, as people made their way home for Shabbat, did so year after year, from 1987 to 1993, until the Intifada was over. Indeed, some continued to protest the occupation long after. Today, there are Women in Black chapters in seventeen different countries on every continent except Antarctica, with an international website as an umbrella for all of these independent organizations. In 2001, Women in Black received the Millennium Peace Prize for Women from the United Nations Development Fund for Women for providing a model of grassroots, silent, nonviolent protest for movements around the world. It is not an exaggeration, then, to say that the Israeli women's movement has provided significant new models of social mobilization that have had a global impact.

This and other forms of mobilization within the women's movement reflect an extraordinary dedication on the part of individual women, sometimes over the course of decades, usually on a purely voluntary basis or for minimal pay. Not only that but despite the fact that their mobilization has not usually hit the national media, to say nothing of the international media, the women's movement has achieved significant structural changes at the level of state and international organizations, changes that we would all recognize as falling within the sphere of "high politics."[23] These include new national laws, particularly relating to violence against women and to women in the labor market, an entire new family court system established in 1995 (the Shalom Court), and UN Resolution 1325, which calls for the equal representation of women and gender issues in major international conflict areas, including the Arab-Israeli conflict.

At the grassroots level, the women's movement has established battered-women's shelters in every major city across Israel. Its rape crisis hotlines have been run since 1987 and, since 1998, organized into a national hotline. This hotline has been managed in five languages, twenty-four hours a day, seven days a week, twelve months a year, decade after decade, in some locations since 1987. The Association for Rape Crisis Centers in Israel reports eight hundred volunteers and sixty professionals working the hotlines in nine centers across the country. Volunteer women do most of this work, usually without pay and often for a decade or more at a time, night and day. They get up in the morning, go out the door, and answer the phones at the hotline offices; other women spend the entire night doing the same thing. This is a level of volunteerism that rivals even major U.S. rights organizations, such as the ACLU and NOW, which have become more bureaucratic over time. It is the degree of commitment to volunteerism at the grassroots level that is one of Israel's hallmark contributions to our available models of how to do social mobilization. The number of volunteers is, indeed, a tiny fraction of the population of the country, although it may be a few thousand women around the country today. Nonetheless, while the total is small, the degree of daily ongoing grassroots activism is extraordinary.

Some women's movement organizations in Israel are more bureaucratic, like social movements that become so well bureaucratized that they look more like interest groups. And there is a creative, if not always relaxed, tension between the two models of organization in Israel. There is also a division of labor between the bureaucratic and the grassroots models. But what all of these organizations share, whether they are bureaucratic, grassroots, or a combination, is an unwillingness to be co-opted into the political establishment. While women's movement organizations may support specific candidates, and the Israel Women's Network in Jerusalem has a whole office and program aimed at teaching women how to run for office, the movement as a whole does not typically field candidates to state office. I believe this insistence on not joining the state and, thereby, not gaining the prestige that would come with that has been critical to the women's movement's successes. It also contributes to the movement's relatively unknown quality. We do not hear about its successes in part because it does not have politicians formally representing it in the Knesset. Even before Yael Yishai wrote *Between the Flag and the Banner* in 1997, bringing our attention to the Archimedean choice that women had been given by the Zionist movement and the early state in Israel, second-wave activists were choosing a new strategy: doing their work quietly, away from the limelight, away from prestige, but also away from the efforts of political parties and state offices to appropriate their daily creative energies and work hours for the agendas of the state or the nationalist movement.

The women's movement has chosen relative obscurity in service of being able to put its daily work hours toward what Yishai calls "the Banner," that is, those issues they see as most critical to the slow but steady achievement of women's rights in Israel. They have chosen "doing daily battle," as Mernissi calls it, as their model of organizing rather than joining institutions that would seek to do battle for them—but in the process turn their agendas, if history is any indicator, from women's rights to issues ostensibly more significant to the nation-state.

Mernissi used the phrase "doing daily battle" to refer to Moroccan women's efforts in the 1980s to get through the day on a daily basis, to feed their children on maybe sixteen cents per hour for an eight- to ten-hour shift of weaving carpets, and perhaps to increase their wages and achieve a higher degree of human dignity in the process. They engaged, she argued, in a form of *sumud*, daily holding on or tenacity, in the face of deeply problematic structural conditions. These conditions included the new reality already in the 1980s, when Mernissi wrote *Doing Daily Battle*, that everyone had to work to feed the family and a disparity in male and female views of their own roles in the family, access to contraception, and access to education. For Mernissi, the primary struggle for women in 1980s Morocco, though, was economic: the basic struggle to survive and feed one's family. Women in the Israeli women's movement are also engaging in a form of *sumud*, or doing daily battle, albeit in a more developed context. Quietly, without fanfare or limelight, they are choosing to work on those issues they see at an organizational level as most needed in the demographic that they are serving. Some volunteers I have worked with since the early 1990s have been doing this work for three and four decades without stop. They have shifted important structural conditions for women (e.g., laws regarding rape, violence against women, labor, and some issues relating to personal status), and they have had some success in changing public opinion on critical issues, such as violence against women, although the word "feminist" remains a very dirty word in some circles in Israel as elsewhere.

Historical Lessons from the First Wave

Yael Yishai noted that the Israeli women's movement has been faced with a choice from the prestate era and throughout the history of the state: the flag or the banner—that is, to choose between the needs of the nation and the needs of women.[24] The two choices, historically, were presented to women's movement organizations and leaders as opposed to each other. Women's needs, it was suggested, would be achieved after the more pressing needs of the nation and the nation-state had been met.

Women who arrived in the pioneering years typically came with highly cultivated socialist sensibilities, in which equality between men and women as builders of the state-to-be was understood to be a given.[25] Feminist women who arrived in those years and after came with strong norms of gender equality and, indeed, with far greater degrees of individual freedom than the middle- and upper-class compatriots they had left behind in Europe.[26] This included living as independent, individual women without need for the sanction of family, particularly male family members, to engage in everyday actions or major life decisions. Nonetheless, given these women's highly tuned expectations of absolute equality, they found that conditions in pioneering Palestine did not meet their goals. Much has been written, for example, of women's marginalization within the kibbutz system, where women were typically relegated to kitchen, child care, and other "traditional" women's work.[27] It is not clear whether men at the time perceived this work to be a matter of "relegating" women, but women perceived it that way. Indeed, women at the time seem to have perceived child care, child rearing, and traditional work around care of home and family to have reached such a low level of social stature and respect that many women within the kibbutz system were adamantly opposed to taking on the full-time care of their own children.[28] They saw it as demeaning to women and as socially unvalued labor. While some men expressed horror at children being unattended by their own mothers and highlighted the lofty role that kitchen work and mothering held in their eyes, women noted the extent to which, in their view, men disdained their abilities as well as traditional women's work related to home and family.

Feeling marginalized within the kibbutz system, Ada Maimon and others established the Women's Worker's Union in 1911. At the same time, a short-lived women's kibbutz was established in Kinneret to respond to the frustration of women who were refused work as farm laborers, both inside and outside the kibbutz system. Outside the kibbutz, farmers appear to have objected to women who wanted to live and work independently of any family ties; inside the kibbutz, they argued that women do not produce as much as men in certain types of labor and thus handicap the viability of the kibbutz. Kinneret provided agricultural training for women and a farm on which they could live and practice their trade. It was not generally supported by the wider Zionist movement and lasted only six years; however, it did have an impact on the development of "women's branches" within the agricultural sector. It was an experiment designed to demonstrate women's capabilities to do just the work that men argued would needlessly handicap the kibbutz, since women were physically not as strong as men. The argument that women should not do certain labor because they would not produce the same results in the same time and would therefore harm the kibbutz—a capitalist efficiency argument—appears to have been shocking to the socialist sensibilities of these women. Deborah Bernstein has argued that the economic factors driving decision making on who would engage in what work on the kibbutz were, ironically, the result of the labor movement's sense that it had to prove its viability in the context of a larger capitalist stage.[29]

The women's workers' movement itself experienced marginalization within both the Zionist movement and its major institutional organ within prestate Palestine, the Histadrut. At the Histadrut's first convention in 1920, the Women's Workers' Union did not run a party list, since it did not see itself as a party. When only four women were elected to offices in the Histadrut, Maimon and the Women's Worker's Council (WWC) threatened to run their own party list in the next election if women were not represented on the Histadrut council. The Histadrut leadership conceded and created something close to a quota system for women representatives.

The WWC within the Histadrut was founded in 1921. In the years before the establishment of the state, the Histadrut leadership, and particularly David Ben Gurion, were critical of its potentially separatist tendencies. In addition, they also may have used the WWC as an excuse to suggest that women's labor issues were now the problem of the WWC and not the wider organization. In short, the leadership of the Histadrut directly called into question the loyalty of women, who were categorized as either "radicals" or "loyalists,"[30] in keeping with Yishai's analysis of the pressing demand that the women's movement choose between loyalty to party/state/nation or to the platform of women's equality, which was considered a special interest.

The first wave of the women's movement continued to work, in small numbers and tirelessly, in the face of these conditions throughout the British Mandate and into the 1950s. The first Israeli Knesset could boast eleven women members. By 1959, that number declined to nine. Not until 1992 did the Knesset see eleven women members again. This corresponded with a general decline in the first wave of the women's movement, which dissipated a great deal in the 1950s. While specific Knesset members brought bills to the Knesset regarding gender issues in the 1950s and 1960s, they were largely unsuccessful. The issue of gender at the political level was largely null during these years. During this period, Golda Meir made great symbolic strides for women in Israel as one of the first woman prime ministers in the world. She was arguably the first woman prime minister in a Western-modeled state, Indira Gandhi in India and Sirimavo Bandaranaike in Sri Lanka serving as prime ministers before Meir in Israel. We now have a long list of women prime ministers on most continents around the world. Meir, more than only for Israel, then, was an early role model for women around the world. Meir was both revered and controversial in the women's movement in Israel, however, as she preferred the flag, when it came to politics, rather than the banner.[31]

As with the demand that women choose between the flag and the banner in Israel, Mernissi argues that by bringing in foreign ideas of women's empowerment, a feminist is seen as a traitor to the nationalist cause. That nationalist formulation implies that the normative view of the nation is somehow not the equal purview of women.

The women's movement did not emerge again until the second wave, which began in 1970. The second wave, with its emphasis on grassroots and other work that eschews participation in the state, saw another notable shift, as the number of women Knesset members passed the crucial number of eleven that had been seen in the first Knesset. By the eighteenth Knesset, Israel could boast twenty-four women members of the Knesset.

It is within this historical context that the second wave of the Israeli women's movement has chosen to engage the state, yes, but not to join it. It has engaged in a division of labor between more bureaucratized organizations, which deal directly with social and state elites, and more grassroots organizations, which typically keep their daily volunteer labors in the trenches of local society and local municipalities where national elites rarely go.

Ethnic Politics within the Israeli Women's Movement: Women's Common Standpoint or Specificity/Identity-as-Difference?

While the Israeli women's movement has succeeded in making major changes to the political and social fabric of the country through the microlevel mobilization mentioned earlier, it has not been without its own internal dilemmas, particularly relating to ethnic relations within the movement. Movement leaders and members responded to some of these problems by explicitly turning to feminist theory, leading to a substantive and theoretical debate.

During the 1980s, the movement was strongly influenced by feminist standpoint theory and theories of "sisterhood is global."[32] These emphasized what women share, highlighting a common standpoint in which all women, regardless of political and ethnic differences, should be united in the struggle against male domination in society and state. By the late 1990s, the movement turned strongly to political mobilization based on an "identity-as-difference" strand of feminist theory,[33] in which political and ethnic divides became the rallying points for organizational structures as well as political action. The result was a fracturing of the movement that culminated in more than a decade of difficulty in maintaining coalition work across ethnic and other lines of differentiation.[34]

The move from feminist standpoint and sisterhood-is-global in the 1980s to identity-as-difference by the end of the 1990s corresponds, temporally, with trends in feminist theory more broadly. In the 1970s and 1980s, feminist theory tended to emphasize women's common oppression within society and politics as well as in more specific arenas such as business, religion, and scientific inquiry.[35] Often referred to as expressing "identity politics," that is, the similar identity that women share as women, these works cited patriarchy as the common source of an ongoing process of marginalizing women. For them, it was patriarchy that made it difficult for individual women to break barriers in education, economic independence, and ostensibly private social institutions such as marriage. This type of identity politics centered on what women share as women and how they differ from men. Feminist standpoint theory was offered in the early 1980s as highlighting a special insight into patriarchal power relations. Recognition of this common women's insight, which emerged from the common experience of being subject to patriarchal power in its various permutations, was presented as marking a way out of the conundrum of women's marginalized status. For example, Nancy Hartsock argued that recognizing what women held in common would provide a basis for mobilizing women from the grassroots to the family to the highest levels of the political system.[36]

In the 1980s, women's organizations in Israel, as in the United States, began to seek out diverse memberships along ethnic and other lines, in part on the basis of the logic of standpoint theory. If women shared a common insight on patriarchal power relations, then it stood to reason that mobilizing more women across various other lines of identification would help feminist goals. According to that logic, one of those goals should be to encourage a "sisterhood-is-global" ethic within and across women's movements around the world.[37] Indeed, by the mid- to late 1980s, seeking out Arab women members within Israel and coalitions between Israeli and Palestinian Arab women in the occupied territories became a high priority in Israel.[38] New members brought their own interests and ideas. And by the early 1990s, some members were arguing for a shift in focus to attention to ethnic politics, differentiation, and varying agenda-setting needs and interests of the different communities *within* the movement. These ideas coalesced into arguments for a politics of identity-as-difference, which stood in competition with the logic of feminist standpoint. Identity-as-difference emphasized the different needs, agenda-setting priorities, and interests of the subcommunities within the movement. As movement leaders read these theories and taught or advocated them to their memberships, they became the foundation for organizing political activities within organizations and across the movement.

A new theoretical trend that emphasized a second type of identity politics had clearly emerged by the 1990s, corresponding to the timing of this new empirical challenge in the Israeli women's movement. This was characterized by a focus on personal (individual-level) identity and differences among women. Women of color, lesbians, women from working-class backgrounds, and others began to argue that the "feminist standpoint" offered in the 1980s provided a particularly white, middle- or even upper-middle-class account of women's lives in society and politics.[39] These postmodern accounts suggested that general discussions of "women" as a larger category ran the risk of essentializing women; that is, they criticized what they saw as the positing of women as a reified *it*, seeing all women as the same, where the model of a woman was based on a wealthy, white notion of womanness. Scholars such as Shane Phelan emphasized differing relational moments through which an individual woman's identity varies by context.[40] They saw the account of white, elite women as not only limited in scope but also inaccurate. Like the Arab and Mizrachi (Middle Eastern–descended Jewish) women in the Israeli women's movement, who claimed to be marginalized personally and with regard to their agendas, this body of theoretical work emphasized a politics of identity-as-difference. Indeed, since the fracturing of the women's movement along these lines in the late 1990s, women's movement members have published significant academic works on Mizrachi women and other aspects of ethnic identity within the Israeli women's movement.[41] By the early 1990s, key movement leaders became explicit advocates of theories that emphasized identity-as-difference, which they sought to use as a basis for a new form of political organization and mobilization.

As a microcosm of society, the Israeli women's movement provides a fascinating social scientific "case" through which to view the state and society. With the ever-present backdrop of the Arab-Israeli conflict, Israeli national identity, as fostered by the state, has focused on a militarized and very specific form of "masculinized" identity.[42] While the State of Israel has sought to put itself forth as a singular, unified society, at least among the Jewish population, that identity has been highly contested within the Israeli women's movement. In this way, the women's movement has been similar to other sectors of Israeli society, in which the image of a unified nation has been a subject of conflict and dissent.[43]

The women's community that was most comfortable with the feminist standpoint approach, with its emphasis on women's commonality, was Ashkenazi (European-descended) Jewish women. By contrast, Palestinian (Israeli citizens) and Mizrachi women argued strongly for emphasizing difference in the formulation of the movement's specific mobilization strategies. This difference in approach reflected in some ways the context of the Israeli national image fostered by the state. That is, over time, some dominant Ashkenazi elites had cultivated a unitary "Israeli" identity based on ties to European culture, Western socialist or liberal values, and common resistance to surrounding Arab states and Palestinian resistance organizations. This unified picture of national identity also included the image of a physically strong "new Jew,"[44] a masculinized Israeli citizen performing regular military service and carrying *his* weapons on public buses on *his* way to serve the nation with *his* national service of reserve duty. The image of the ideal national citizen performing *his* communal duty included scant, if any, recognition of women in military service, nor certainly the possibility of a feminized (or multiplicity of feminized) options available to be an ideal national citizen. In the context of this particular emphasis on national community, which erased women to a great extent and Arabs to an even greater extent and which viewed Mizrachi Jewish populations with suspicion, the communally oriented notion of women's common standpoint strained the sensibilities of women from marginalized groups within Israeli society. They sought attention to their specific identities, agendas, and needs within what they saw as a powerfully communal, militarized, and Ashkenazied context. Women argued that the women's movement in particular should be free of such hierarchical and community-specific power dynamics.

These tensions of identity politics in the Israeli women's movement reflect quite strongly Joel Migdal's suggestion that the values and norms of state and society are not consensus driven but, rather, *contested*.[45] The

Israeli state, as with most states, has endeavored to construct an image of national unity suggesting a particular national identity to structure both state and society. This process is predicted by Migdal's approach.[46] The construction of this image has been documented from the individual level to the societal level. For example, it works to cultivate a homogenized national identity that would blur differences among the ethnically varied Jewish populations that immigrated to Israel, initially under the rubric of Labor Zionism.[47] State agencies also encourage Jewish reproduction through awards to mothers who would have ten or more children,[48] and secular and religious leaders have united to support specific policies regarding in-vitro fertilization in the context of the same "demographics war."[49] This construction of the national image has also included a policy of ethnically stratified military service, in which most Arabs are not allowed to participate in or gain the benefits of this national service,[50] as well as the efforts of certain state agencies and officials to control minority religious institutions.[51] Most of the women I have interviewed rejected almost all these constructions of "Israeliness" by the state. However, some aspects of it were challenged more overtly than others. For example, there was much agreement in defining Jewish "dominance" in the context of the Arab-Israeli conflict, but Ashkenazi-Mizrachi questions of "dominance" raised significant ire and dissent. Nonetheless, the identity and difference debates within the Israeli women's movement reflected a real contest over many dimensions of "Israeliness" as well as what should count as "feminist"—and perhaps "Israeli feminist-ness"—in this context of ongoing civil and national warfare.

As the First Intifada began in 1987, the Israeli women's movement was mobilized on the logic of feminist standpoint theory: women must unite and mobilize together against their often violent male compatriots to overcome patriarchy in society and politics. Through at least 1993 and 1994, international funding agencies such as the Ford Foundation tended to emphasize projects that united women across ethnic lines, particularly in the context of Israel and Palestinians. This foundational theory had a profound impact on the women's movement in Israel, which engaged in a massive effort to unite women across Arab and Jewish lines both within Israel and across the Green Line, extending into the occupied territories.[52] In 1998, two years before the beginning of the Second Intifada, the foundational theory underlying women's mobilization changed to one based on what Phelan has called a second politics of identity, which emphasizes difference.[53] This type of identity politics was reinforced by changes in funding, which restructured women's organizations themselves, particularly creating new organizations along ethnic lines. These changes occurred as the result of specific women's movement leaders who championed this theoretical logic within those funding agencies. In contrast to the efforts of the late 1980s and early 1990s, the women's movement since 1998 has seen a logic of ethnic separation. By the middle of the first decade of the twenty-first century, collaboration among Jewish and Arab organizations that had previously engaged in a great deal of work together had nearly ceased. Organizations that were ostensibly mixed ethnically tended to work separately rather than collaborating across ethnic lines, with some organizations more successful than others at overcoming these tensions. Across the women's movement as a whole, however, separation along ethnic lines became the most common model for structuring organizations and for grassroots types of political mobilization. (As mentioned, this latter model is the predominant form of political mobilization for the movement.) National-level political mobilization, which reflects a smaller part of everyday women's movement activities across the country, saw coalition work across ethnic lines but significantly less than in the earlier period, in which theories of feminist standpoint and sisterhood-is-global had predominated. This ethnic separation within the Israeli women's movement has extended beyond Arab-Israeli lines to include Ashkenazi, Mizrachi, Ethiopian, Russian, and Arab groups, as well as groups based on other identifiers, such as lesbian and Jewish Orthodox organizations. This story of ethnic politics and lines of difference within the Israeli women's movement reflects, in some ways, a microcosm of fissures that remain across Israeli society and politics more broadly to the present.[54] Since 2008, efforts to reinvigorate ethnic coalition work across the movement have increased, with great success in some organizations.

Conclusions

One reason the Israeli women's movement is not always visible is that it has been characterized by a political mobilization strategy that can most aptly be described as microlevel mobilization, that is, mobilization happening at the one-on-one, local, and ground levels of state offices and social communities. Organizations across the country have achieved change through microlevel interactions with municipal leaders and offices, police, rabbinical authorities, and the like. While larger, bureaucratized organizations exist and engage in vibrant and direct work with the national government, the greatest preponderance of work by organizations across the country is centered on this level—daily work or "doing daily battle," as Mernissi described it in another context. This mobilization strategy was an overt choice on the part of some women's movement leaders, who had learned the lesson of the first wave of the Israeli women's movement not to allow themselves to be co-opted into the state. While the state might offer more funding, publicity, and institutional backing, it had also demonstrated a willingness and ability to override women's movement agendas regarding gender in service of ostensibly more important concerns. The second wave of the Israeli women's movement has explicitly drawn on feminist theories such as Mernissi's "doing daily battle," Yishai's *Flag and Banner*, and the wider international debate between feminist standpoint theory and specificity and difference in addressing questions of how to prioritize funding, how to structure its organizations, as well as in its choice of mobilization strategies in a multifaceted, multiethnic movement. The movement, then, offers a fertile site of intersection between theory and practice as well as interesting and effective models for social and political mobilization that may be useful elsewhere in the world.

NOTES

I would like to thank Office of the Provost, University of Florida, for a research fellowship contributing to the research for this chapter; the insightful comments of the editor of this volume and the press; and my research assistant, Joshua Vadeboncoeur, of the Junior Fellows Program, Department of Political Science, University of Florida.

1. Although in the original usage of the term in European Enlightenment philosophy and among early twentieth-century thinkers such as Antonio Gramsci, civil society was seen as the social groundwork on which elites (and only possibly counterelites) built their political regimes (Robert W. Cox, "Civil Society at the Turn of the Millennium: Prospects for an Alternative World Order," *Review of International Studies* 25 [1999]: 3–28), contemporary political scientists use the term to mean, roughly, "independent social activism" (Marcia A. Weigle and Jim Butterfield, "Civil Society in Reforming Communist Regimes: The Logic of

Emergence," *Comparative Politics* 25 [1992]: 1–23), often assuming precisely mobilization among counterelites. Only recently have comparative political scientists reminded us of the extent to which civil society may still be elite driven or elite dominated; see Scott Radnitz, *Weapons of the Wealthy: Predatory Regimes and Elite-Led Protests in Central Asia* (Ithaca, NY: Cornell University Press, 2012). The term is widely used in comparative politics and often includes a dimension of public discourse in addition to social or political activism per se.

2. Michael Bernhard and Ekrem Karakoç, "Civil Society and the Legacies of Dictatorship," *World Politics* 59 (2007): 539–67.
3. Fatima Mernissi, *Doing Daily Battle: Interviews with Moroccan Women*, trans. Mary Jo Lakeland (New Brunswick, NJ: Rutgers University Press, 1989).
4. *Ashkenazi* refers to Jews descended from the Christian parts of Europe (to be distinguished from Jews descended from European parts of the former Ottoman Empire).
5. As used in Israel, the term *Mizrachi* refers to Jews descended from the Middle East, Africa, or Asia. It is often widely used as an umbrella term that includes Jews of the former Ottoman Empire and Sephardi Jews, those populations that trace their descent from Muslim Spain.
6. These debates within the women's movement have been limited to Palestinian women who are citizens of Israel. When Palestinian women from the occupied territories, and later the Palestinian Authority, are addressed in the movement, it has been done in separate discussions and typically among women who mobilize specifically about the Arab-Israeli conflict. Inasmuch as ethnic tensions are discussed later in this chapter, these are debates limited to questions of relations among women within the women's movement who are all citizens of Israel. As a whole, the women's movement has chosen *not* to be mobilized on the Arab-Israeli conflict, although some specific organizations such as Women in Black are exceptions to that trend. The choice not to mobilize or have a specific stance on the Arab-Israeli conflict is one taken by most organizations as more conducive to their work on gender and as opening the door for more women to participate in their gender work.
7. Marina Lazreg, *The Eloquence of Silence* (London: Routledge, 1994); Barbara Gates, "The Political Roles of Islamic Women: A Study of Two Revolutions—Algeria and Iran" (Ph.D. diss., University of Texas at Austin, 1987).
8. Bouthaina Shaaban, *Both Left and Right Handed: Arab Women Talk about Their Lives*, new ed. (Bloomington: Indiana University Press, 2009); Huda Sharawi and Margot Badran, *Harem Years: The Memoirs of an Egyptian Feminist, 1879–1924* (New York: Feminist Press, CUNY, 1987); Nawal el-Saadawi, *The Hidden Face of Eve: Women in the Arab World* (New York: Beacon, 1982).
9. Yael Yishai, *Between the Flag and the Banner: Women in Israeli Politics* (Albany: SUNY Press, 1997).
10. Patricia J. Woods, "It's Israeli after All: A Survey of Israeli Women's Movement Volunteers," *Israel Studies Forum* 19:2 (April 2004): 29–43.

11. Ibid., 37–38.
12. Ibid., 37.
13. Ibid., 38–40.
14. Ibid., 38.
15. Guillermo A. O'Donnell, "Democracy, Law, and Comparative Politics," *Studies in Comparative International Development* 36 (2001): 7–36.
16. Aharon Barak, "The Constitutional Revolution: Protected Basic Laws" [in Hebrew], *Mishpat u-Mimshal* 1 (1992): 9–35.
17. Sammy Smooha, *Arabs and Jews in Israel*, vol. 1 (Boulder, CO: Westview, 1989); Sammy Smooha, "The Model of Ethnic Democracy: Israel as a Jewish and Democratic State," *Nations and Nationalism* 8 (2002): 475–503; Yoav Peled, "Ethnic Democracy and the Legal Construction of Citizenship: Arab Citizens of the Jewish State," *American Political Science Review* 86 (1992): 432–42.
18. Peled, "Ethnic Democracy and the Legal Construction of Citizenship."
19. Israel maintains civil rights for Palestinian citizens alongside legal frameworks that exclude them from rights enjoyed by Jewish citizens; Rebecca Kook, "Dilemmas of Ethnic Minorities in Democracies: The Effect of Peace on the Palestinians in Israel," *Politics and Society* 23 (1995): 309–36.
20. Yael Yishai, "Civil Society in Transition: Interest Politics in Israel," *Annals of the American Academy of Political and Social Science* 555 (January 1998): 147–62.
21. *Hegemonic* is a term that is usually traced, within the social sciences, to the works of Antonio Gramsci and particularly to his notion of cultural hegemony whereby political, economic, and social power elites create the terms of debate that define the way the wider society is able to conceive of the world. Antonio Gramsci, *Selections from the Prison Notebooks of Antonio Gramsci*, ed. and trans. Quintin Hoare and Geoffrey Nowell Smith (New York: International Publishers, 1971).
22. Yishai, "Civil Society in Transition."
23. Fred Halliday, "Hidden from International Relations: Women and the International Arena," in *Gender and International Relations*, ed. Rebecca Grant and Kathleen Newland (Buckingham, UK: Open University Press, 1991), 158–69.
24. Yishai, *Between the Flag and the Banner*, 6.
25. Dafna N. Izraeli, "The Women Worker's Movement: First Wave Feminism and Pre-State Israel," in *Pioneers and Homemakers: Jewish Women in Pre-State Israel*, ed. Deborah S. Bernstein (Albany: SUNY Press, 1992), 184; Deborah Bernstein, "The Women Worker's Movement in Pre-State Israel, 1919–1939," *Signs* 12 (Spring 1987): 454–70.
26. Izraeli, "Women Worker's Movement," 184; and Sylvie Fogiel-Bijaoui, "From Revolution to Motherhood: The Case of Women in the Kibbutz, 1910–1948," in Bernstein, *Pioneers and Homemakers*, 216.
27. Deborah Bernstein, "The Plough Woman Who Cried into the Pots: The Position of Women in the Labor Force in the Pre-State Israeli Society," *Jewish Social Studies* 45 (1983): 43–56.
28. Fogiel-Bijaoui, "From Revolution to Motherhood," 216.

29. Bernstein, "Plough Woman Who Cried into the Pots," 43–56.
30. Izraeli, "Women Worker's Movement," 203.
31. Yishai, *Between the Flag and the Banner*, 35–36.
32. Nancy Hartsock, *The Feminist Standpoint Revisited and Other Essays* (Boulder, CO: Westview, 1998); Robin Morgan, *Sisterhood Is Global: The International Women's Movement Anthology* (New York: Doubleday, 1984).
33. Patricia Williams, *The Alchemy of Race and Rights* (Cambridge, MA: Harvard University Press, 1991); Aida Hurtado, *The Color of Privilege: Three Blasphemies of Race and Feminism* (Ann Arbor: University of Michigan Press, 1996); Patricia Hill Collins, "The Social Construction of Black Feminist Thought," *Signs* 14 (1989): 745–73.
34. Patricia Woods, "Identity-as-Difference or Women's Common Standpoint: Ethnic Politics and Political Fracture in the Israeli Women's Movement," in *The Everyday Life of the State: A State-in-Society Approach*, ed. Adam White (Seattle: University of Washington Press, 2013).
35. Catharine MacKinnon, *Sexual Harassment of Working Women: A Case in Sex Discrimination* (New Haven, CT: Yale University Press, 1979); Catharine MacKinnon, "Feminism, Marxism, Method, and the State: Toward a Feminist Jurisprudence," *Signs* 8 (1983): 635–58; Judith Plaskow, *Sex, Sin, and Grace: Women's Experience and the Theologies of Reinhold Niebuhr and Paul Tillich* (Washington, DC: University Press of America, 1980); Judith Plaskow, *Standing Again at Sinai: Judaism from a Feminist Perspective* (New York: HarperCollins, 1991); Donna Haraway, *Primate Visions: Gender, Race, and Nature in the World of Natural Science* (New York: Routledge, 1989); Sandra Harding, *The Science Question in Feminism* (Ithaca, NY: Cornell University Press, 1986); Hartsock, *Feminist Standpoint Revisited and Other Essays*; Nancy Hartsock, *Money, Sex, Power: Toward a Feminist Historical Materialism* (New York: Longman, 1983).
36. Hartsock, *Money, Sex, Power*.
37. Morgan, *Sisterhood Is Global*; see also Chandra Mohanty, Ann Russo, and Lourdes Torres, *Third World Women and the Politics of Feminism* (Bloomington: Indiana University Press, 1991).
38. See, for example, Simona Sharoni, *Gender and the Israel-Palestinian Conflict: The Politics of Women's Resistance* (Syracuse, NY: Syracuse University Press, 1995).
39. Williams, *Alchemy of Race and Rights*, Hurtado, *Color of Privilege*; Collins, "Social Construction of Black Feminist Thought."
40. Shane Phelan, *Getting Specific: Postmodern Lesbian Politics* (Minneapolis: University of Minnesota Press, 1994).
41. See, for example, Henriette Dahan-Kalev, "Tensions in Israeli Feminism: The Mizrahi-Ashkenazi Rift," *Women's Studies International Forum* 24 (2001): 669–84; Pnina Motzafi-Haller, "Scholarship, Identity, and Power: Mizrahi Women in Israel," *Signs* 26 (2001): 697–734; Amalia Sa'ar, "Contradictory Location: Assessing the Position of Palestinian Women Citizens of Israel," *Journal of Middle East Women's Studies* 3 (2007): 45–74.

42. Tamar Mayer, "From Zero to Hero: Masculinity in Jewish Nationalism," in *Israel Women's Studies*, ed. Esther Fuchs (New Brunswick, NJ: Rutgers University Press, 2005), 97–117; Sharoni, *Gender and the Israel-Palestinian Conflict*; Lesley Hazleton, *Israeli Women: The Reality Behind the Myths* (New York: Simon and Schuster, 1977).
43. Related to Arab-Jewish issues alone, see Joel Migdal, "Whose State Is It Anyway? Exclusion and the Construction of Graduated Citizenship in Israel," *Israel Studies Forum* 21 (2006): 3–27; Ilan Peleg, "Jewish-Palestinian Relations in Israel: From Hegemony to Equality?," *International Journal of Politics* 17 (2004): 415–37; Rashid Khalidi, *The Formation of Palestinian Identity: The Critical Years, 1917–1923* (New York: Columbia University Press, 1997); Gad Barzilai, *Wars, Internal Conflicts, and Political Order: A Jewish Democracy in the Middle East* (Albany: State University of New York Press, 1996); Gershon Shafir and Yoav Peled, *Being Israeli: The Dynamics of Multiple Citizenship* (New York: Cambridge University Press, 2002); Kook, "Dilemmas of Ethnic Minorities in Democracies"; and Peled, "Ethnic Democracy and the Legal Construction of Citizenship."
44. Sandra M. Sufian, *Healing the Land and the Nation: Malaria and the Zionist Project in Palestine, 1920–1947* (Chicago: University of Chicago Press, 2007); Mayer, "From Zero to Hero."
45. Joel Migdal, *State in Society: Studying How States and Societies Transform and Constitute One Another* (New York: Cambridge University Press, 2001), 5.
46. Ibid., 16, 19.
47. Mitchell Cohen, *Zion and State: Nation, Class and the Shaping of Modern Israel* (New York: Columbia University Press, 1992).
48. Jacqueline Portugese, *Fertility Policy in Israel: The Politics of Religion, Gender, and Nation* (Westport, CT: Praeger, 1998); Hazleton, *Israeli Women*.
49. Susan Martha Kahn, *Reproducing Jews: A Cultural Account of Assisted Conception in Israel* (Durham, NC: Duke University Press, 2000); see also Rhoda Ann Kanaaneh, *Birthing the Nation: Strategies of Palestinian Women in Israel* (Berkeley: University of California Press, 2002); and Portugese, *Fertility Policy in Israel*.
50. Peled, "Ethnic Democracy and the Legal Construction of Citizenship."
51. Rebecca Rubin Peled, *Debating Islam in the Jewish State: The Development of Policy Toward Islamic Institutions in Israel* (Albany: SUNY Press, 2001).
52. Sharoni, *Gender and the Israel-Palestinian Conflict*.
53. Phelan, *Getting Specific*.
54. Kook, "Dilemmas of Ethnic Minorities in Democracies"; Peled, "Ethnic Democracy and the Legal Construction of Citizenship"; Smooha, *Arabs and Jews in Israel*, vol. 1; see also Sarab Abu-Rabia Queder, "Permission to Rebel: Arab Bedouin Women's Changing Negotiation of Social Roles," *Feminist Studies* 33:1 (2007): 161–87; Shalva Weil, "Ethiopian Jewish Women: Trends and Transformations in the Context of Transnational Change," *Nashim* 8 (Fall 2004): 73–86; and Henriette Dahan-Kalev, "You're So Pretty—You Don't Look Moroccan," *Israel Studies* 6 (2001): 1–14.

PART III

Religion

6

Modern Orthodox Feminism

Art, Jewish Law, and the Quest for Equality

PAULA J. BIRNBAUM

Although recent descriptions of Israeli Orthodoxy have emphasized its patriarchal character, less attention has been given to feminist efforts within the Orthodox community. These have been evident in theology, religious practice, and scholarship. In this chapter, I focus on evidence of similar trends in the visual arts in order to demonstrate both the diversity within the Israeli Orthodox community and how it may evolve.

In January 2012, an exhibition of Jewish feminist art titled *Matronita* opened at the Mishkan Le'Omanut in Ein Harod, a kibbutz museum in northern Israel. Cocurated by Dvora Liss and David Sperber, *Matronita* was the first major museum exhibition in Israel of Jewish feminist art by women who identify as religious and observe traditional Jewish customs (*halacha*). *Matronita* is a term that appears in the Talmud to refer to a woman who engages in discussions with the rabbinic sages and possesses the right to question authority, so the exhibition's title refers to a woman of high social and moral status. The works in the exhibition ask provocative questions regarding the dissonance between Haredi (ultra-Orthodox) interpretations of Jewish law and modern life that are timely for women in Israel today. Among the themes the artists explore are women's relationship to religious education, ritual, and text; modesty and gender segregation; family purity laws around menstruation (*niddah*) and ritual immersion (*mikveh*); hair covering; and Jewish legal debates around marriage, divorce, adultery, rape, and infertility. *Matronita* was well received by the secular community in Israel and the Israeli art world. Smadar Sheffi of *Haaretz* was one of many who noted the timeliness of the exhibition in light of recent threats to gender equality from

Israel's fast-growing Haredi population, which is seeking to expand religious-based control and segregation in the public realm.[1]

By promoting works questioning Jewish laws around the regulation of the female body, *Matronita* contributes to the legacy of what is known in the field of art history as "institutional critique." Initiated in the 1960s and 1970s by conceptual artists including Hans Haacke, Daniel Buren, Andrea Fraser, and Marcel Broodthaers, this movement sought to expose the ideologies and power structures underlying the display, circulation, and discussion of art and cultural practice.[2] Many works first associated with institutional critique were set within the museum as a means to initiate public awareness of the authoritarian and hierarchical aspects of the art world. *Matronita* offered a similar public forum within a museum space to engage in social critique by promoting the work of religious Israeli women taking a critical stand toward religious institutions. Rather than tackling the ideologies and power structures of the art world, these artists are questioning Jewish law from their perspective as observant women.

Many who criticized *Matronita* did not actually go to see it; it appears they were unwilling to engage in a dialogue about the shifts that are presently taking place in Israeli society around gender issues in religious communities. Anat Chen, a curator and instructor of art at Emunah College, a religious school for young women in Jerusalem, wrote a letter to her students explaining why she refused to take them on a school-funded trip to see *Matronita*. Chen, who did see the exhibition, represented or, more accurately, misrepresented it to her students as "a bad exhibition, on curatorial and artistic terms . . . that perpetuates the stereotype of the religious woman as someone who has no spiritual and cultural world of her own, and is only concerned with going to the *mikveh* every day."[3] Clearly the work in this exhibition touched a nerve, perhaps for fear of exposing young, religious women art students to the open-ended questioning of the patriarchal authority of Jewish law. In fact, when I recently lectured on the work of some of the *Matronita* artists publicly in an American university context, several Orthodox audience members severely criticized me for presenting work that questions Jewish law.

This exhibition and the work produced by three participating, self-defined religious Israeli artists—Hagit Molgan, Hila Karabelnikov-Paz, and Andi Arnovitz—offers a productive vehicle for exploring the controversial discourse about gender and sexuality in the religious sphere. My goal is to provide case studies as a means to highlight how both the exhibition and the individual works in it engage in explicit institutional critique of the religious establishment in Israel. I show how these artists create imagery of the religious female body that addresses the complexities of being an observant Jew and a feminist living in Israel today. My work is based primarily on interviews with the artists along with my own interpretations of their work in light of recent shifts taking place in contemporary Israeli society and the research of the *Matronita* cocurators Dvora Liss and David Sperber in the accompanying exhibition catalog.[4] The artists in this study do not represent the full spectrum and diversity of Israeli Jewish women who identify as religious/observant; each belongs to a distinct Modern Orthodox community with its own particular customs and interpretations of Jewish law.

Grounded in feminist theory as well as Michel Foucault's theories of power and the body, this chapter explores how these artists negotiate their own attitudes toward Orthodox rituals and texts that seek to control, manage, and monitor the female body and the way it functions in Israeli society. These women are part of a growing community of Israeli artists who are engaged with the discourse of "religious feminism" in Orthodox Judaism.[5] This movement, initiated by Israeli and American scholars including Tova Hartman, Tamar Ross, and Chana Kehat, seeks to improve the religious, legal, and social status of observant Jewish women. By critically questioning the limits of Jewish law that often remain unchallenged in Israeli society, Molgan, Karabelnikov-Paz, and Arnovitz courageously grapple with Haredi interpretations of traditional Judaism's patriarchal subordination of women.

Before we look at individual case studies of each artist's work, I would like to provide more contextual background on the field of religious feminist art as it relates to recent conflicts between the religious and secular populations in Israel as well as to the larger art world. In some ways, Israel can be considered a leader in women's rights. Israel elected Golda Meir in 1969 as one of the democratic world's first female heads of government. Women lead the Israeli Supreme Court and two of the nation's main political parties, and women are drafted into military service. Israel is also known to have some of the world's toughest laws against sexual harassment and rape.[6] However, a host of recent incidents suggest that the Haredim are engaging in militant tactics to impose their priorities not only inside their own communities but also in public institutions as well as in public spaces.[7] The media's extensive coverage of ultra-Orthodox male harassment of women and girls regarding "modest dress" in religious communities, gender segregation on public buses and sidewalks, and women's right to sing (even in the army, a secular organization), dance, pray, and even receive professional awards in public has elicited public outrage.[8] Conflicts over who controls the female body may become more prevalent in the future if demographic studies predicting that the Haredim could grow to 40 percent of the Israeli population by 2059 turn out to be correct.[9]

However, alongside the conflicts between the secular and the Haredim, the Orthodox feminist voice has become quite strong and has introduced significant changes to religious life in Israel today. The *Matronita* exhibition marked a milestone for the field of religious feminist art both in Israel and internationally by focusing on women's questioning of the Orthodox establishment and the interpretation of Jewish law. Related exhibitions, such as *The Sexuality Spectrum*, curated by Laura Kruger for the Hebrew Union College Museum in New York in 2012–13, followed suit.[10] These exhibitions offer proof that a diverse group of Israeli as well as international visual artists and writers are presently articulating a powerful and public critique and Orthodox feminist aesthetic.

While international interest and scholarship on Israeli art has increased since the time of the Second Intifada (2000), museum and gallery exhibitions have prioritized work by secular artists that addresses national identity and geopolitical conflict as prevailing themes.[11] In contrast, Israeli artists who take up issues of gender, sexuality, and religion have been perceived as less significant in light of the reality of the volatile politics of the region.[12] *Matronita* cocurator David Sperber has written extensively about how religious Jewish art has received little critical attention and is rarely displayed in secular museums and galleries both in Israel and abroad.[13] Feminist artists who examine and critique the role of women in religious doctrine have thus been doubly marginalized and are largely absent from the canon of Israeli art. These artists have not attracted the same degree of interest as those engaged in the struggles of national identity and political conflict, and their concerns are often perceived as less pressing. Sperber and Liss, both of whom come from within the religious community and know the world of *halacha*, set out to challenge this omission by assembling a broad range of religious women artists from Israel and abroad making contemporary, cutting-edge work.[14] Their exhibition and related scholarship challenges the long-accepted dichotomy between art and religion in Israeli art institutions and asks what religious feminist art can teach us in light of the current crisis between the religious and secular in Israeli society.

By turning now to the works of three contemporary Israeli artists—Hagit Molgan, Hila Karbelnikov-Paz, and Andi Arnovitz—we can gain a nuanced understanding of the complexity of gender issues in a religious population whose customs elicit both curiosity and censure from the secular world. How do these religious artists' works respond to attempts by Haredi sectors to impose their strictures both inside and beyond their own communities? How does their work engage in institutional critique of the religious establishment in Israel?

Molgan, whose installation and video work has focused on the rituals of family purity, offers explicit criticism of the patriarchal submission of women to *halacha*.[15] She has taken great risks in expressing her views as an artist and faced extensive criticism from her own religious community. Hila Karabelnikov-Paz has been producing large, colorful canvases constructed from multicolored masking tape that document her life as both a participant and observer of religious life. Her work offers self-reflexive questioning of her own identity as a religious woman and professional artist with access to both communities. Andi Arnovitz is an American émigré who constructs garments, artist books, and installations using needle and thread, discarded prayer-book pages, and other forms of text to both question and critique the role of women in Jewish law, history, and culture. Her work explores what the artist describes as the "politics, myths, and challenges of the woman within Judaism" as well as the cultural and political challenges faced by Israeli women in the twenty-first century.[16] All three artists turn to the visual as a means to embrace one of the central tenets of Judaism: to question and point to conflicts and ambiguities. Let us now consider how their work engages in productive dialogue on the controversial discourse on gender and religious doctrine in contemporary Israeli society.

Hagit Molgan and the Abject Body

Hagit Molgan (born 1972) offers a powerful example of an observant Israeli woman's artistic response to the patriarchal control of women's sexual and reproductive resources. She grew up in what she describes as an ultra-Orthodox family in Petaḥ Tikvah and is a member of the religious Kibbutz Sa'ad, located just north of Gaza.[17] Molgan first began exploring religious feminist issues in her work largely outside the institutional framework of the Western feminist art movement, as a master of fine arts student at the School of Art (Hamidrasha) at Beit Berl College. She describes how as a young child she was confounded by the Mishnah: "For three sins women die in the hour of giving birth: for carelessness in keeping *niddah* [laws of menstrual purity], challah [removing a portion of dough as tithe to the priesthood], and [Shabbat] candle-lighting" (*Shabbat* 2:6). Her artistic practice has developed in response to the first of these sins—*niddah* or family purity laws, which mandate physical separation (primarily regarding sexual intimacy) of a married couple during menstruation and for an additional seven "clean days" afterward, during which the woman is still forbidden to have sexual contact with her husband. During the week following menstruation, an observant woman checks herself internally to make sure that bleeding has ceased, culminating in the purificatory ritual of *mikveh* (submersion).

For many Orthodox and ultra-Orthodox women in Israel, the "intimate corporeal drills of the *niddah-mikveh* ritual sequence" offer what the cultural historian Susan Sered has described as "collective narratives of gender and purity."[18] Sered has also argued that the religious discourse of fertility is in fact linked to multiple institutions in Israel—from the rabbinate to the Knesset to the military—that position demography and motherhood as the defining feature of Israeli female citizenship.[19] While the modern notion of menstruation as a normal and healthy physiological process is regularly taught as part of family and sex education programs in most Israeli schools (except for Haredi schools), traditional Jewish conceptualizations of menstrual purity and their link to reproductive health continue to influence many women.[20]

Molgan's video *Five Plus Seven*, 2004 (figure 6.1), offers a conceptual critique of the counting of days that accompanies *niddah*. The video features seven women wearing white dresses to symbolize purity. A cut-out square exposes their stomach and navel, thus emphasizing fecundity. The artist explains that the square shape is intended to resemble "an internal screen inside women's bodies—like a TV screen or a computer screen—that reveals the double standard of the gaze and what it means to be looked at while negotiating one's identity and self-perceptions as a woman."[21] The women march in a row methodically, stepping alternatively into vats containing red and clear water, the soles of their feet remaining stained red even after immersion in the clean water. Molgan first conceived of the piece in 2001 as part of her master of fine arts exhibition, with the intention of isolating the *niddah* rituals and exposing them to the secular Israeli art world: "I wanted to show how we are explored, examined by men who check and recheck us all the time. I was inspired by the work of Barbara Kruger and the neon text that she hung around New York. I felt it was the same text I found in the *siddur* [prayer book] referring to myself as a woman. The gazing look of the man will always come after me and keep me in check, especially when I'm doing the laws of *niddah*."[22]

Figure 6.1. Hagit Molgan, *Five Plus Seven* (2004).

Molgan draws an interesting parallel between her own work and Kruger's, isolating the relationship between the text of Jewish law and the observant woman reader of the prayer book who is intended to follow such directives without questioning them. Because of the controversial nature of this project, Molgan had great difficulty finding a site to film the video as well as Israeli women willing to act in it (all but one of the participants are American, and the film was shot at night to keep the location a secret). None of the students or teachers who worked with Molgan at Hamidrasha/Beit Berl College at the time knew what the film was about. Only her teacher, the artist Yair Garbuz, asked her privately when critiquing her final project if she was one of the women. "'I didn't know where to bury myself,' she says. 'It wasn't for reasons of modesty that I was afraid to admit it, it was because I didn't want to reveal that I am an active participant in this humiliating ritual.'"[23]

Molgan's *Five Plus Seven* was, in fact, part of her first public exhibition, *Not Prepared* (*Ani Lo Mukhanah*), based on her graduate thesis at Beit Berl College. Curated by Ziva Yellin and shown at the Kibbutz Be'eri Art Gallery in 2004, the exhibition elicited a strong critique from the religious community of the region and the artist's own kibbutz community.[24] Most of the works in the exhibition were made of *bedikah* or examination cloths, small pieces of white cotton cloth that observant women must use to check for bleeding following menstruation.[25] The rites and rituals of *niddah* vary depending on the religious community and its particular interpretation of *halacha* and its requisite practices; in Molgan's religious kibbutz, "The examination must be carried out twice a day. You wind the cloth around your finger, so that a tail of cloth remains, and you place it into the vaginal canal. If the cloth comes out stained, you put it into a bag and send it to the rabbi of the kibbutz, through a friend, so as to maintain anonymity. The rabbi is supposed to confirm that the cloth is clean for seven days. If after a few days the cloth comes out stained, you start the count again."[26]

Molgan covered the gallery walls with these white cloths, stained some of them with red marks, and created a grid symbolizing the five impure days and seven clean days. Viewers were invited to stamp the cloths with a Badatz *kashrut* seal in red ink (Badatz is the religious institution that supervises kosher food products), noting the similarities between different types of purification in Jewish law. According to the

Haaretz critic Dana Gillerman, while the "men visiting the exhibition took up the suggestion, the women refused."[27] Two white *tallitot* (prayer shawls) hung on an adjacent wall as symbols of patriarchal control, their openings resembling the shape of both female and male sexual organs. Molgan's project clearly intended to highlight the way that Jewish law positions women and female sexuality as unclean, impure, and in need of male regulation.

Molgan's *Not Prepared* exhibition shares its documentary-style critique of purity laws with the work of Helène Aylon (born 1931), a pioneering American, formerly Orthodox, Jewish feminist artist, although Molgan was not familiar with Aylon's work at the time.[28] In Aylon's video installation pieces *My Bridal Chamber* and *My Clean Days* (2001), prominently featured in *Matronita*, the artist covered a bed with white handkerchiefs symbolizing inspection cloths, juxtaposed with a wall-sized projection of the monthly calendars that document Aylon's day-to-day "cleanliness" during the ten years of her marriage. The marital bed and menstrual chart were accompanied by a tape-recorded reading ("five days, seven days, ritual bath . . . five days, seven days, ritual bath . . .") that questions the policing of intimacy in Jewish law.

Molgan has acknowledged the influence of the Israeli artist Yocheved Weinfeld's 1976 performance of her piece known as *Menstruation* at the Debel Gallery in Jerusalem. In this ceremonial piece, also inspired by Jewish purity laws, Weinfeld sat passively in the gallery while a series of violent actions were performed on her body; these included blocking her mouth, cutting her hair, cleaning her genitalia, cutting her dress, and applying makeup.[29] According to Gannit Ankori, Weinfeld "used her own body, her Jewish heritage, and the female experience as materials for creating art."[30] Weinfeld is a "foremother" of Israeli feminist art, and her work has inspired younger Israeli artists like Molgan to use visual art to explore how Jewish law degrades women by promoting the dichotomous division of purity and impurity with regard to the Jewish female body.

Molgan's work, like Weinfeld's, can be connected to the tradition of secular American and European feminist artists, scholars, and theorists who began exploring the role of menstruation in cultural constructions of femininity in the late 1960s and 1970s. Carolee Schneemann and Judy Chicago, both secular American Jews, actively engaged with menstrual blood as a material in their art to explore cultural taboos about menstruation and female embodiment in a secular context.[31] Scholars have turned to the writings of the cultural theorists Mary Douglas and Julia Kristeva to support their interpretations of such work through theories of abjection, in which female bodily fluids, including menstrual blood, are perceived as cultural symbols of pollution, contamination, and, in Kristeva's case, the repression of the maternal body.[32] While Weinfeld was exhibiting and performing her work in Israel at the same time as her American counterparts, the issues for her and for the younger Molgan are distinct. As an observant Jew from a traditional background, working in an Israeli kibbutz outside a network of feminist artists, Molgan's engagement with the theme of *niddah* is necessarily quite different from that of the first-generation American feminist artists.

While the secular Israeli art community was very supportive of Molgan's 2004 exhibition, the religious community largely was not.[33] A few women from her kibbutz approached her and said that they had never been able to talk with anyone about their disdain for this ritual practice and that they were going to stop using the inspection cloth. On the other hand, many others expressed strong disapproval and refused to speak with her. Some even wrote personal letters to Molgan stating that if she had forgotten the laws of *niddah*, they would be happy to teach her again. Others claimed she had taken God's name in vain, and still others told her they believed that the Jewish people had survived the Holocaust because of their adherence to family purity rituals. In short, the majority of the members of her own religious community felt that Molgan's work and exhibition were unacceptable.

In response to the difficult reception of her 2004 exhibition, Molgan stopped working for several years, severely affected by the negative reception of her work among so many Orthodox men and women. After learning of Molgan's work and experience, the American curator Nina Felshin invited her to serve as an artist in residence at Wesleyan University in Middletown, Connecticut. With an artist's residency funded by the Israeli government, Molgan recreated *Not Prepared* in the Davison Art Center at Wesleyan over a two-month period in 2005–6. While she described this experience as liberating, the Israeli government in fact refused to offer public acknowledgment of their sponsorship of Molgan's residency, likely due to the controversial nature of her work in Israel.

Molgan and her family are presently "on sabbatical" from their kibbutz near Gaza, living in Jerusalem, and it is unclear if they will return. She has rented a studio and is producing new work in video about gender issues and religious life from an Israeli perspective. She has chosen to make all of her work publicly available on YouTube, showing her interest in cultivating an international audience for her work.[34] Molgan remains observant and admiring of many aspects of Jewish law, but the critical nature of her work has led her and her family to contemplate permanently giving up their place in kibbutz life. Her story illustrates how difficult it is for women from within the religious community in Israel to publicly question rituals that they feel are humiliating, but also how productive one can be in the face of adversity.

Hila Karabelnikov-Paz and the Religious Gaze

Hila Karabelnikov-Paz's (born 1981) images of Orthodox Jews engaged in everyday activities offer ambivalent questioning of gender roles and customs in contemporary Israeli society. Raised in the religious neighborhood of Bnei Brak by a family that supports women's achievements, Karabelnikov-Paz's practice has been informed by years of study at both religious grade schools and secular art schools, including the School of Art (Hamidrasha) at Beit Berl College and Bezalel Academy of Arts and Design. Her access to both communities gives her a unique perspective and artistic voice. She describes her work as representing the complexity of women's daily experiences from both within and outside the religious community: "I'm standing in a tough place in between nonreligious and religious worlds; I see things from two sides, and it keeps me thinking."[35]

Karabelnikov-Paz creates large, brightly colored, mosaic-style canvases of both religious and secular life in contemporary Israel. Her early works depict members of the Bnei Brak community in crowded street scenes, shopping in the market in preparation for Shabbat or joyfully engaged in rituals related to different Jewish holidays (Yom Kippur, Sukkot, Purim, Lag Ba'Omer, and many others). She often inserts her own red-haired self-portrait at the edge of the canvas, her direct gaze suggesting her dual roles as both a participant in religious community life and a silent observer or critic of that life. "I tell my own story, about myself, through the images of all of these people in the community."[36]

Karabelnikov-Paz's technique also melds tradition and modernity. She constructs her works with multiple layers of multicolored masking and insulating tape, wallpaper, and stickers, overlaying them with glue and varnish to create bold imagery of religious and secular Israeli life. Her finished works offer richly textured images of diverse members of Israeli society, with each work resembling a brightly colored mosaic. While the artist's technique evokes a Roman artistic tradition that took root centuries ago in the Middle East, the ephemeral and modern attributes of her materials emphasize their contemporaneity.[37]

Karabelnikov-Paz has created a series of works relating to the theme of the *mikveh* that offer an interesting counterpart to Molgan's critique of purity laws.[38] In *Mikveh 1*, 2010–11 (figure 6.2), the viewer is invited into the intimate experience of ritual immersion with a close-up view from behind of an isolated figure whose naked body is nearly fully submerged under water. The artist uses her technique of layered masking tape to emphasize the luxurious and reflective quality of the blue tones of the water against the figure's pale skin and the light and dark bath tiles. Although the sensual image suggests private revelation and pleasure in a timeless ritual, the metal plumbing calls attention to the sterility and modernity of the setting in which such acts are performed. In *Mikveh 2*, 2010–11 (figure 6.3), Karabelnikov-Paz emphasizes the experience of solitude of the *mikveh*; the figure appears in private revelation, her body wrapped in one white towel and her head completely covered by another. In yet a third work in which no figure is present, Karabelnikov-Paz attempts to personalize the small, tiled room of the *mikveh* by covering the neutral-colored tiles with her own colorful garments and belongings. In all of these works, the artist reflects with both nostalgia and a certain degree of criticality on her own personal experience of family purity rituals: "There is a fine line between simply *swimming* in a *pool* and sinking into water for *purification*, water covering everything yet covering nothing."[39]

Karabelnikov-Paz took part in a multimedia group exhibition in 2013 curated by Raz Samira, titled *A Tale of a Woman and a Robe: Ritual Immersion of Female Converts* (Tel Aviv, Zaritsky Artists House), in which she further investigates her own ambivalence toward the *mikveh* rituals by focusing on the theme of women who convert to Judaism.[40] As part of the conversion process, a woman must submerge herself in water with

Figure 6.2. Hila Karabelnikov-Paz, *Mikveh 1* (2010–11).

Figure 6.3. Hila Karabelnikov-Paz, *Mikveh* 2, 2010–11.

a cloth over her head in front of three *dayanim* or rabbinic judges, while they ask her if she truly wishes to convert or if someone is forcing her to do so. In this series, the artist shows how the *balanit*, or woman in charge of maintaining the *mikveh* as a kosher site, is deemed powerless in the face of the three male judges. Karabelnikov-Paz claims, "Her witnessing is made void."[41] This series and collaborative exhibition brings to the fore timely debates about the Orthodox feminist desire for women to serve as official "witnesses" of many important rites of passage in Judaism, including conversion, which is prohibited by Jewish law.

Karabelnikov-Paz's work can be contextualized within a larger tradition of religious Israeli and American feminist artists who examine the *mikveh* as a site of self-exploration, empowerment, and critique. Mierle Ukeles, an Orthodox Jewish American artist, was the first to create such a project in her 1977 performance of *Mikva Dreams* in Franklin Furnace in New York, published in the American feminist art journal *Heresies*.[42] In the published piece, Ukeles includes a photographic self-portrait shot from behind, her body draped in a white sheet before a large body of water, her long dark hair hanging down her back, surrounded by the repetition of the text in all capitals: "IMMERSE AGAIN." In the accompanying artist statement, Ukeles describes her experience of submersion as "a taste of heaven" that offers "an experience of rebirth as a married woman and mother."[43] Rather than concealing her body, hair, and sexuality, as is the norm in Orthodox Jewish culture, Ukeles does just the opposite. Her piece subverts this ritual meant to enhance a woman's fertility in preparation for sexual contact with her husband and turns it into a private moment of revelation. Ukeles's artistic interpretation of the *mikveh* ritual can be viewed as part of the larger first-generation American feminist art movement's goal to reclaim the female body as a means for liberation.[44]

Ukeles's celebration of *mikveh* culture has influenced subsequent generations of religious Jewish American and Israeli artists that include Karabelnikov-Paz. For example, the American artist Janice Rubin's *The Mikvah Project* (2001), a traveling exhibition of photographs and interviews, offers a romantic view of the collective experiences of an anonymous group of women and the important role the *mikveh* plays in their lives. The women's faces are not included in the photographic portraits, while the interviews reveal a range of *mikveh* experiences, from that of joy in monthly purity rituals to healing from sexual abuse. Karabelnikov-Paz stands out as one of several observant Israeli female visual artists recently showcased in *Matronita* who are engaged in making their questions and ambivalence about such rituals visible to the public.[45] Her *mikveh* imagery not only offers her own private experience of this particular ritual as it relates to female sexuality but also exposes the artist's feelings of ambivalence and isolation as well as frustration about the power dynamics created by the Orthodox institutions that govern such rituals. By representing a range of observant Israeli women's attitudes toward the laws

Figure 6.4. Hila Karabelnikov-Paz, *6 Women, Sheraton Beach* (2012).

and practices of purity rituals, Karabelnikov-Paz thus moves the discussion from her own individual private body to a collective one of religious women's sexual and reproductive agency and questioning.

In another recent series, titled *Sheraton Beach*, 2012 (figure 6.4), Karabelnikov-Paz engages with the discourse of *tzniut* (modesty) in the Orthodox Israeli community from a feminist perspective.[46] Featured in a solo exhibition in 2012 at Braverman Gallery in Tel Aviv, this series was billed as offering its secular audience a glimpse of a "microcosm of the urban Orthodox and religious Jewish community." The artist's subject is popularly known as the "religious beach" in Tel Aviv. While secular Israelis refer to the beach as *Ḥof Ha-datiyim* or the Separated Beach, Karabelnikov-Paz strategically chose a different title:

> The original name is based on the Sheraton hotel which is a significant landmark in the area and I used it because it describes that whole section

> of the promenade, of which the separate beach is a part, emphasizing the fact that it's not as separate as one might think/like it to be. You can be a non-religious hiker and it will still be part of your view. Rather, you can be a non-Jewish tourist and see the whole "separate" and supposedly hidden beach from your window in the Sheraton hotel. In short, you can't put something in plain view and tell everyone not to look at it. It'll make people peep and paint pictures.[47]

The religious beach is one of thirteen public beaches along the coast of Tel Aviv, connected by a promenade, and almost all are crowded with people in the summer months and equipped with lifeguards and other facilities. Whereas other beaches remain open in all directions, a large tin wall deliberately separates the religious beach from the beaches adjacent to it. Those who wish to enter the beach must first pass through a heavy rubber curtain that hangs on the entrance door, where a large sign announces that women are allowed in only on Sunday, Tuesday, and Thursday and men only on Monday, Wednesday, and Friday.

In this series, Karabelnikov represents the activities that occur at the religious beach during the days it is open only to women. While some works represent the entire beach from a distance, with little attention given to the figures, others offer close-up views of the bodily gestures and expressions of individual women bathers. Their bodies are nearly fully covered in the richly patterned and colorful clothing and head scarves typically worn by the women of Bnei Brak. The women play in the sand, converse in a group, wade at the shoreline, and swim. The series features a sense of intimacy between the female bathers, who appear relaxed, self-absorbed, and unaware of an external gaze. In some works, their activity is portrayed as intimate and sensual, their wet clothing clinging to the very body parts, such as buttocks and breasts, that they are expected to hide. Karabelnikov-Paz gives agency to her religious bathers, emphasizing their humanity and individuality, while alluding to their sexuality in certain cases.

As both an insider and an outsider in the Bnei Brak community that regularly frequents this beach, Karabelnikov-Paz described the reactions she has received from the secular public: "If the women don't want to be seen, then why are you painting them?"[48] In response, she described her close identification with the paintings' subjects as well as her desire to visually capture and share the tender, human, and at times humorous interactions of a community that elicits such curiosity from the secular public. However, when the artist presented this series to a group of religious Israeli schoolchildren, she was not surprised that "they did not ask questions; they were submissive and accepting of their life, point blank."[49]

Galia Yahav, a secular Israeli feminist artist and art critic for *Haaretz*, was critical of Karabelnikov-Paz's *Sheraton Beach* series when it was exhibited in Tel Aviv. She denigrated the artist's mosaic technique as "only a charming technical trick that with folkloric colors and uncritical decoration creates socio-ethnic souvenir postcards."[50] Yahav claimed the artist was "unaware" of how her work engages with Western art history and its preoccupation with the theme of women bathing or that she is engaging with gaze theory.[51] "Gaze theory" and the notion of "the male gaze" are terms that were introduced by film theorists in the 1970s to explain the voyeuristic way in which male viewers of art and visual culture look at and objectify women.[52] In my view, the artist is quite aware that she is inserting herself within an art-historical tradition of masculine mastery and feminine display. She is playing with the fact that, as a religious woman artist who is in fact a member of the very community she depicts, she has a unique vantage point of straddling both worlds of object and subject. The relaxed poses and gestures of the bathers might be interpreted as suggesting the artist's identification with a feminine fantasy of bodily liberation from both the secular male gaze of art history and the religious male gaze of her own Orthodox community that insists on women covering their bodies. The question of whom Karabelnikov-Paz identifies as her audience is also crucial, as her work is largely patronized by the secular Israeli art world. These interpretations take on heightened meanings in light of the contemporary context of the Haredim's increasing insistence on ever greater gender segregation and modesty for religious women in Israel. It is as if Karabelnikov-Paz is debating whether religious women can ever really escape becoming the object of desire both within and outside their community.

In another work in this series, *The Runner, Sheraton Beach*, 2012 (figure 6.5), the artist seems to confront gaze theory quite directly. In this piece, the partition wall shields the religious female bathers from the gaze of a bare-chested, secular male jogger wearing sunglasses and

Figure 6.5. Hila Karabelnikov-Paz, *The Runner, Sheraton Beach* (2012).

headphones. His exposed skin is presented in contrast to the women's clothed bodies. In response to this work, Galia Yahav seems to contradict her earlier assessment: "since he is the only indication of male presence in this area, he is also the presence which generates all the rituals and restrictions and the reason for having a separate 'women only' beach."[53] In another work portraying the same beach at sunset (figure 6.6), Karabelnikov-Paz covers the entire canvas with the mesh pattern of a wire fence, offering what the critic Uzi Zur of *Haaretz* described as an "apocalyptic" scene of both "female paradise" and the "ghetto life" of "imprisoned women."[54] Evident in all the works in this series is a critical commentary on both the positive and negative aspects of gender segregation and the laws of modesty in the religious community surrounding Tel Aviv. The beach functions as a very public and accessible space that highlights the divisions between female and male as well as holy and secular.[55]

Hila Karabelnikov-Paz's work offers a productive entrée for dialogue regarding the most recent conflicts surrounding modesty and gender segregation in Israel's Haredi communities. As someone with access

Figure 6.6. Hila Karabelnikov-Paz, *Sunset, Sheraton Beach* (2012).

to both religious and secular worlds, she produces imagery that subtly addresses her simultaneous pleasure and ambivalence toward many different aspects of traditional Jewish culture and law. She modernizes traditional Orthodox notions of modest dress for women; for example, while she always covers her head in public, she might wear a beret or stylish hat rather than the traditional scarf. Now living with her family in a small apartment in Tel Aviv, Karabelnikov-Paz enjoys a modern lifestyle while continuing to observe religious rituals and traditions. When she first entered the graduate program in fine arts at Bezalel Academy of Arts and Design in 2011, she explained that she nonetheless found it very difficult to share with her classmates that she comes from the Bnei Brak community.[56] The power of Karabelnikov-Paz's work lies in her ability to celebrate certain aspects of Jewish law that build community while critiquing the male-controlled legal systems that regulate Jewish women's bodily experience.

Andi Arnovitz: Body, Text, Ritual

The work of the American-born Andi Arnovitz (born 1959) engages with needle and thread to address recent tensions in Israeli society that exist within religion, gender studies, and politics. Themes in her work of interest to this study include, but are not limited to, Jewish legal debates around marriage, divorce, adultery, rape, and infertility, as well as political conflict. Based in Jerusalem, Arnovitz immigrated to Israel in 1999 from Atlanta, where she had enjoyed a successful career in advertising. Her background informs her extensive use of text as a means to offer social critique and questioning of the traditional texts of Judaism.[57] Arnovitz is also part of a generation of female artists engaged with craft-based techniques and garment production who ask questions about gender in society. Her family owned a fabric store, and growing up, she was "surrounded by women whose chief occupation was sewing."[58] Arnovitz collects textiles and embraces embroideries and other works created by women from diverse cultures, including the work of Bedouin, Druze, Palestinian, and Ethiopian women residing in Israel.

In a series of recent works titled *Coats of the Agunot* (figure 6.7), Arnovitz takes on the problematic issue of the *agunah* (chained woman) who, according to Jewish law, cannot remarry due to her spouse's refusal to grant permission by means of a *get* (Jewish writ of divorce).[59] Without her husband's consent, the woman's status is frozen: she is unable to remarry or have a new partner, and any future children are considered illegitimate. In response, she must take her case to the rabbinic court, where male rabbis rigidly defend the Jewish legal interpretation of the bond of marriage, regardless of mitigating factors such as spousal abuse or criminal behavior. For this series, Arnovitz researched and received permission to reproduce hundreds of Jewish marriage contracts (*ketubot*) from the National Library of Israel's World Repository of Ketubot. The artist describes how for many centuries women had little means for creative expression, and the creation of elaborate marriage certificates offered a vehicle for them to engage in artistic practice. As part of her process in honoring these women, Arnovitz photocopied, tore, manipulated, and sewed together thousands of small fragments of paper photocopies of the *ketubot* to create a series of "cumbersome coats that she must wear continuously."[60] These brilliantly colored and richly textured life-size

Figure 6.7. Andi Arnovitz, *Coat of the Agunot* (2010).

paper coats thus prohibit a woman's mobility. The act of sewing all of the pieces of a woman's marriage certificate symbolizes the fact that she is literally bound to every word. Arnovitz chose to sew the sleeves, hems, and collars shut, with each work becoming a "straitjacket where women are trapped by the paper—literally and figuratively, since her *get* is also a piece of paper—and she is left hanging, evidenced by the hanging threads."[61] The artist explains her choice of paper as material for the *Agunot* series: "It is created out of paper because it is paper (her *ketubah*) that entraps her and paper (her *get*) that will free her."[62]

As a body of work, Arnovitz's colorful coats are meant to be symbolic of all women who are in this very difficult legal situation. The statistics on the "*agunah* problem" in Israel vary depending on who is reporting them; many cases remain unresolved, as they are dismissed by the rabbinic courts, leaving the women in long-term limbo.[63] Anat Zuria's film *Mekudeshet* (*Sentenced to Marriage*, 2004) chronicles the lives of four young, observant Israeli women in this situation who over a period of two years struggle to obtain a divorce with the help of female Orthodox rabbinical advocates, without success. Ronit and Schlomi Elkabetz's more recent film *Gett: The Trial of Viviane Amsalem* (2014) further emphasizes the futile nature of this process by focusing on the protagonist's repeated interactions with the rabbinic court system, as days become weeks, months, and eventually years. Arnovitz's series of coats, like these two films, expose the archaic process of divorce for Jews married in Israel, where there is no option of a civil marriage and divorce is dealt with according to traditional Jewish law. In one of the final scenes of Zuria's film, Tamara, a former art student and mother of four, creates a haunting assemblage piece in which she aggressively inserts thumbtacks into her torn wedding photograph, pinning it to an unfinished piece of wood. Tamara proclaims that she would rather move on with her life and pursue a career in the arts than continue her legal appeal. For the filmmaker (who is also an exhibiting artist), art becomes a place of healing and also a vehicle for exposing the injustices that religious orthodoxy can promote. Arnovitz's series of coats, each with its own rich textures, colors, and hanging threads, is thus part of a recent body of work produced by contemporary Israeli female artists who are initiating important dialogue about the empowerment of observant women who are bound to religious law.

Another issue of great importance taken up by Arnovitz is that of alleged infertility and the Israeli religious establishment's stake in women's bodies. In a series of works that includes *Counting Your Eggs* and *4% of Us*, 2011 (figure 6.8), the artist comments on what is known as "*halachic* infertility," in which observant women cannot conceive because their ovulation cycle does not conform to the rigid counting of days prescribed by the Jewish laws of *niddah*.[64] As we saw in Molgan's *Five Plus Seven*, most Orthodox Jewish women abstain from sexual contact with their partner for five days of menstruation plus another seven days before going to the *mikveh*, for a total of twelve days. Women who ovulate during this period of abstention are thus unable to conceive if they observe Jewish law. Most of those who experience "*halachic* infertility" could easily become pregnant if they were able to have sexual contact earlier in their cycle. In *4% of Us*, Arnovitz fills a found wooden box with hundreds of tiny paper and clay figures in the form of a fetus, a metaphor for literally counting the "lives lost" by *halachic*

Figure 6.8. Andi Arnovitz, *4% of Us* (2011).

infertility due to patriarchal control over the laws of family purity. According to Susan Sered, "These women then turn to male rabbis who give orders to consult certain doctors, which infertility drugs to take, which prayers to say, which *mitzvot* [commandments] to do, etc."[65] In Israel, all women, regardless of religious background, are entitled to two state-funded in-vitro fertilization therapies; and many religious women, although not actually infertile, have few options but to pursue this route despite health risks involved in these treatments. Arnovitz's work is thus critical of what Sered describes as Israel's "hierarchical and dogmatic model of interaction between menstruating, sick or infertile women and the religious establishment."[66] The artist took her title from Dr. Danny Rosenak, an obstetrician/gynecologist in Jerusalem who "has determined that we have lost 4% of the Jewish people" over the millennium due to the inflexibility of the rabbis and the issue of *halachic* infertility.[67] Through this series, Arnovitz thus shows how visual art can serve to make important political claims about how codified religious law in Israel regulates the female body in oppressive ways.

In 2012, Arnovitz was commissioned by the Ein Harod Museum of Art to create a site-specific piece for the *Matronita* exhibition, titled *A*

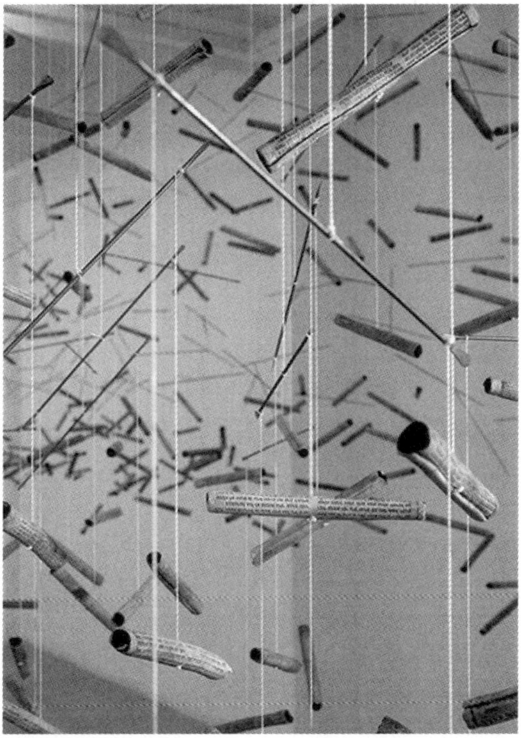

Figure 6.9. Andi Arnovitz, *A Delicate Balance* (2012).

Delicate Balance (figure 6.9). This fourteen-foot installation forces visitors venturing toward the museum's Judaica wing to navigate hundreds of small rods of iron, suspended from the ceiling and filling an entire corridor, on which are balanced pairs of fragile clay scrolls that are also suspended, mobile-like, from the ceiling. Careful examination reveals that the pairs of scrolls balanced on each rod contain texts that are in fact related to each other. "One scroll is the *halachic* source for an Israeli law, a rule, a governing point of view, and the other scroll is what happens in real life."[68] For example, a scroll stamped with an article about the return of the former Israeli soldier Gilad Shalit, who was imprisoned by Hamas for over five years, is paired with a source text describing the commandment of the "return of the captive." Another scroll pairs an article about the corruption scandal of former Israeli prime minister Ehud Olmert with the source text for the "laws of bribery." The piece brings together much of the artist's questioning of the power and meaning of Jewish law in contemporary Israeli society as well as the implications for observant women. The latest research about infertility is paired with the laws of *niddah*, and contemporary studies of the domestic abuse of Israeli women are paired with religious laws dealing with adultery. Arnovitz explains: "The title refers to the very delicate balancing act that the state of Israel does day after day in order to exist. Israel is a country in which constant and endless intersections of Judaism (*halacha* specifically), real-life, and the individual meet. Often one seems to carry more weight than the other: sometimes *halacha* carries more importance and overrules the concerns of the individual, sometimes the individual deliberately breaks with *halacha*, and sometimes real life creates havoc with both the individual and the system."[69]

Pieces of the installation are intended to break if handled roughly as "a deliberate reference to what happens in Israel when the state and the individual come into conflict without being sensitive to the other's needs and priorities."[70] Because of the central placement of this installation in the passage from one gallery to the next, Arnovitz compels the visitor to engage with the pervasiveness of religious law in contemporary Israeli society and to contemplate what it means to resist it, both personally and collectively.

Conclusion

The Ein Harod Museum of Art that commissioned Arnovitz's installation and organized *Matronita* must be credited for promoting public awareness of religious feminist art that questions the status quo in Israel. Part of a movement of kibbutz museums that sprang up in the 1930s in communal agricultural settlements, it was in fact one of the very first kibbutz art museums in Israel.[71] It is also among the earliest museums to consistently showcase work by noncanonical Israeli artists, including women and artists of diverse cultural backgrounds.[72] Directed by Galia Bar-Or, the museum offers a productive space for dialogue about important areas of political and social conflict in Israel today. While *Matronita* threatened some people, it showed that certain Israeli museums like Ein Harod's Museum of Art are offering a venue in which to engage in productive dialogue and to question the authority of the religious establishment.

Both the exhibition itself and the individual works discussed here engage in institutional critique by exposing the ideologies and power structures of the religious establishment. In many ways, what these religious feminist artists are doing is institutional critique in its current incarnation, which, according to recent scholarship, is no longer taking place exclusively within the museum but going outside it.[73] The Vienna-based artist group Wochen Klausur writes in "From the Object to Concrete Intervention" (2005), "Art should no longer be venerated in specially designated spaces. . . . Art should deal with reality, grapple with political circumstances, and work out proposals for improving human coexistence."[74] All three artists in this study have sought out creative outlets both inside and outside the traditional frame of the museum and art market to question Haredi sectors in Israel that take steps to impose their strictures beyond their own communities. Hagit Molgan shows her work on YouTube and is one of many artists turning to the Internet "as a tool and site for interventionist critique."[75] Of the three artists in this study, Molgan has perhaps taken the biggest risks and faced the harshest criticism for her work, resulting in her choice to leave her religious community. She remains observant and states, "I believe in the system, but some of the laws need to be questioned again."[76] Karabelnikov-Paz expresses some of the tensions in straddling both religious and secular worlds in her work, and one wonders if she feels mutually welcome in both worlds. While she sells her work to secular collectors at a commercial gallery in Tel Aviv as a means to support her family, she is not heavily invested in the marketable aspect of her work ("I'm not doing this to sell"). She turns to social networks like Vimeo to promote her work, and she also regularly presents to religious schoolchildren from her community in an effort to expand their thinking.[77] Of the three artists, Arnovitz, an American émigré, is the most secure in her place. Her work has been shown in Europe, Israel, Canada, and the United States and is in numerous international collections, including the Library of Congress, the Israel National Library, and museums in the United States and Israel, foreign ministries, foundations, and private collections. She describes her collectors as generally religious women who are "committed to Judaism,"[78] and many of them are Americans. She, too, makes her work readily available on the Internet, engages in artist residencies, and is a strong voice in the international Jewish feminist art community.

With a wide-reaching public audience, these three Israeli artists of different generations and backgrounds engage in institutional critique to expose some of the challenges and constraints facing religious women in Israel today. Their work instigates productive dialogue and contributes to an emerging field of religious feminist art that is taking shape both inside and outside Israel. For example, to protest a little-known religious Jewish sect led by a Haredi woman named Bruria Keren in Beit Shemesh—where some women and girls cover themselves in head-to-toe black burqas and do not speak in public—Arnovitz made a piece that exposed the similarities between fundamentalist Jewish women and fundamentalist Muslim women. She created a large digital print of Adam and Eve and covered Eve's body in entirety with green leaves to symbolize physical nullification. This work stands in direct dialogue with that of contemporary Muslim women artists such as Shamsia Hassani, a street artist living in Kabul, Afghanistan; the Pakistani Aisha Khalid; and Yemeni Boushra Almutawakel—all of whom offer visual critiques of the burqa in Islamic culture by emphasizing both physical containment and invisibility in some cases, as well as empowerment in others.[79] Fundamentalist women in Jewish and Muslim societies share certain experiences in that both groups live according to contemporary extremist interpretations of the laws of ancient, patriarchal religious legal systems that view women's modesty as the symbol of righteousness and purity. With women's rights a continued threat in the Islamist-dominated governments of the Arab Spring, religious feminist artists worldwide are exhibiting work via the Internet and digital media that exposes issues around fiercely enforced cultural dictates of modesty, purity, stereotyping, and multiple oppressions of women. In the case of contemporary Muslim women artists, their work also often engages with power dynamics between East and West, the global aftermath of 9/11, and Islamophobia.

Matronita can thus be productively situated as part of a larger global phenomenon in which women artists of Jewish, Christian, Muslim, Hindu, and other religious faiths and backgrounds courageously use art as a form of social protest both within and outside their communities. These artists use institutional critique to expose extremist dictates that severely constrain freedom and prohibit female agency for religious women. As modern Orthodox women working in Israel, Arnovitz,

Molgan and Karabelnikov-Paz all view part of their mission as artists to challenge the radicalization of the most extreme factions of the Haredim and to reaffirm what they identify as the compassionate aspects of Jewish law.

NOTES

I would like to thank the following colleagues for their feedback on this essay in various stages: Kim Anno, Alla Effimova, Tirza True Latimer, Ruth E. Iskin, Lawrence Raphael, Jordana Moore Saggese, Rachel Schreiber, and Jennifer Shaw.

1. Smadar Sheffi, "Jewish Look at Roots of Feminism," *Haaretz*, March 9, 2012. Sheffi, a prominent art critic from *Haaretz*, pointedly described *Matronita* as "one of those exhibitions that expresses and even defines the spirit of the times. It was curated well before the 'exclusion of women' made headlines, alongside crazed proposals to prohibit women from singing in state ceremonies. In this regard, the exhibition seems to offer a counterpoint to these backward phenomena. But most of all, the work in the present exhibition reflects the profound change in the self-consciousness of religious Jewish women over the last two decades."
2. See Alexander Alberro and Blake Stimson, eds., *Institutional Critique: An Anthology of Artists' Writings* (Cambridge, MA: MIT Press, 2009); Julia Bryan-Wilson, "A Curriculum for Institutional Critique, or the Professionalization of Conceptual Art," in *New Institutionalism*, ed. Jonas Ekeberg (Oslo: Office for Contemporary Art, 2003), 89–109, reprinted in *Beck's Futures* catalog (London: Institute of Contemporary Art, Summer 2004), 8–19.
3. Thanks to Andi Arnovitz for sharing this letter of March 2012 with me and to Stav Pelti-Negev for her translation.
4. *Matronita: Jewish Feminist Art* (Ein Harod, Israel: Mishkan Le'Omanut/Museum of Art, 2012). See Dvora Liss, "Tzena Ure'ena," in ibid., 198–181; David Sperber, "Feminist Art in the Sphere of Traditional and Religious Judaism," in ibid., 164–141; David Sperber, "The Abject: Menstruation, Impurity and Purification in Jewish Feminist Art," in ibid., 142–117 (page numbers are in reverse in this bilingual publication). Both curators contextualize the work of the twenty artists featured in *Matronita*, including Molgan, Karabelnikov-Paz, and Arnovitz, along with other Israeli, American, and European colleagues, in light of the rich dialogue between feminist art practices and questions specific to the role of women in Orthodox Judaism. See also the videotaped panel discussion of the exhibition, "Matronita 2012: The Groundbreaking Jewish Feminist Exhibition," with Andi Arnovitz, Helène Aylon, Dvora Liss and Doni Silver-Simons, moderated by Anne Hromadka on March 25, 2015, at the 2015 Conney Conference on Jewish Art at the University of Southern California: http://conneyproject.wisc.edu/videos-2015/.
5. Tali Berner, "Religious Feminism: Origins and Directions," in *Matronita: Jewish Feminist Art*, 181. Some of the key texts relating to this movement in relation to Orthodox Judaism are Yael Israel-Cohen, *Between Feminism and Orthodox Juda-*

ism: Resistance, Identity, and Religious Change in Israel (Leiden, Netherlands: Brill, 2012); Tova Hartman, *Feminism Encounters Traditional Judaism: Resistance and Accommodation* (Hanover, NH: Brandeis University Press, 2007); Tamar Ross, *Expanding the Palace of Torah: Orthodoxy and Feminism* (Hanover, NH: Brandeis University Press, 2004); Tamar Ross, "Modern Orthodoxy and the Challenge of Feminism," in *Jews and Gender: The Challenge to Hierarchy* (Studies in Contemporary Jewry 16), ed. Jonathan Frankel (New York: Oxford University Press, 2000), 3–38; Chana Kehat, *Feminism and Judaism: From Collision to Regeneration* [in Hebrew] (Tel Aviv: Ministry of Defense Publishing House, 2008); Tamar El-Or, *Educated and Ignorant: Ultraorthodox Jewish Women and their World* (Boulder, CO: Lynne Rienner, 1994; published in Hebrew, Tel Aviv: Am Oved, 1992). See also *Women and Judaism: New Insights and Scholarship*, ed. Frederick E. Greenspahn (New York: NYU Press, 2009).

6. Despite these advances and the egalitarianism of the founding socialist ideals, feminist historians argue that advances toward gender equality have historically been low priority in Israel due to the constant struggle for sovereignty and military control. An overview of the feminist movement in Israel is not in the scope of this essay. Among the many sources of interest, see Nahlo Abdo, *Women in Israel: Race, Gender and Citizenship* (London: Zed Books, 2011); Esther Fuchs, ed., *Israeli Feminist Scholarship: Gender, Zionism and Difference* (Austin: University of Texas Press, 2014); Esther Fuchs, ed., *Israel Women's Studies: A Reader* (New Brunswick, NJ: Rutgers University Press, 2005); Ruth Halperin Kaddari, *Women in Israel: A State of Their Own* (Philadelphia: University of Pennsylvania Press, 2003); Hanna Herzog, *Gendering Politics Women in Israel* (Ann Arbor: University of Michigan Press, 1999); Yael Azmon and Dafna N. Izraeli, eds., *Women in Israel* (New Brunswick, NJ: Transaction, 1993); Barbara Swirski and Marilyn Safir, eds., *Calling the Equality Bluff: Women in Israel* (Oxford, UK: Pergamon, 1991).
7. The nation was shocked in December 2011 by images on prime-time television of a modern Orthodox eight-year-old girl from the religious community of Beit Shemesh crying after she was spat on and insulted by adult men belonging to a sect of ultra-Orthodoxy who accused her of "immodest" dress. A demonstration attended by thousands followed, and Prime Minister Benjamin Netanyahu and President Shimon Peres responded.
8. The group known as the Women of the Wall continue to pray and work for the full equality and access to religious freedom at the Western Wall, including freedom to pray in peace, as a group, out loud, with *tallit* (prayer shawl), *tefillin* (phylacteries), and Torah. The Freedom Rider Project organized by the Israeli Reform movement sends women to sit at the front of bus routes between Haredi towns to ensure that the January 2011 Supreme Court ruling that forbade public bus companies from enforcing segregation is upheld. While conflicts regarding gender discrimination in the Israeli religious community have only recently been featured in the international press, scholars of Israeli feminism have been re-

searching such debates over the past four decades and have produced a rich body of scholarship on this subject.

9. These projections were released in 2012 by the Israeli Central Bureau of Statistics, quoted in Mati Wagner, "The Ultra-Orthodox on the Warpath," *Commentary* 133:2 (2012): 33.
10. *The Sexuality Spectrum* exhibition was on view at Hebrew Union College Museum, New York, NY, from October 10, 2012, to June 28, 2013. The exhibition featured "over fifty international contemporary artists exploring a broad range of subjects, including the evolving social and religious attitudes toward sexuality; issues of alienation, marginalization, and inclusion; the impact on the family, child-rearing, and life stages; violence and persecution; AIDS/HIV; and the influence of the LGBTQI community on the Jewish and larger world." See the online exhibition catalog at http://huc.edu/flipbook/2012/the-sexuality-spectrum/. In May 2011, Irene Gordon curated an exhibition at the Jerusalem House of Quality of work by members of Studio Mi'shelakh (A Studio of Your Own), a collective founded by Tsipi Mizrahi to provide support and communal studio space to religious Orthodox women artists starting their careers.
11. For example, the exhibition *Dateline Israel: New Photography and Video Art*, organized in 2007 by the Jewish Museum in New York, featured work by artists that reveal "a range of contemporary attitudes about Israel as a political and cultural construction" and was well received for its presentation of the themes of contested land and the rights and needs of Israelis and Palestinians who have "outgrown the utopian model of the nation's settlement and statehood." Andy Grunberg, "Beyond Boundaries, within Borders," in *Dateline Israel: New Photography and Video Art*, ed. Susan Tumarkin Goodman (New Haven, CT: Yale University Press, 2007), 5.
12. In response to a 1994 exhibition of feminist art, *Meta-Sex* (Tel Aviv: Ein Harod Museum of Art and Bat Yam Museum), curated by the Israeli Tami Katz-Freiman, Katz-Freiman quoted one such colleague, Katherine David, the curator of *Documenta X* (1997), who felt that the feminist work on display was "not political enough." See Tami Katz-Freiman, "'Bad Girls'—The Israeli Version," in *Jewish Feminism in Israel*, ed. Kalpana Misra and Melanie S. Rich (Hanover, NH: Brandeis University Press / University Press of New England, 2003), 169n1.
13. See David Sperber, "Israeli Art Discourse and the Jewish Voice," *Images: Journal of Jewish Art and Visual Culture* 4:1 (2010): 109–31; David Sperber, "Feminist Art in Traditional and Religious Judaism," *Zeek: A Jewish Journal of Thought and Culture*, April 4, 2012, http://zeek.forward.com/articles/117543/.
14. Liss is curator of Judaica at the Museum of Art, Ein Harod, and a member of the religious kibbutz Shluchot. Sperber is an art historian and critic from a family of prominent rabbis and historians.
15. Ruth Halperin-Kaddari, "The Halachic Trap: Marriage and Family Life," in Fuchs, *Israeli Feminist Scholarship*, 158–82.

16. Andi Arnovitz, "Andi LaVine Arnovitz: Feminist Artist Statement," Elizabeth A. Sackler Center for Feminist Art, Brooklyn Museum, http://www.brooklynmuseum.org/eascfa/feminist_art_base/andi-lavine-arnovitz.
17. Kibbutz Sa'ad was established in 1947 by the Bnei Akiva religious Zionist youth movement.
18. Susan Sered, "The Ritualized Body: Brides, Purity, and the Mikveh," in Fuchs, *Israel Women's Studies*, 150.
19. Susan Sered, *What Makes Women Sick? Maternity, Modesty and Militarism in Israeli Society* (Hanover, NH: Brandeis University Press / University Press of New England, 2000).
20. Susan Sered's "The Ritualized Body" offers an insightful overview and interpretation of the origins of the *niddah-mikveh* rituals and the implications for contemporary practice.
21. Interview with the author, July 2, 2012.
22. Ibid.
23. Dana Gillerman, "Making an Exhibition of Ritual Purity," *Haaretz*, February 4, 2004.
24. Ibid.
25. Molgan bought the inspection cloths (which are also called *edim*, or "witnesses") in the grocery store in her kibbutz; at the time, a pack of eighteen cloths cost six new Israeli shekels. I am grateful to Andi Arnovitz for providing the following sources for the *bedikah* cloth in Jewish law: Lev. 15:28—a woman counts for herself and then becomes purified; Isa. 64:5—the word *edim* is used; *b. Nid.* 16ab, 58ab, 68ab—all discuss circumstances and methods of checking; *Shulchan Aruch, Yoreh Deah* 196:6—the use of a soft white cloth is described in detail.
26. Gillerman, "Making an Exhibition of Ritual Purity."
27. Ibid.
28. See Helène Aylon's memoir, *Whatever Is Contained Must Be Released* (New York: Feminist Press at the City University of New York, 2011); also Alison Gass, "The Art and Spirituality of Helène Aylon," *Bridges* 8:1–2 (2008): 12–18.
29. See Gannit Ankori, "Yoheved Weinfeld's Portraits of the Self," *Woman's Art Journal* 10:1 (1989): 22–27.
30. Ibid., 23.
31. See Sperber, "The Abject," 129–124, for an insightful discussion of "art and menstrual impurity." See also Anna M. Chave, "Normal Ills: On Embodiment, Victimization and the Origins of Feminist Art," in *Trauma and Visuality in Modernity*, ed. Eric Rosenberg and Lisa Saltzman (Hanover, NH: University Press of New England, 2006), 132–57; and Lisa Bloom, *Jewish Identities in American Feminist Art: Ghosts of Ethnicities* (New York and London: Routledge, 2006).
32. See Mary Douglas, *Purity and Danger* (New York: Routledge, 1969). Julia Kristeva describes abjection as "that state of uncertainty between subject and object that consciousness conceives as abject—state of uncertainty regarding the *identity* of the self and the *other*." Julia Kristeva, "Pouvoirs de l'horreurs," *Tel Quel* 86 (1980): 50.

33. Interview with the author, July 2, 2012.
34. See http://www.youtube.com/user/hagitmolgan.
35. Interview with the author, July 3, 2012.
36. Ibid.
37. Nurit Banai, "Hila Karabelnikov—Tel Aviv," *Art Papers* 31:4 (2007): 74–75.
38. David Sperber has traced the significant presence of the *mikveh* in international Jewish feminist art in "The Abject," 124–118.
39. Quoted in ibid., 120, from his interview with the artist.
40. The exhibition took place April 18 through May 11, 2013, at the Zaritsky Artists House, Tel Aviv. See Raz Samira and Nurit Jacobs-Yinon, eds., *A Tale of a Woman and a Robe* (Tel Aviv: Zaritsky Artists House, 2013).
41. Interview with the author, July 3, 2012.
42. Mierle Laderman Ukeles, "Mikva Dreams—A Performance," *Heresies* 2:1 ("The Great Goddess," 1978): 52–54. In 1986, Ukeles exhibited an installation on the *mikveh* theme at the Jewish Museum in New York. For more on Mierle Ukeles and her *mikveh* series, see Bloom, *Jewish Identities in American Feminist Art*, 52.
43. See Mierle Laderman Ukeles, "Mikva Dreams—A Performance."
44. See Sperber, "The Abject," 122; and Bloom, *Jewish Identities in American Feminist Art*, 52.
45. For example, see Susan Sered's review of the Israeli filmmaker Anat Zuria's film *Purity*, 2004, in *NASHIM: A Journal of Jewish Women's Studies and Gender Issues* (2004): 263–65.
46. See Hartman, *Feminism Encounters Traditional Judaism*, 45–61; Zvi Triger, "The Self-Defeating Nature of 'Modesty'-Based Gender Segregation," *Israel Studies* 18 (2013): 19–28; Ricky Shapira-Rosenberg, *Excluded, for God's Sake: Gender Segregation in Public Space in Israel* (Jerusalem: Israel Religious Action Center, 2010).
47. Email correspondence with the author, January 19, 2013.
48. Interview with the author, July 3, 2012.
49. Ibid.
50. Galia Yahav, "Hila Karabelnikov-Paz: Sheraton Beach," *Haaretz*, March 12, 2012, trans. Stav Palti-Negev.
51. Ibid. For a range of critical responses to Karabelnikov-Paz's *Sheraton Beach* series, see Hila Shkolnik-Brenner, "Hila Karabelnikov-Paz," *City Mouse Magazine*, April 15, 2012. While the literature on bathers and feminist art history is vast, see in particular Linda Nochlin, *Bathers, Bodies, Beauty: The Visceral Eye* (Cambridge, MA: Harvard University Press, 2006).
52. The term "male gaze" was coined by Laura Mulvey in her seminal "Visual Pleasure and Narrative Cinema," first published in *Screen* 16 (Autumn 1975). Mulvey is known for her role in establishing a psychoanalytically grounded body of literature on gaze theory in cinematic studies that focuses on representation and sexuality and its relationship to the dominance of the male power structure within patriarchal society.
53. Yahav, "Hila Karabelnikov-Paz: Sheraton Beach."

54. Uzi Zur, "Days of the Women Apart," *Haaretz*, March 16, 2012.
55. One might productively compare Karabelnikov-Paz's series to the contemporary work of the secular Israeli-American photographer Michal Ronnen Safdie, who for four years engaged in a project in which she took hundreds of photographs of women at the religious beach in Tel Aviv. Safdie's series, titled *Sunday, Tuesday, Thursday*, was exhibited at Andrea Meislin Gallery, New York, in March 2012. See Eric Herschthal, "Not Your Typical Beach Days," *Jewish Week*, February 21, 2012. Also of interest is the work of the American secular artist Gillian Laub, who for ten years has photographed people of diverse ages and religious and cultural backgrounds (including Arabs, Orthodox Jewish women, American teenagers, Russian and Ethiopian immigrants, and Filipino and Chinese workers) on the Tel Aviv beaches. See Gillian Laub's photo essay "Tel Aviv Beach: One Photographer's Enduring Oasis," *Time-Lightbox*, October 10, 2011, http://lightbox.time.com/2011/10/10/israeli-beach-gillian-laub/#1. See also Gillian Laub, *Testimony* (New York: Aperture, 2007), which features portraits of Israelis and Palestinians.
56. Interview with the author, July 3, 2012. Karabelnikov-Paz received her master of fine arts from Bezalel Academy of Arts and Design in 2013.
57. For an excellent overview of Arnovitz's career and practice, see Dvora Liss, "Tear / Repair," in *Tear / Repair: Andi Arnovitz*, exhibition catalog for *Tear / Repair*, Brandeis University, spring 2010, and Yeshiva University, summer–fall 2010 (Jerusalem, 2010).
58. Ibid., 4. Arnovitz also collects and exhibits colorful textiles, jewelry, and pottery from Uzbek, Turkish, and other Middle Eastern, Asian, and African cultures that inspire her work in her home.
59. The literature on divorce and the *agunah* problem in Israel is vast. See Ruth Halperin-Kaddari, "The Halachic Trap: Marriage and Family Life," in Fuchs, *Israeli Feminist Scholarship*, 165–67; Susan M. Weiss and Netty C. Gross-Horowitz, eds., *Marriage and Divorce in the Jewish State: Israel's Civil War* (Waltham, MA: Brandeis University Press, 2012).
60. Interview with the artist, July 1, 2012.
61. Ibid.
62. Ibid.
63. It is unknown how many women in Israel are *agunot*. Israeli rabbinic courts have released numbers that many activists, including Mavoi Satum, an *agunah* advocacy agency in Israel, believe are too low to be credible. See Sam Sokol, "Rabbinical Court: 4.7% Rise in National Divorce Rate," *Jerusalem Post*, January 29, 2013.
64. See Tsipy Ivry, "Halachic Infertility: Rabbis, Doctors, and the Struggle over Professional Boundaries," *Medical Anthropology: Cross Cultural Studies in Health and Illness* 32:3 (2013): 208–26.
65. Sered, *What Makes Women Sick?*, 17.
66. Ibid.
67. Andi Arnovitz, "Works: *4% of Us*," Andi Arnovitz's website, http://andiarnovitz.com/work/4-of-us. For background on Dr. Rozenak's claims, see Yair Ettinger, "Be Pure or Be Fruitful," *Haaretz*, December 6, 2010.

68. Andi Arnovitz, unpublished artist's statement.
69. Ibid.
70. Ibid.
71. Galia Bar-Or, *"Hayenu mehayevim omanut": Binyan tarbut ke-binyan hevrah: Muze'onim le-omanut be-kibbutzim 1930–1960* ("Our life requires art": Culture building as society building: Art museums in kibbutzim, 1930–1960) (Beer-Sheva, Israel: Ben-Gurion University of the Negev, 2010).
72. See Sorin Heller, "Shaping Identity in Peripheral Museums in Israel" (Ph.D. diss., Anglia Ruskin University, 2010). Heller has categorized the exhibition themes of the Museum of Art, Ein Harod, as focused on the following categories: "Preoccupation with art within the kibbutz movement; preoccupation with women's identity issues, history of Israeli art, preoccupations of Israeli society, refugees from Nazi Europe and new immigrants, contemporary art issues (mostly focused on Israeli art), and photography" (218–19).
73. See Alexander Alberro, "Institutions, Critique, and Institutional Critique," in Alberro and Stimson, *Institutional Critique*, 15, for a discussion of what he calls "Exit Strategies" to characterize the recent work of artists who engage in "tactical media strategies to intervene effectively in an array of fields that are far removed from the institutions of art."
74. Ibid.
75. Ibid., 17.
76. Interview with the author, July 2, 2012.
77. Interview with the author, July 2, 2012.
78. Ibid.
79. There is extensive literature on imagery of the *burqa* and the veil in contemporary Islamic art and culture. See Sahar Amer, *What Is Veiling?* (Chapel Hill: University of North Carolina Press, 2014); Kristen Gresh, *She Who Tells a Story: Women Photographers from Iran and the Arab World* (Boston: MFA Publications, 2013); Valerie Behiery, "Alternative Narratives of the Veil in Contemporary Art," *Comparative Studies of South Asia, Africa, & the Middle East* 32:1 (2012): 130–46; David A. Bailey and Gilane Tawadros, eds., *Veil: Veiling, Representation, and Contemporary Art* (Cambridge, MA: MIT Press, 2003). See also *Muslima: Muslim Women's Art & Voices*, a global online exhibition from the International Museum of Women, which debuted online in March 2013 and ran through December 2013 and remains accessible at http://muslima.imow.org/about.

7

Jewish Ideological Killers

Religious Fundamentalism or Ethnic Marginality?

MICHAEL FEIGE

Evolution and Revolution in Settler Society

In a fictional theater play called *Chevlei Mashiaḥ* (the suffering before the messiah is assumed to arrive), author Motti Lerner tells of a West Bank settler family encountering a crisis.[1] Shmuel, the father and head of the family, has brought his wife and children to Samaria and became a community leader. Through the play, he fights a losing battle against the government, which reaches an agreement with Jordan and the Palestinians to evacuate the settlers. (The play was first performed in 1987, when such an agreement seemed viable.) The family is not representative of the entire settler community but only of a certain group, the National Religious ideological settlers.[2] Different male and female members of the family represent more radical or moderate views regarding the neighboring Arabs and the morality of the Jewish settlement project. Benny, Shmuel's son-in-law, joins a group that places explosives in the mosque on the Temple Mount, blowing it up and killing Muslims. The emerging peace agreement is shelved, and the settlements are saved, while Israel prepares for the inevitable war.

The national drama is played through the National Religious settler family, especially the conflict between the moderate father and the radical son-in-law. Benny uses the terminology that brought the settlers to the West Bank in the first place in order to justify his radicalism: "See how this nation sinks in slumber, . . . how it deteriorates. . . . You should ask who started the route that will force the people at long last to wake up from this slumber. You should ask how we can stop the disintegration. . . . True. There will be a war. But since when are we afraid of wars? If we have no other way, we shall get stronger through war."

His father-in-law, not able to comprehend, asks how Benny would know that the end result would not be worse, a forced arrangement that will cost not only the settlements but also Jerusalem, where the terrorist act took place. Benny again uses his father's own theology to counter his claims: "Don't try to frighten me with Holocaust and destruction [*shoah veḥurban*]. This step shall succeed even if there will be casualties. It will succeed because it is done according to the wishes of God Almighty, shall He be blessed. That is why we did it. . . . And now you can take the phone and call the police. Please do."

Benny is relentless in insisting that blowing up the mosque and killing Muslims is in line with the logic of the settlement project, as embodied by his devastated father-in-law: "You know that in your heart you justify what I have done. . . . You know that it is justified to rebel against the kingdom in order to fulfill a higher mitzvah. That purifying the Temple Mount is explicitly such a mitzvah. And what did we do by canceling this vile peace treaty? We did not fulfill a mitzvah? Even when you called us to come and settle here, we followed you to fulfill a mitzvah."

Shmuel answers as his family, along with his life's work, disintegrates before his eyes: "God Almighty . . . We settled here to force God to complete redemption?! To force Him?! I have never uttered such blasphemy. . . . To rattle God with dynamite?! . . . With prayer!!! With trying!!! Little by little, step by step, heel after toe. We came here to fulfill the mitzvah of settling the land. If this profanity came out of this, if for this mitzvah blood will be shed, we should never have come here."

While this play is a dramatic invention, it is loosely based on actual historical occurrences. In the early 1980s, the so-called Jewish Underground did target the mosques on the Temple Mount, hoping to bring forth salvation. The group was apprehended before it could complete its plot but after it had committed several terrorist acts against Palestinians; its members were sentenced to long terms in jail, though they were released within a few years. While the group was small and enjoyed little support among the settlers, arguments like the one portrayed in the play actually took place, for example, in jail between the members of the Underground and the disappointed friends coming to visit them. Yoel Bin-Nun, a settler from Ofra, criticized the acts, claiming that redemption would come only through gradual evolution, through slowly settling hills and settling in the hearts of Jewish Israelis. Yehudah Etzion, his next-door neighbor who shared his vision and struggle for two decades and now was among the leaders of the Underground, responded that it was time for revolution.

The questions of whether settlement in the West Bank will lead necessarily to violence and whether the settlers will respond to threats on their communities and on their entire project have occupied Israelis for some time and have various manifestations. For example, young settlers enthusiastically join the Israel Defense Forces, and many become officers in the top units. Can they be trusted with the mission to evacuate settlements, including their own homes? Will their protest remain within the acceptable civil realm in a democratic society? In which direction will they point their weapons? Who will they listen to, their right-wing radical rabbis or their officers? Those questions remain yet without answers.[3]

Lerner's play, written in the 1980s, reflected the fears of Israeli society of that period. While those threats have not subsided, the main thrust of right-wing violence came from other directions, not anticipated by Lerner. The play shows how the violence erupts from the core group of the ideological settlers, using its own terminology of salvation. As it turned out, the Jewish Underground, especially with respect to its attempt to bring forth hasty redemption, was an isolated case. When the settler project was threatened, much of the violence came from the ethnic fringes and the marginal subcultures around the settler community.

In this chapter, I discuss the two most notorious political crimes done during the 1990s: the Cave of Machpelah massacre perpetrated by Baruch Goldstein and the assassination of Prime Minister Yitzhak Rabin committed by Yigal Amir. Goldstein, a resident of Kiryat Arba and a physician by profession, donned his army uniform from his reserve service, entered the mosque at the Cave of Machpelah, and shot twenty-nine Muslims dead while they were praying. When he stopped firing, he was killed by the worshipers. Amir, a Bar Ilan student from the city of Herzliya, waited for Rabin after a peace rally in Tel Aviv and shot him dead. He was apprehended, brought to trial, and sentenced to life imprisonment.

There are differences between the two occurrences: Goldstein's act was indiscriminate terrorism against a random group of Muslim prayers in a mosque, while Amir's was a political assassination targeted at a specific leader in a secular setting. Goldstein was killed, while Amir survived, though that is only a technicality: there is no indication that Goldstein's act was meant to be suicidal, while Amir took into account that he might be killed in the act. Goldstein's victims were Palestinians, while Amir's victim was an Israeli Jew. However, this difference, I contend, is not of the substantial importance that it may seem. When Amir was waiting for Rabin to approach, he was joking about the demonstration of left-wingers being mostly Arabs (which they were not). Rabin had been portrayed in right-wing demonstrations with an Arab keffiyeh on his head. For the extreme right wing, he was considered a traitor to his nation, therefore symbolically passing to the side of the Arabs.

Those facts lead to the more important commonalities. Both murderous acts came in the wake of—and as a response to—the Oslo Accords and the signing of the agreement between Israel and the PLO. Both murderers were religious, and, according to their understanding, both were protecting the settler community in their acts, while not belonging to the mainstream core group that they were protecting. Both were disavowed by the settler leadership and are considered, to use the settlers' favorite metaphor, bad weeds in an otherwise healthy flowerbed. The attempt by the settlers to put as much distance as possible between themselves and those killers was not uncritically accepted in Israeli society and among its leaders and elite: following Goldstein's act, there were discussions of evacuating the Jewish community of Hebron, and following Amir's act, the settlements, as well as other national-religious institutions, were placed under severe public attack. Until today, however, the two killers have been seen by the settlers, including most of their political and spiritual leaders, as an aberration rather than as symbolizing an acceptable option, though in the extreme fringes, they are hailed as national heroes, including with acts of semireligious veneration.

The cases discussed here are the best known, yet other Jewish terrorists also came from the social, ethnic, and political fringes of the settler society:[4] Yona Avrushmi, who in 1983 threw a grenade into a Peace Now demonstration, killing the activist Emil Grunzweig and injuring eight others; David Ben-Shimol, who in 1984 shot a missile into a Palestinian bus in Eastern Jerusalem, killing one; the two settlers from the Jewish Underground who physically shot Palestinians in the Islamic College in Hebron and were apprehended in 1984; Eden Natan-Zada, who killed four Israeli Arab citizens in 2005; Yaakov Teitel, who was arrested after killing a Palestinian taxi driver and a shepherd and placing a bomb at the door of the left-wing intellectual Zeev Sternhell in 2009. Almost all Jewish ideological killers have a story that places them at the margins of the settler society; in that, Goldstein and Amir are no exception.

In what follows, I explain why the religious murderers came from the fringes and the marginal subcultures of the settler society and not from the core, as "predicted" in Motti Lerner's dramatic play. I start with a presentation of the basic groups in question, namely, fundamentalists in Israel and especially Gush Emunim, which established the ideological settlements in the West Bank. From there, I describe and place the two crimes in context. Finally, I compare and draw conclusions regarding the social location from which Israel's most notorious murderers have arrived.

Religious Fundamentalism in General and in Israel: Some Definitions

While the term "fundamentalism" originated in the United States with regard to Christian evangelicals, it has been widely used in other contexts regarding other religions. Literally, "fundamentalism" means going back to the fundamentals of belief, as "radicalism" means going back to its roots. Fundamentalism characterizes all great religions in the modern age and can be understood as a religious response to secularism, consumerism, and globalization; it takes a different character according to social and cultural context.[5] Jewish fundamentalism in Israel holds similarities with other forms of fundamentalism, but it also has unique features, originating from the depth of Jewish traditions, the backdrop of Zionism, and the circumstances of a state situated in the volatile Middle East.

In the Israeli context, the term "fundamentalism" is used for various communities, each searching for its own roots, historical traditions, and religious fundamentals. The ultra-Orthodox (Haredim) believe in the eventual coming of the messiah, though not through the political vehicle of Zionism.[6] Shas, representing traditional and ultra-Orthodox Jews of Sephardic origin, has a cultural agenda of returning the glory of Sephardic Judaism.[7] In this chapter, I concentrate on one specific type of fundamentalism, the one that views the State of Israel as part of a process of divine salvation and therefore demands certain policies regarding Israel's borders and sovereignty. The National Religious version of religious radicalism, connected to the Gush Emunim movement and its offshoot groups, holds to my mind special importance due to its connection to the basic premises of Zionism and its demand to restructure Israeli society according to its principles.[8]

The drive for a messianic future came from religious sources, but it was also highly connected to the principles and discourse of Zionism itself. National movements promise salvation and connect their narrative to sacred history, and Zionism is no exception. Zionism offered itself as a continuation, even culmination, of Jewish history and as such made use of the traditional messianic discourse. While Zionism was understood as the return of the Jews to being active historical agents, it also signified "the end of history," with what was assumed to be the ultimate return of the Jews to their historical homeland.[9]

While freely using religious imagery and terminology, Zionism was basically a secular national movement, and for much of the twentieth century its dominant political parties, Labor and Revisionists alike, marginalized religion, religious groups, and religious interests. The advance and success of Zionism generated an existential crisis among religious Jews, having to do specifically with its pretensions of redemption and salvation. To the surprise and even dismay of many religious Jews, the so-called national salvation was brought about by secular leaders and secularized groups.[10]

Some Jewish streams of thought shunned away from defining Zionism in terms of religious salvation and thereby solved, or at least encountered and belittled, their dilemma. The ultra-Orthodox, for example, declared Zionism to be either a historical example of false messianism or entirely irrelevant to the future redemption, which was expected to arrive through divine intervention. Many religious Zionists accepted the national narrative and did attribute sanctity to the national movement and the state but did not necessarily connect it to the religiously promised salvation of the future.

As the Zionist zeal was waning among secular Zionists, religious Zionism offered its own version of messianism. The most important proponent of messianism for the National Religious camp was Rabbi Avraham-Yitzhak HaCohen Kook, who lived, worked, and died before the establishment of the state. He was followed by his son, Zvi Yehudah HaCohen Kook, who taught at his father's yeshiva, Merkaz HaRav, in Jerusalem. Generations of young National Religious students passed through the yeshiva and were deeply influenced by its teachings. They became the political and ideological nucleus that was to create and lead Gush Emunim and to offer an alternative messianic interpretation of Zionism.

The "Kookist" ideology/theology centers on the concept of redemption; yet unlike other religious messianic beliefs, it incorporates Zionism and the state as integral parts of its dialectical logic. According to its belief, salvation is already in the process of arriving and is obvious for everyone to see through his or her eyes. The proof is the blossoming of the land of Israel, attesting to the divine decision to return the people of Israel to their land and bring about salvation. The tools of God's will are not necessarily the true believers; they can rather be the Zionist pioneers, Israel Defense Forces soldiers, and Jews arriving in the land of Israel in general. Most may define themselves as secular; yet according to Kookist political theology, they fail to comprehend their sacred role in the religious order of things.

This theology gained national importance in the wake of the 1967 Six-Day War and the evolution of the debate over the future of the territories occupied by Israel. Followers of the teachings of Rabbi Kook were not the first or the only ones to claim that the newly acquired territories should remain in Israel's possession indefinitely, but they brought a deep religious belief that the historical events of 1967 were part of a process of divine salvation and that therefore any territorial compromise would be tantamount to religious transgression.[11] They also supplied thousands of highly motivated young men and women and a systematic program of settling in the territories in order to stop any governmental attempt to avert what they regarded as the pathway leading to national salvation. The disciples coming out of the Merkaz HaRav yeshiva who followed the teachings of Rabbi Kook formed the core of the Gush Emunim movement, whose main goal was to keep the territories, especially Judea and Samaria, under Israeli rule; and their main strategy was settling the land. The return to the ancient holy places was accompanied with a demand pointed at reconnecting the modern Israeli society to its destiny and ancient roots.

The practice of settling on the hilltops of Judea and Samaria, starting in the mid-1970s, was attempted initially without governmental consent. After the rise to power of the right-wing Begin government in 1977, there was much more cooperation between the Gush Emunim settlers and the Israeli authorities. Still, the settlers' project, while gaining in strength, was rejected by large portions of Israeli society, not to mention the international community. The main points of contention were claims that the settlers were blocking the possibility of peace and compromise and that the territory on which they settled belongs, or should belong following negotiations, to the local Palestinians. The violent eruptions between the settlers and the Palestinians also kept the legitimacy of the settlers' newfound homes in constant doubt. In any case, the divine-salvation passion of the religious-fundamentalist group of Gush Emunim supporters was not accepted by secular Israelis as a legitimate political goal.

Currently, the West Bank settlers (excluding Eastern Jerusalem) number approximately four hundred thousand people living in about 120 villages and towns. Of them, only about half are National Religious, and only a portion of those are hard-core ideologically minded settlers. The rest—among them secular Israelis and ultra-Orthodox—came to the settlements following financial incentives given by Israeli governments and due to the proximity to the large urban centers of Tel Aviv and Jerusalem. The growth of the settler community can be seen as a great success of Gush Emunim and the ideological settlers, yet through the years, they have also suffered some substantial setbacks, which they have failed to reverse even after intense political struggle. The evacuation of Sinai in 1982, the Oslo Accords of 1993 and the disengagement from the Gaza Strip in 2005 were among the most traumatic events in the settlers' history, all brought about by Israeli governmental decisions. In their struggle against these decisions, the settlers were treading on the verge of illegality but were very reluctant to alienate the Israeli public through radical violent acts.[12]

This is where distinctions between fundamentalists become important. Generally speaking, the ideological settlers do their utmost to create the image of civility and good citizenship. According to their conception, they wish to establish Israeli law in the territories where they live and therefore hesitate to undermine that law. Their theology encourages them to cooperate with secular Israeli Jews and with the state, which they consider to be sacred. Furthermore, their existence in their chosen hostile environment and their aspirations for the future are dependent on a strong Israeli state, sympathetic to their cause.

The Israeli public does not always understand or accept the fine distinctions that the settlers make between law-abiding protest and radicalized struggle. Most left-wing Israelis consider the basic existential decision of the settlers to reside in a place that is not formally part of Israel as inherently illegal and immoral. They add that, under a thin veil of legality, the settlers abuse the human rights of the local Palestinians, who in any case are not Israeli citizens. The claims of the settlers that they are law-abiding citizens is either outright rejected or ridiculed as an example of the flaw of the ethnocratic Israeli state.[13] The settlers, however, contend that they often compromise out of respect for legality, for the decisions of the democratic majority, and for the sanctity in which they hold the Israeli authorities, especially the army. Being Israeli citizens, they demand their civil right to protest governmental decisions within the acceptable frameworks.[14]

Radicals, coming from within the camp or from its fringes, do not accept these premises. They claim that the appeasement of other Israelis will only bring more calamities on the West Bank settlement project, and in any case, since the issues involve the religious dictum of never forsaking the sacred land, there is no room for compromise, not with Israelis and definitely not with Palestinians. On the way to salvation, respecting Israeli civil law and social norms is considered a luxury that true believers cannot indulge.

Regardless of what many Israelis may think, most settlers are an integral part of the Israeli political community. They mainly try to achieve their aspirations through accepted political channels, even though they often stretch what is considered legitimate. In that sense, they are not much different from fundamentalists in other democracies—the United

States is a prime example—who try to advance their agenda through the parliamentary system, using legitimate political means and with constant struggles against the extreme fringes. The question that I am dealing with in this chapter is who are those who would cross the lines and become political deviants; the two cases brought here are the most radical of them all.

Baruch Goldstein: The Making of a Jewish Terrorist

Baruch Goldstein was born in 1956 in Brooklyn, New York, as Benjamin Kappel Goldstein.[15] He came from an Orthodox family, with some pedigree to known Hasidic rabbis. While the family resided in a secular neighborhood and his father worked in the educational bureau, Benjamin was sent to the Yeshiva of Flatbush religious day school. He studied at Yeshiva University and finished with distinction in 1977. He went on to receive medical training at Albert Einstein College of Medicine.

Goldstein became a dedicated supporter of Rabbi Meir Kahane and joined the Jewish Defense League (JDL). The main actions of the JDL were protecting elderly Jews in New York's poorer neighborhoods, assaulting young African Americans and Latino Americans, and best known, high-profile provocative acts against Soviet agencies in the context of the struggle to let Jews leave the Soviet Union. Initially Rabbi Kahane's assertive actions enjoyed popularity among American Jews (his slogan "Never Again" was taken from the Warsaw Ghetto uprising), yet with the dubious legality of some of his acts, he was eventually prosecuted in US courts. When Kahane immigrated to Israel, he became an extreme right leader, holding a theology that called for the eviction of non-Jews from Israel and establishing a movement and a party called Kach.[16] Goldstein shared his views, as can be seen from a letter to the editor published in the *New York Times*:

> Disparity of birth rates, associated with a declining Aliyah, assures Israel of an Arab majority in Israel (70 years?) unless steps are taken to prevent this from occurring. Ceding the "West Bank" to the "Palestinians" would, therefore, not solve the problem. . . . It would serve only to further jeopardize Israel's security and betray a Biblical trust.

> The harsh reality is: if Israel is to avert facing the kinds of problems found in Northern Ireland today, it must act decisively to remove the Arab minority from within its borders.[17]

On Goldstein's graduation from medical school, he immigrated to Israel and joined the Israel Defense Forces. As a military doctor, he declared that he would not treat non-Jews, including Druze Israeli soldiers. He was always open and candid about his extreme right and racist views.

Goldstein married Miriam and changed his name to Baruch. The marriage ceremony was accompanied by a statement: they wanted to get married on the Temple Mount but were not allowed to do so and therefore settled for the gate leading to the place. Meir Kahane was the rabbi performing the rite.

The couple settled in Kiryat Arba, the Jewish settlement overlooking Hebron, and had four children. Years later, one of the children became the subject of controversy. He joined the Israeli air force and trained to be a pilot. The argument raged in the Israeli media regarding whether the son of a notorious father who committed the worst hate crime in Israel's history should be allowed to patrol the skies of Israel with a fighter jet loaded with missiles.

On Baruch Goldstein's release from the army, he continued to serve when called to reserve duty. He found work as a regional physician in Kiryat Arba and was a highly respected member of the community. While the majority of the nearby population was Palestinian, under the segregated conditions of the region, Goldstein was not required to accept non-Jews. He was called often to treat Israeli soldiers and civilians, including his next-door Jewish neighbors, who had been injured in terrorist acts. His dedication earned him an appreciative letter from the regional chief army doctor, Arie Eldad (later an ultrarightist member of the Knesset). His acquaintances later testified that encountering the horror of terrorism—they mentioned especially the death in his arms of his friend Mordechai Lapid and his son—left a deep psychological scar.

Goldstein remained a devoted supporter of Meir Kahane and a member of his Kach party, though he was never one of the known radical activists. He appeared in the party list for the eleventh Knesset in 1984, and the party proudly publicized having a respected member of the medical profession on its list. Rabbi Kahane was elected but without enough votes for Goldstein to enter the Knesset. By the next election, Goldstein was still on the list, yet Kach was declared a racist party and according to a new law was barred from participating. Goldstein, however, was elected to the Kiryat Arba municipality, where he represented the Kach point of view. In 1990, Meir Kahane was assassinated by a Palestinian in New York, which for Goldstein was another personal trauma begging for revenge. He helped to erect a public park in Kiryat Arba commemorating Kahane's name, a park where he was eventually buried. His leaving the local political sphere was also due to racist sentiments—he was opposed to Russian immigrants coming to Kiryat Arba for fear of their not being Jewish.

The 1992 elections that brought Yitzhak Rabin to power and afterward the Oslo Accords came as a shock to the settlers in the West Bank. Goldstein expressed his discontent with the most blatant symbolism possible, wearing a yellow star patch on his shirt bearing the word "JUDE." Defining himself as a victim persecuted by Nazis—transformed in his mind into the Israeli government—for him legitimated retaliation.

No one can say why Baruch Goldstein "snapped" when he did on February 25, 1994. Maybe the holiday of Purim had something to do with the choice of date. On Purim, Jews celebrate the reversal of fortunes, and the legendary tale ends with a massacre of the enemies in the Persian kingdom. Purim is also the holiday of masquerade; and while Goldstein was a reserve officer, donning his army uniform on that day was putting on a costume. The Purim symbolism added another mythical layer on an act of biblical resonance.

At five a.m. Goldstein left his fellow Jewish prayers at the Hall of Abraham and moved to the Hall of Isaac, where hundreds of Hebron Muslims were praying on their knees, their backs turned to the door. He threw a grenade and started firing until his weapon jammed and he was beaten to death with fire extinguishers. Twenty-nine worshipers were killed and 125 injured. In the following eruption, twenty more Palestinians were killed.

Beyond the initial horror in Israel and the world over this massacre, there were discussions in the government about removing the Jewish settlers from Hebron. Eventually the results were a much stricter segregation between Jews and Palestinians in the Cave of Machpelah and in the region in general. Radical Muslims vowed revenge, and Hamas attributed the consequent suicide attacks on Israeli buses to retaliation for Goldstein's act. The renewed cycle of violence was among the main reasons for the end of advancements in the peace process, and in that respect, Goldstein may have achieved his goal.

Goldstein did not explain his deeds. There may be an element of personal revenge, retribution, and retaliation for the death of Kahane and Goldstein's encounters with victims of terrorism in his vicinity, yet the true cause of the act went to the grave with the killer. Regardless of personal motivations, the mass murder committed by Goldstein has to be understood against the backdrop of the history of Jewish Hebron as it is interpreted by the settlers. While the entire ideological settlement in the West Bank is based on principles of memory and return, Hebron is exceptional in the multiple layers of memory and the earnestness of return. Goldstein's action resonates on much more than simply retaliation and revenge for the Palestinian terrorist acts he encountered and the death of his father figure Meir Kahane; the symbolic and mythological connections were understood instantly by the Jewish residents of the area.

According to the Bible, the city of Hebron is the place where the three patriarchs and three of the matriarchs were buried. Tradition places the burial site in the monumental building, sacred to Jews and Muslims alike, where Goldstein chose to commit the massacre. Hebron is also the town from which King David moved the capital city to Jerusalem. A traditional Jewish community lived in Hebron—one of the four holy cities in the Land of Israel—until it was brutally wiped out in the massacre of 1929. The events of Tarpat ("1929" in Hebrew letters) are a formative memory for the Jews in Hebron, and they view their penetration to the city as exercising a Jewish right to return. To their mind, the local Palestinians are the heirs of the murderers who have not paid the penalty for their crimes or even apologized. The Jews see their right to build their life there as irrefutable, based on religious, ancient mythical, and recent historical memories. According to the settlers, the local Palestinians have no right to Hebron, as their people and religion have no collective right on the Land of Israel in general; their case is further weakened by the Tarpat massacre.[18]

Living in Hebron or nearby Kiryat Arba, the Jews see the much larger Palestinian population and its right to pray in the Cave of Machpelah as a glaring injustice, a thorn in their eye, and the wrong order of things.

They actively try to transform the situation, though not through the extreme measures taken by Goldstein. However, Goldstein's act was well understood within this context. The writing that (literally) appeared on the walls of Kiryat Arba in the days following the massacre was "there are many physicians in Hebron," referring sarcastically to both Goldstein's profession and the need to address what the settlers define as a pathological state of affairs. After the murder, a story circulated that the local Palestinians had been gathering weapons in order to commit a second massacre, which was foiled by Goldstein's act.

In the symbolic world of Hebron, Baruch Goldstein is seen by many people as a saint, even by some who condemn what he did. At his gravesite, it was possible to pray with the *tallit* of the *tzaddik* (holy man). Miriam Goldstein sued the Israeli authorities, demanding that her husband's killers be brought to justice and that he be considered a victim of terrorism, a status that holds benefits in Israel. A book titled *Baruch Hagever* (blessed be the man), which was published in his memory, brought about debates in the Israeli public sphere regarding the limits of free speech.[19]

The Cave of Machpelah massacre was an attempt to close historical accounts going back millennia or, at the very least, to the Tarpat massacre and the terrorist acts of late. Closing circles, settling accounts, and returning to the sacred place were exactly what the settlers of Hebron claimed they wanted to do and the raison d'être for their arrival. Goldstein, in his act, therefore embodied the deep logic of Hebron. If that is the case, then I shall try to answer why it was Goldstein who committed this massacre.

Yigal Amir: The Making of a Political Assassin

There is a direct line connecting the two notorious murderers who emerged in the wake of the Oslo Accords, even though they never met. Yigal Amir attended Goldstein's funeral, which had a decisive impact on his decision to turn to radicalism. Rather than expressing remorse for the dead Palestinians, he felt deep sympathy with the suffering of the settlers, which, according to his interpretation, led inevitably to Goldstein's act of despair. He explained to the Shamgar Committee investigating Rabin's assassination,[20]

> I went to the funeral. I wanted first of all to learn. I never met this public, so I wanted to go and see. I said to myself that if a man gets up and sacrifices his life, then probably this public is under stress, anxious about something. So I went there and watched all the thousands that were there in the funeral. I saw the love they had for him, and I understood that the issue is not simple. I talked to people and started to realize that what we have here is not just an extremist fanatical public. It is a public that fights for the people. Values are very important to them, and many other things, but they are ostracized and radicalized.

Yigal Amir was born in 1970 as one of eight children to an ultra-Orthodox (Haredi) Yemenite family in Neve Amal, an eastern suburb of Herzliya.[21] Shlomo, his father, was a Torah scroll writer (*sofer stam*), and his mother, Geula, was a kindergarten teacher. Yigal Amir grew up as an ultra-Orthodox Yemenite boy in an ethnically and religiously diverse neighborhood, and his mixed encounters and hybrid identity became a main characteristic of his biography.

The Amirs sent their children to the ultra-Orthodox school nearby, characterized by mainly religious studies, segregation between genders, and low, if any, observance of Israeli national holidays. Amir went to high school in Yeshivat Ha-Yishuv Ha-Chadash (lit., the yeshiva of the new community), an ultra-Orthodox school located in north Tel Aviv. From there, he went on to study in Yeshivat Kerem Be-Yavneh (lit., the orchids in Yavneh), a *yeshivat hesder*, which combines religious study with army service. After studying in the yeshiva for a year or two, students are required to join the army and then finish their studies. Amir was enlisted into the army in August 1990 as part of the *yeshivat hesder* arrangement. He served for a year and a half in a unit of the Golani brigade consisting of mainly religious soldiers, before returning to finish his studies at the yeshiva. He then went on a short educational mission to teach Hebrew in Russia and was assigned to Riga, Latvia.

Amir went on to university and chose Bar-Ilan, which defines itself as a religious university based on the American model of Christian universities and colleges. He went on to study law. In one of the strange ironies of this story, a picture of him studying in the library appeared in one of the university's publications. A young Mizrachi law student, toiling over books in the serene atmosphere of the university library, was the kind of publicity that Bar-Ilan cherished. After the assassination, the picture came back to haunt the university, which neglected to notice that it was publicizing itself through the image of a notorious murderer.

Amir could be seen in his career up to that point as a mobile Mizrachi, moving up the social ladder of the National Religious community. Though he kept his black skull cap, going to Bar-Ilan and studying law were indicators of an attempt to integrate within the general Israeli society. However, this story of upward mobility and integration in the Israeli middle class was about to take a fateful twist.

At the university, Amir became politically involved. The Rabin government had just come to power, and National Religious university students were agitated and active, participating and initiating protest demonstrations against the government. Amir took an active part and found his favorite extracurricular activity in joining and leading groups to the West Bank and Gaza Strip settlements.

In addition to his political involvement, his romantic affairs were important, as they had influence on what was to come and shed interesting light on his development toward religious and political radicalism. Amir was attracted to young Ashkenazi women and had special deep relationships with some. His best known attempt at romance was with Margalit Har-Shefi, a twenty-year-old law student at Bar-Ilan who grew up in the settlement of Beit-El. She belonged to one of the more aristocratic families of the National Religious camp, her uncle and aunt Benni and Emuna Elon being influential leading figures in the settlers' camp. Later, when Amir was discussing with police investigators the way he and Har-Shefi met, he revealed his "pick-up line": "I don't start with a girl easily. First we talk ideology. I am a great admirer of Goldstein, so to know a girl I ask one question: What do you think of Goldstein? The answer reveals to me if the girl is shallow or deep, meaning attractive to me."[22] Seemingly, Har-Shefi confronted Amir, especially when he claimed that Rabin should be eliminated, telling him that he was insane and that she would inform the authorities. Amir was, in all probability, attracted to Har-Shefi romantically, while she claimed never to have considered him as a romantic partner. After a few months of friendship, they parted ways. At this point, Amir started planning in earnest how to carry out his plan and kill Rabin.

During Amir's years as an activist, he belonged to what can be considered a fringe counterculture consisting of some family and friends. His brother Haggai and his friend Dror Adani were later convicted as accomplices and sent to jail, as was Har-Shefi.

Amir came close to Rabin on a few occasions but either backed down or failed at the last moment. On the evening of November 4, 1995, Yigal Amir took his gun and went to a rally in support of Rabin's policies at a plaza in Tel Aviv (now called Rabin Plaza). He waited patiently near the steps, trying not to attract attention and allowing government ministers, including Shimon Peres, to pass him by. As Rabin was approaching his car after the end of the rally, Amir sneaked behind him and shot him in the back three times, mortally wounding Rabin and injuring his bodyguard. Amir was immediately apprehended.

The events of that evening are a traumatic watershed moment in Israeli memory. Like Goldstein's act, Amir's hammered another nail into the coffin of the Oslo Accords and peaceful negotiations between Israel and the Palestinians. Within a few months, the Israeli right, hostile to the Oslo Accords, came to power. Rabin became an Israeli and international hero of peace, and an elaborate cult developed around his image, including a national day of remembrance. Amir was positioned as the demonic villain.[23]

Amir's murder trial lasted from January 23 to March 27, 1996. When his figure and biography were first revealed to the public, Israeli audiences, media, and the judges were critical, even shocked, at his demeanor, his smile, and his lack of remorse or regret. In his defense, he used religious reasoning, claiming that he implemented a *din rodef*, the right to stop a criminal before he commits further crimes. He stressed that his motivation was not vengeance but an attempt to avert future disaster from following Rabin's policies. The enraged public was looking for further culpable parties, especially religious figures that influenced or directed Amir toward his decision. While Amir claimed that he had religious justification, and the theological discourse of the preceding years was inflammatory, no rabbi was willing to take responsibility or publicly support Amir's violent act. Amir was found guilty and sentenced to life imprisonment. His subsequent appeals were rejected. The Knesset passed a law barring the pardon for any assassin of a prime minister.

The story of Yigal Amir does not end with his incarceration. He is Israel's most famous prisoner and still holds great fascination for the Israeli public. To some fringe ultraright groups, he is a hero, and to many Israelis, especially of left-wing orientation, he is the embodiment and incarnation of their greatest anxiety—a threat to the Israeli state institutions emerging from within. Faced with a lifetime in jail, Amir needed to reinvent his image in an attempt to remain relevant to Israeli society even from within solitary confinement. He married Larisa Trembovler, an older Russian immigrant divorcée; and after a long legal battle and hunger strike, the prison authorities allowed her conjugal visit rights. In October 2007, Larisa gave birth to a son.

A few days after the assassination of Rabin, a young, angry Israeli arrived at Baruch Goldstein's tomb at Kiryat Arba and in front of cameras vandalized the shrine. He realized that the two murderous acts were connected. Both derailed Israel from a certain political path. Since then, there have occasionally been further talks between Israelis and Palestinians, yet the memory of the two violent events loom large as a warning to the violence that may erupt—either toward Palestinians or toward the decision makers—if Israel ventures to compromise.

The Marginal Fundamentalist

As is evident from the two biographies presented here, both Baruch Goldstein and Yigal Amir were marginal figures among the West Bank settlers, each for a different reason. One was an immigrant from the US and the other a Mizrachi, unlike most settlers and especially their leadership, who are mostly of veteran Ashkenazi origin. Both grew up in households leaning to ultra-Orthodoxy. Their religious education at early age did not include an intensive study of the teaching of Rabbi Kook, and they never adopted this specific political theology with any enthusiasm.

This point about political theology is of utmost importance for two reasons. One is the content of the ideology/theology that informed Gush Emunim, the engine behind the settlement project. It legitimated the settlement act yet also set limits to what was morally acceptable. This ideology claimed that salvation is apparent and visible in our time, and even if there are discrepancies between the glorious future and the disappointing present, they are only a temporal delay in the divine process. The ideology of the rabbis Kook, father and son, portrayed the state, its institutions, and its secular leaders as sacred vehicles through which God brings about redemption. Believers of these ideas can sustain tensions and discrepancies, believing them to be only temporal. Therefore, they have built-in inhibitions against exercising excessive violence against the state and its representatives.

The second reason for the importance of the Kookist worldview is that, while it invited all Jews to join in the sacred project of redeeming the people and the land, it marginalized those who were not familiar with its intricacies. The ideology/theology supplied a language, a discursive regime, with which to discuss issues of Zionism, settlements, Palestinians, and evacuations. Those who learned the sacred teachings and understood their complex meaning were privileged in the sense of being able to comprehend the salvation process in its entirety and to connect to the primary logic that motivated the settlement project. The Ashkenazi National Religious group that studied the Kookist books in schools, youth movements, and yeshivas and kept those books in its homes used this knowledge as its main symbolic capital in marginalizing those who, like them, believed in maximalist Zionist expansion and an exclusively Jewish state but based that belief on other logics and motivations.

New Jewish immigrants such as Goldstein and young Mizrachi Jews such as Amir, who did not belong to the traditional National Religious elite, were enthusiastically invited to join the project, as they were seen as living proof that the ideology held appeal for Jews regardless of ethnic background. At the same time, however, the same ideology marginalized them, kept them away from leadership positions, and restricted their social networks. In response, they often did what marginal groups in other times, places, and contexts have done: they tried to excel and prove their worth in what they felt was the pivotal mission confronting the dominant camp.

In the struggle of Goldstein and Amir for what they felt was the good of the people of Israel, for the future of the settlements, and against the Oslo Accords, they did not share the inhibitions of their friends, because they did not feel that the Kookist ideological system applied to them. The idea that salvation was predetermined regardless of setbacks was seen as a dangerous path. For Goldstein, the perceived pathology of Hebron, where Arabs have rights that are reassured and reestablished by the Oslo Accords, was an unacceptable premise. Without the Kookist optimistic historical overview, he could not see how deteriorating circumstances are actually the suffering leading to salvation. Amir saw Rabin as a mortal threat to the future of the Jewish people and an urgent danger to Israelis on both sides of the Green Line. The concept that Rabin and his government were in any sense sacred and should not be physically harmed was, for Amir, just an inexplicable expression of weakness. While he admired the leadership of Gush Emunim and the ideological settlers for their suffering and bravery, Amir also despised them for what he interpreted as an unwillingness to follow their own convictions. In his interrogation, he stated that he felt that they could not do what he did because they were still intimidated by their desire to be liked by the rest of Israelis. Both Goldstein and Amir were not occupied by such desires to be liked, though they fostered hopes that future generations will appreciate their deeds.

For Goldstein, who was politically socialized under the guidance of Meir Kahane, the world was divided between Jews and non-Jews, and all non-Jews were defined as enemies. Many of the established arrangements of Israel as a democratic liberal state were unacceptable to him, as they were unacceptable to his mentor: Arabs as citizens, Druze as soldiers, multiple versions of Jewish religiosity, negotiation with former national enemies, and so forth. The settlers of the West Bank, emerging from within Israeli society and accepting a theology that calls for patience, had a different mind-set that did not lead to murder.

For Amir, being of Yemenite origin and ultra-Orthodox in his upbringing probably also influenced his judgment. The Yemenite community in Israel was extremely critical of the treatment it received during its immigration in the early state years, and the stories of stolen children, reflecting on the Orientalist attitudes in Israel against Yemenites, are a scar that has not healed to this day.[24] The ultra-Orthodox, for their part, are critical and suspicious of the secular state for wanting to enforce secular education on children, not to mention betraying the age-old teachings of Jewish tradition. Amir belonged to two identity communities that hold bitter memories of the way they were treated in the past and are critical of the way they are still treated today. Upon joining a third community, Amir took the National Religious admiration of the state and its leaders with more than a grain of salt.

Some qualifications have to be made regarding the argument connecting ethnic marginality and violence. The first is that, indeed, there were killers who came from the inner circles of the Ashkenazi community, like the ones depicted at the opening of this chapter in Lerner's play. However, their narration of their violent acts is distinctly different from that of the killers coming from the ethnic margins. They supply one of two explanations for their violent acts: One is that violence holds a deep theological meaning of hastening redemption and can be logically deduced from the Kookist belief system. They therefore find themselves in elaborate theological discussions against their friends from the same camp, sometimes next-door neighbors, regarding the best way to connect deeds in the mundane world to the divine scheme. In the acts of the so-called Jewish Underground, exposed in 1986, its Mizrachi members did most of the actual killing yet never theorized about their acts. The leaders, especially Yehudah Etzion, entered into long discussions on their way to jail as to the pros and cons of bringing redemption through radical violent acts. The need for elaborate explanations discloses the working of moral considerations, based on the basic theology of the camp, even though theology may eventually develop toward giving legitimacy to murder.

The second explanation given by core members of Gush Emunim when they kill Arabs is that their violence is retaliatory in nature, a necessary response to a life-threatening situation. While critics from the Israeli peace camp claim that settlers evoke violence and then react with great force, the settlers explain many occurrences in which Palestinians are killed in self-defense or as a contextual response to a local problem, such as, to take an example from the southern Hebron region, a quarrel among shepherds on grazing grounds. The importance of this argumentation is that violence as such is not justified as a legitimate means of serving political purposes and hastening salvation. To sum up this point, I am by no means claiming that veteran Ashkenazi settlers of the core Gush Emunim group do not exercise violence in their relations with their social environment but that when they do, it is explained either under lofty theological discourse or as a response to a localized incident.

The illegitimacy of violence against Jews and Arabs among the ideological West Bank settlers started to change with the appearance of a second and third generation of settlers, whose education, though influenced by the teachings of Rabbi Kook, are also influenced by more radical and less intellectual approaches. Those are the generational margins of Gush Emunim, some of whom are called "the youth of the hills" and reside in "illegal outposts." They define their violent actions as retaliation, either to local events in the West Bank or to events that reach media attention, and are called a "price tag." The basic generational experience of the youth growing up in the settlements is of a terrorist threat constantly hanging over their heads and the violent death of people close to them. For them, the Palestinian presence is not a theological issue but a burning practical problem demanding quick, radical solutions. Furthermore, the State of Israel is considered by them to be a taken-for-granted—yet most problematic—reality, which no longer enjoys the same sanctity as it did in the eyes of their parents. The issues that mobilized the ethnic fringes of Gush Emunim are now appearing with a vengeance in the homes of veteran settlers in the form of their children.[25]

Another important qualification to the thesis presented here is that not all, or even most, immigrants from Western countries or Mizrachi Jews who joined the settler camp are deviants or for that matter even more radical than veteran Ashkenazi settlers are. Most of the notorious killers to come out of the Israeli right wing do share this distinction, but overall most Jewish immigrants and Mizrachim who have joined the settlers' ranks have been well absorbed and accepted. Actually, many American immigrants are known for their relative moderation in comparison to other settlers.[26]

Theologically and ideologically, the rift between veteran Israelis and new immigrants and between Ashkenazim and Mizrachim is played down among the National Religious believers. While the ultra-Orthodox Jews have religious restrictions as well as ethnic qualifications that bring bitterness and hostility to their relationships with all "others," the National Religious camp and especially the West Bank settlers have a strong ideological inclination to include all Jewish groups in their midst. Their ideological platform of Jewish exceptionalism and bringing redemption to the people cannot survive alongside overt exclusion and inner-group preference, not to mention racist attitudes. Therefore, Jewish immigrants and Mizrachi Jews have a good chance of being accepted into the settler community, including close friendships and marriage. Among young settlers, the ethnic differences seem to matter very little, if not to disappear altogether. Research on Mizrachim in Israel shows that most are becoming part of a large, homogeneous Jewish middle class, and the settler society is no exception.[27]

As for Israeli society in general, and even to a greater extent, social integration and melting-pot ideology were of great importance to the National Religious camp and especially Gush Emunim. Again, like the general national community, religious Zionism succeeded in the absorption of many people but left wide margins of people committed ideologically to the ethos of the camp yet frustrated by their difficulties with social and economic integration. The State of Israel cannot shrug off its responsibility for its disenfranchised citizens, but the settlers in the West Bank can and often do. Their ethnic margins are given the Durkheimian role of marking the boundaries of the collective. The settlers often explain to their Israeli critics that their community is peaceful and moral and cannot be responsible for the "wild weeds" that grow on their fringes. Disavowing all responsibility for the killers further strengthens the inclination not to encounter the ethnic problems that trouble the settler community and even to deny its existence.

The dangers that political criminals such as Goldstein and Amir pose to a democracy are evident; they also pose danger to the group from which they emerge and whom they claim to represent. If the settlers are to flourish and to strengthen their foothold within Israeli society—even if their eventual goal is to transform its core values—they need to control to a large extent violent outbursts that may be seen to be representative of the entire camp. However, religious fundamentalists have a problem in dealing with their radicals, as they are seen to represent the message with its greatest purity and without compromise. After failing to stop radical acts from occurring, the mainstream fundamentalist group needs to do damage control, which usually would mean clarifying the distinction between itself and the rogue individual. Therefore, while Goldstein targeted random Palestinians and Amir targeted the Israeli prime minister, they pose a threat—maybe even mainly—to the camp they support. The political left tries to glue both Goldstein and Amir to the political right in general and especially to the West Bank settlers.

The right tries to distinguish itself from the killers and to present Goldstein as a deranged individual and Amir as an act-alone killer. The settlers, therefore, define them as not truly belonging to the group.

I have tried to show how radicalism, often leading to political deviance and murder, emerges from fundamentalist religion, and even when fundamentalism is institutionalized as part of the legitimate political system, its complex structures of inclusive and exclusive practices bring about violent and illegal consequences. They may be marginalized by the core fundamentalist group, but they are also too numerous and important not to deserve academic scrutiny. Motti Lerner, in the play described at the beginning of this chapter, was right to spot the danger of how groups and individuals might act when the settler vision is threatened; but the social location of the propagators turned out to be different than he anticipated. Baruch Goldstein and Yigal Amir remain as a warning sign to the West Bank settlers and to Israeli society in general.

NOTES

1. Motti Lerner, *The Suffering of the Messiah* [in Hebrew] (Tel Aviv: Or-Am, 1988). The translations, taken from pages 99–103, are all mine.
2. The National Religious (Zionut Datit or Dati Leumi) are a distinct group of religious Orthodox in Israel, identified by knitted skull caps. They make up approximately 10% of the Israeli population and politically tend to hawkish positions. They support the West Bank settlement project and constitute half of the West Bank Jewish population.
3. For academic discussions on this dilemma, see Stuart Cohen, *The Scroll or the Sword? Dilemmas of Religion and Military Service in Israel* (London: Harwood Academic Press, 1997); Etta Bick, "Rabbis and Rulings: Insubordination in the Military and Israeli Democracy," *Journal of Church and State* 49 (2007): 305–27; Motti Inbari, *Messianic Religious Zionism Confronts Israeli Territorial Compromises* (Cambridge: Cambridge University Press, 2012).
4. The claim regarding the importance of terrorist countercultures at the fringes of the settler community has been made by Ami Pedahzur and Arie Perliger, *Jewish Terrorism in Israel* (New York: Columbia University Press, 2009). My argumentation takes a different route.
5. On fundamentalism, see, for example, Bruce B. Lawrence, *Defenders of God: The Fundamentalist Revolt against the Modern Age* (San Francisco: Harper & Row, 1989); Karen Armstrong, *The Battle for God: A History of Fundamentalism* (New York: Knopf, 2001); Gabriel A. Almond, Scott R. Appleby, and Emmanuel Sivan, *Strong Religion: The Rise of Fundamentalism around the World* (Chicago: University of Chicago Press, 2003); and the five volumes of *The Fundamentalism Project*,

ed. Martin E. Marty and R. Scott Appleby (Chicago: University of Chicago Press, 1991–94).

6. On the ultra-Orthodox in Israel, see Samuel C. Heilman and Menachem Friedman, "Religious Fundamentalism and Religious Jews: The Case of the Haredim," in *Fundamentalism Observed*, ed. Martin E. Marty and R. Scott Appleby (Chicago: University of Chicago Press, 1991), 197–264.
7. On Shas, see Yoav Peled, "Ethnic Exclusionism in the Periphery: The Case of Oriental Jews in Israel's Development Towns," *Ethnic and Racial Studies* 13 (1990): 432–43.
8. On Gush Emunim and the West Bank ideological settlers, see Gideon Aran, "Jewish Zionist Fundamentalism: The Bloc of the Faithful in Israel," in Marty and Appleby, *Fundamentalism Observed*, 265–344; Ian Lustick, *For the Land and the Lord: Jewish Fundamentalism in Israel* (New York: Council on Foreign Relations, 1991); Ian Lustick, *Unsettled States, Disputed Lands* (Ithaca, NY: Cornell University Press, 1993); Idith Zertal and Akiva Eldar, *Lords of the Land: The War over Israel's Settlements in the Occupied Territories, 1967–2007* (New York: Nation Books, 2007); Michael Feige, *Settling in the Hearts: Jewish Fundamentalism in the Occupied Territories* (Detroit: Wayne State University Press, 2009); and Gadi Taub, *The Settlers* (New Haven, CT: Yale University Press, 2010).
9. On Zionism and messianism, see Amnon Raz-Krakotzkin, "From Covenant of Peace to Holy Temple," *Theory and Criticism* 20 (2002): 100–110; and David Ohana, *Political Theologies in the Holy Land: Israeli Messianism and Its Critics* (London: Routledge, 2009). In the context of Gush Emunim, see Gideon Aran, "A Mystic-Messianic Interpretation of Modern Israeli History: The Six Day War as a Key Event in the Development of the Original Religious Culture of Gush Emunim," *Studies in Contemporary Jewry* 4 (1988): 263–75.
10. Avi Ravitzki, *Messianism, Zionism, and Jewish Religious Radicalism* (Chicago: University of Chicago Press, 1996).
11. On the Greater Israel ideology, see Arye Naor, *Greater Israel: Theology and Policy* [in Hebrew] (Haifa, Israel: Haifa University Press; and Lod, Israel: Zemorah Bitan, 2001).
12. On how the settlers encountered crisis, see Motti Inbari, *Messianic Religious Zionism Confronts Israeli Territorial Compromises* (New York: Cambridge University Press, 2012).
13. The criticism over the legality and morality of the settlers' actions are widespread, and I refer here to only two websites of the organizations mainly dedicated to exposing those acts: Peace Now (peacenow.org.il/eng/) and B'tselem (www.btselem.org/).
14. The questions of legality and legitimacy among the settlers have been discussed by Ehud Sprinzak, "Elite Illegalism in Israel and the Question of Democracy," in *Israeli Democracy under Stress*, ed. Ehud Sprinzak and Larry Diamond (London: Lynne Rienner, 1993), 98–173. An important case regarding the self-limitation of the settlers, at least according to their own definitions, arrived with the 2005 disengagement from the Gaza Strip. Thousands of settler supporters were con-

centrated in moshav Kfar Maimon, encircled by the army. The settler leadership decided not to force an encounter and left the area peacefully. They claimed that they avoided confrontation against state agencies out of their deep attachment to the state, even if it enabled the implementation of the disengagement as planned. It is impossible to know if the motivation was indeed civil or if a different decision would have changed the course of events. However, the settlers present the "Kfar Maimon decision" as proof of good citizenship. See Anat Roth, *The Secret of Its Strength: The Yesha Council and Its Campaign against the Security Fence and the Disengagement Plan* [in Hebrew] (Jerusalem: Israel Democracy Institute, 2005).

15. This biographical portrayal is taken from various sources, mainly Pedahzur and Perliger, *Jewish Terrorism in Israel*; Richard Lacayo, "The Making of a Murderous Fanatic," *Time*, March 7, 1994; *Commission of Inquiry—Massacre at the Tomb of the Patriarchs in Hebron*, June 26, 1994 (the Shamgar Report). Excerpts of the Commission of Inquiry report can be found on the Ministry of Foreign Affairs website: http://www.mfa.gov.il/mfa/aboutisrael/state/law/pages/commission%20of%20 inquiry-%20massacre%20at%20the%20tomb%20of%20the.aspx.
16. On Rabbi Kahane, the Jewish Defense League, and Kach, see Robert I. Freedman, *The False Prophet* (London: Faber and Faber, 1990); and Yair Kotler, *Heil Kahane* (New York: Adama, 1986).
17. Baruch Goldstein, "Israel Needs No New Enemy State at Its Border," *New York Times*, July 9, 1981.
18. On the Hebron settlement and a discussion of the massacre from different viewpoints, see Feige, *Settling in the Hearts*, chap. 7; and Jerold S. Auerbach, *Hebron Jews: Memory and Conflict in the Land of Israel* (Lanham, MD: Rowman & Littlefield, 2009).
19. *Baruch Hagever*, ed. Michael Ben-Horin (Jerusalem: Shalom al Yisra'el, 1995).
20. Chief Justice Meir Shamgar headed investigative committees after both Goldstein's massacre and the Rabin assassination.
21. While there is no systematic biography of Yigal Amir, there are newspaper reports that abounded after the assassination and chapters in books dedicated to Amir's act, such as Michael Karpin and Ina Friedman, *Murder in the Name of God: The Plot to Kill Yitzhak Rabin* (New York: Metropolitan Books, 1997); and Pedahzur and Perliger, *Jewish Terrorism in Israel*. My depiction is based on those sources. For more information about his biography, see my article, "Yigael Amir: The Making of a Political Assassin," in *Struggle and Survival in Palestine/Israel*, ed. Mark Levine and Gershon Shafir (Berkeley: University of California Press, 2012), 384–98, in which some of the ideas discussed in this section appeared in an earlier form.
22. Karpin and Friedman, *Murder in the Name of God*, 120.
23. Much has been written on Rabin's commemoration; see Yoram Peri, ed., *The Assassination of Yitzhak Rabin* (Stanford, CA: Stanford University Press, 2000); and Vered Vinitzki-Seroussi, *Forget-Me-Not: Yitzhak Rabin's Assassination and the Dilemmas of Commemoration* (Albany: SUNY Press, 2009).

24. Yemenites in Israel claim that in the first weeks after their arrival in Israel in 1949–50, many of their babies were snatched and given to veteran families for adaption. Several state commissions have not produced conclusive evidence for either side, yet the belief is strong and persisting.
25. Maybe the threat anticipated in Motti Lerner's play, that the young generation is poised for violent radicalization, will materialize in the future. On the youth of the hills, see Feige, *Settling in the Heart*, chap. 12.
26. On immigrants from English-speaking countries to the West Bank settlements, see Sara Yael Hirschhorn, "Operation 1000 for the Settlement of Jewish-American Immigrants in the Occupied Territories," *Israel Studies* 19:3 (2014): 81–107.
27. Uri Cohen and Nissim Leon, "The New Mizrahi Middle Class: Ethnic Mobility and Class Integration," *Israel Journal of Israeli History* 27 (2008): 51–64.

PART IV

Identity

8

Israeli Fiction

National Identity and Private Lives

NEHAMA ASCHKENASY

This chapter's two-pronged goal is to identify new directions in literary theories adopted by Israeli critics to appraise both current fiction and literary history and to highlight some of the recent fictional representations of Israel, which have been received with special interest by both the reading public and the academic community. As we will see, these representations reflect Israel's ongoing reconsideration of its relationship to both the Jewish past and the Zionist ideology out of which the country was born. Delving into Israeli writers' thematic preoccupations, as well as their imaginative landscapes and literary strategies, opens a window to the cultural and sociopsychological spirit of the Israeli people and identifies the major currents in the national frame of mind. The critical approach and the fiction itself are both propelled by changing ideological and sociopolitical attitudes. Together, they offer an avenue into Israel's search for identity and its current focus on reassessing the ideological status quo or cultural norm prevalent in the first several decades of the state.

Post-Zionism and the Issue of Canon Formation

The most conspicuous or remarkable developments in the arena of fiction and its critical reception are interconnected, originating from a general sense that Israeli culture has progressed into the "postmodern" era. In the particular case of Israel's cultural and political history, this is reflected in a "post-Zionist" attitude to the state and the nationalist ideology that gave birth to it.[1] The move by a new generation of intellectuals to deconstruct the Zionist grand story has led to the call to reassess the accepted literary canon, which was the product of the critical establishment during the first several decades of the state. Spearheaded most prominently by Hannan Hever, these critics claim that the body of works accepted as representing Israel's cultural norms and concerns had been propelled by writers' commitment to Zionism's overarching grand vision of the return of the people to their land (the Zionist metanarrative) and dictated by the dominant Zionist ideology.[2] Hever and his followers call for reshuffling the established canon by post-Zionist criteria, as some people would argue, or by no idea or ideology other than literary criteria.

To evaluate the novelty of this approach, we will contrast it to the critical paradigm of Gershon Shaked, the leading figure in Hebrew literary criticism until his death in 2006. Shaked's monumental five-volume *Hebrew Fiction* assumed that the "Zionist metaplot" was the ideological and psychological framework for the works of Hebrew writers, even those who later began to question some of Zionism's basic ideas.[3] This metaplot was also the fundamental tenet of Shaked's own investigation of Hebrew literature and the benchmark of his critical inquiry.[4] In fact, the very vocabulary that Shaked and others employed to distinguish between generations of Hebrew writers points to the close relationship between the scholarly criteria applied to the study of literature and the nation's journey from the struggle for the land to the establishment of the state and beyond—thus the terms *dor ba'aretz* (the native generation), sometimes also dubbed "the generation of the Palmach" (*dor ha-palmach*, the acronym for the legendary prestatehood elite military combat unit), or "the generation of the War of Independence" (*dor milḥemet ha-shiḥrur*) and "the generation of the state" (*dor ha-medinah*), that is, the wave of writers who came to maturity after the founding of the state. Shaked's term for the writers of Amos Oz's generation, *gal ḥadash* (a new wave), as well as the title of his next study, *gal aḥar gal* (wave after wave) implies a moving forward within the history of the state.[5] These terms signify the convergence of the literary world—the fiction and the scholarly canon makers—with the Zionist project. Using Israeli wars to define the rise of a new generation of writers is not limited to Shaked and his contemporaries. A critic of a younger age group has suggested classifying the writers born in the 1950s and therefore of military age during the 1973 war as "the generation of Yom Kippur."[6]

Indeed, perhaps no other literature of the twentieth century was as rooted in national crises or revolutionary ideologies as Hebrew literature and its accompanying scholarship. Hebrew writers felt exceptionally committed to the revival of Jewish nationality, the secularization of Jewish life, and eventually the establishment of a state. Fiction both mirrored and brought into sharp relief the changing identities of the Jew, from the pious ghetto dweller to the secular Hebraist and nationalist and later to the Palestine-bound Zionist (bypassing, initially, the victim of the Holocaust in Europe) who turned into the "new Jew," the heroic fighter for political independence in Palestine. This image continued to evolve in modern Israel into that of the disillusioned citizen, facing the discrepancy between the Zionist romantic vision and the everyday reality of numerous social ailments and a constant state of siege, and of the morally conflicted individual trying to reconcile the Zionist ethos with the treatment of the Palestinians and other issues of inequality and injustice. A kind of unspoken contract, an implicit covenant if you will, was established very early between the Hebrew writer and the community, with the former undertaking the role of accompanying, mirroring, translating, and critiquing the progression of the Zionist idea in all its transmutations and transformations, as well as reflecting the materialization of the Zionist idea in time, territory, and politics. Hebrew literature also saw itself as the moral compass of the people, pointing out ethical weaknesses or doubts and unease in the national subconscious while serving as the harbinger or pathbreaker of new sensitivities and sensibilities. These roles are reflected in the works of canonic writers such as the prestatehood Yoseph Hayim Brenner as well as of the literary voice of the generation of the war, S. Yizhar, and the Israeli-born Amos Oz and A. B. Yehoshua, to mention a few. To use the lexicon of contemporary critics, the canonical literary works took part in the building of a new nation and in promoting nationalist-patriotic sentiments in the people.

The scholarship of modern Hebrew and Israeli literature, led most prominently by Gershon Shaked and his disciples, became bound by this implicit contract: it endorsed the Zionist metanarrative and adopted it as its critical foundation, tracking the literary works as they reflected external realities, pointed to hidden trends, and eventually criticized openly and even overturned some of the basic tenets of the Zionist idea and the

Jewish state. An earlier generation of critics had been locked in a debate as to whether the godless, secular Zionist writers represented a revolution in Jewish history or its natural culmination, some claimed in the form of secular messianism.[7] The next generation of scholars, Shaked, Dan Miron, and others, already assumed the dual face of secular Hebrew literature as both revolutionary and the culmination of an age-old tradition. Shaked's description of S. Y. Agnon, the outstanding chronicler of eastern European Jewry and the early pioneers in Palestine, as the "revolutionary traditionalist" is significant. Essentially invalidating the critical approach of traditionalists such as Baruch Kurzweil and Dov Sadan, the new generation of scholars turned their critical look more sharply on the Zionist idea in all its complexities and permutations.[8] Yaron Peleg's assessment of Shaked's entire critical oeuvre as manifesting the mind of a "dialectical Zionist" is telling and accurate.[9] While Shaked never compromised on aesthetic considerations in his interpretive approach, he nevertheless embraced the Zionist project as the sociohistorical basis for his critique, examining the relationship of each generation of writers with it. Contradicting Shaked and his school, Hever and his followers no longer see the Zionist idea as a yardstick of critical evaluation; they argue that their precursors' admission or exclusion of literary works into the canon was a matter of Zionist power politics, rendered irrelevant in today's climate. Writing against the Zionist metanarrative, these critics aspire to correct literary historiography and move beyond the nationalist commitment as a canonical norm.

"Hebrew," "Jewish," "Israeli"?

The move by current critics to unsettle the accepted Hebrew canon and to release literary criteria from their Zionist/nationalist foundation has brought to the fore another issue, that of the boundaries of Hebrew literature. The implicit Zionist premise was that the literature produced in the new country would be written by Jews in the state's official language, Hebrew, and thus be heir to European Hebrew literature—born of the Enlightenment and later championing the Zionist mission. The moniker "Hebrew literature" also embedded Hebrew writings in Israel within another continuum, the linguistic/literary tradition originating in the early Hebrew masterpiece of the ancient homeland, the Bible, through the entire spectrum of Jewish history, leading eventually to Modern Hebrew, restored to a living, spoken language. Notwithstanding the commitment of Shaked and his generation to the State of Israel, they preferred to call the literature produced in Israel "Hebrew" rather than "Israeli," assuming, perhaps, that it was safer or more accurate to place this literature within the time-hallowed continuum of Hebrew writ or within the equally important movement of Jewish nationalist revival than to tie it to the geopolitical quandary. Shaked suggested that "perhaps it is easier to define who is a Jew than who is an Israeli."[10] Similarly, it seemed easier at first blush to define "Modern Hebrew literature" than "Israeli literature," because it seemed that the latter might be fraught with problems of identity, while "Hebrew" was assumed to be identical with "Jewish."

This premise was shaken when Israeli Arab writers, such as Atallah Mansour (b. 1934) and Anton Shamash (b. 1950), began to tell the Arab story in the Hebrew language, uncoupling Hebrew literature from its implied Jewish distinctiveness and claiming the language as the conduit of their own Arab identity.[11] Shamash's famous novel *Arabesques* became known for its masterful use of the Hebrew language to express the predicament of Israeli Arabs in the Jewish state.[12] With Hebrew thus co-opted by non-Jewish residents of the state and with Israeli literature becoming gradually multilingual, the search for a definition of Israeli Jewish literature has become more complex. Dan Miron has suggested the need for an inclusive, new literary paradigm that encompasses the diverse Jewish literatures produced today globally in multiple languages and that should be "open ended, never tie itself to a specific Jewish canon, and be ever ready to apply itself to whatever literary corpus experienced as 'Jewish' in the most inclusive sense of the term."[13] Presumably, contemporary Israeli-Jewish literature written in Hebrew or in any other language, together with Yiddish literature, Jewish American, and other Jewish literatures published worldwide, would thus be lumped together in a fluid, broad "Jewish" corpus.

Yet burying Israeli literature in this all-encompassing, loosely delineated "Jewish" literature is definitely not a solution for Israeli literary critics, who are still shuttling between "Hebrew literature" and "Israeli literature" to identify Jewish literature published in contemporary Israel. The term "Israeli literature" means different things to different scholars.

Thus, Shaked, in his 1999 anthology of translated fiction titled *Six Israeli Novellas*, which includes native and foreign-born writers, clearly implies that by "Israeli literature" he means a "major national literature," another way of saying Hebrew, Jewish, and Zionist.[14] Yet if the label "Israeli fiction" connotes a "national literature," then again the Israeli Arabs who write in Hebrew, like the popular Sayed Kashua, born in 1975, whose darkly humorous works explore the split personal and national identities of an Israeli Arab,[15] or who, like the late Emil Habibi, write in Arabic but partake in the Hebrew translation of their own works are excluded. These Israeli Arabs, some with prominent Israeli careers, may have a legitimate claim to identifying themselves as Israeli; Habibi was a member of the Knesset and a recipient of the prestigious Israel Prize. Conversely, we may ask if the entire literary corpus of Aharon Appelfeld, also represented in Shaked's anthology, can be termed "national," given that it is anchored either in the pre-Holocaust European Jewish community or in a post-Holocaust unspecified zone, not so much a location as an asylum for the emotionally scarred.

Further, given that even Israeli Jewish authors currently write in many languages, Hannan Hever offers a broad, multilingual, multiethnic, and multicultural definition of "Israeli literature." He suggests that "Israeli literature" is any literary document, including popular writings, literary criticism, and children's stories, produced in Israel since the creation of the state, including translations from other "Israeli languages," such as Yiddish and Arabic, and "other foreign languages," such as, presumably, English or Russian.[16] Shaked and others still continued in the 1990s to use the label "Hebrew literature" for the works of native-born writers like Oz and Yehoshua, who came of age after the birth of the state. For Hever, however, the demarcation line between "modern Hebrew literature" and "Israeli literature" is 1948, the establishment of the State of Israel, after which any literary text published in Israel is "Israeli." Hever's thinking is clearly propelled by postcolonial denunciation of any cultural, ethnic, or linguistic hegemony. He explicitly negates the notion that only a narrative written in Hebrew is "Israeli," contending that the Hebrew language is rooted in Zionism and Judaism and that such a criterion would exclude, or in fact has excluded, those who did not see themselves as fully participating in Judaism or Zionism. Obviously, underlying Hever's argument is the rejection of the premise, vastly held by Israeli literary critics until the past two decades or so, that Israeli literature is the direct heir to Modern Hebrew literature, which began in Europe during the eighteenth- to nineteenth-century Jewish Enlightenment (Haskalah), or, indeed, that it is the offshoot of the long Hebrew tradition that originated in the ancient Israelite culture. In this thinking, Hebrew thus loses its supremacy as the language that mirrors and is organically meshed with Israeli culture; instead, it is cut down to size, becoming just one of the many languages that express today's multinational, multiethnic Israeli reality.

Minority Voices Move to the Center

It is no surprise that with the loosening and reshuffling of hitherto near-sacred boundaries of ideology, language, and national identity, minority voices have gained momentum, some a central position, in the new Israeli literary scene. The postmodern temper rejects overarching systems of any kind or the privileging of one voice over the other and insists on the fractured nature of reality, of the self, and of what had been called national identity. Thus, narratives hitherto considered marginal and therefore insignificant, such as fiction's preoccupation with women's social or emotional issues, have become an inextricable element in the Israeli culture, equal to issues of political and national significance and placed at the heart of a society searching for a redefinition of its identity.

One of the major developments of the past two decades or so in Israeli life and letters is the influx of women writers into the literary scene as well as the centrality accorded them by the scholarly community. The influences of both postmodernism and modern feminist thinking freed women writers to claim legitimacy for their own narratives, which had heretofore been considered "minor" or "subjective." Within this new framework, the fragmentation of the self is no longer a psychotic female symptom but the epitome of the postmodern state of mind, with its sense of the erosion and flattening of the individual in a discombobulated universe. Further, female protagonists' tendency to sympathize with any minority or build consensus or mend that which masculine power has damaged, prevalent in contemporary women's writings, is now perceived as reflective of the national psyche as a whole and not only the female condition. Thus, Amalia Kahana-Carmon (b. 1926),

Yehudit Hendel (b. 1926), Shulamit Hareven (1931–2003), Rachel Eytan (b. 1931), Shulamit Lapid (b. 1934), and Ruth Almog (b. 1936), initially marginalized, began to enjoy public and critical accolades in the late 1970s. Women writers have also become bolder in their choice of narrative themes, breaking normative boundaries and no longer shying away from themes such as lesbian relationships, love affairs with Palestinian men, or conceiving the Israeli territory within a post-Zionist system. Some of the names representing these trends are Savyon Liebrecht (b. 1948 in Germany), Michal Govrin (b. 1950), Shifra Horn (b. 1951), Nava Semel (b. 1954), Zeruya Shalev (b. 1959), Ronit Matalon (b.1959), Orly Castel-Bloom (b. 1960), and Yehudith Katzir (b. 1963). The progress of Israeli women writers from marginality to the epicenter of contemporary culture and their assimilation into the canon by the scholarly establishment are major new trends of the past two decades or so.[17]

Another group that has moved from the margin to the mainstream is Sephardi writers, who are breaking the borders of the established canon, heretofore Ashkenazi dominated; among them are Sami Michael, Amnon Shamosh, Shimon Ballas, Dan-Banaya Seri, and Ronit Matalon. Several Sephardi writers had already been regarded as canonical, such as, in an earlier generation, the Palestine-born Yehuda Burla, who depicted the lives and cultural practices of the Sephardi community in the prestatehood era. Of the "new wave" generation, A. B. Yehoshua, also of a Sephardi family, has been a major literary figure in Israel and internationally, greatly esteemed by the scholarly community and the general public alike. Yet the new Sephardi writers are more of a wave than isolated cases; they explore more closely the conflicted Sephardi identity against the background of this community's characteristics, traditions, and experience, both in Israel and the Diaspora, thus challenging Ashkenazi-European dominance with regard to thematic focus and cultural tenets. In fact, a growing number of scholars have recently called for broadening the Euro-centeredness of Hebrew literary historiography and for investigating the Arab cultures and customs needed to understand Sephardi writers, including those born in Arab countries and in Israel. They also point out the difficult choices that Sephardi writers have had to make when attempting to establish themselves within an Ashkenazi sociocultural hegemony and a literary environment still steeped in European/Enlightenment thinking.[18]

Recently, Israeli-based fiction in languages other than Yiddish or Arabic, such as English and Russian, have also gained a following and added another facet to the cultural and linguistic diversity of the current Israeli scene.[19] Russian Jewish literature is also making its mark on Israeli fiction, often exploring the Russian immigrant's encounter with Israeli reality with humor and an inventive synthesis of the Russian and Hebrew languages.[20]

Holocaust Writings and the National Memory

Another discernible turn in Israeli culture and letters is the transformation in the status of writings about the Holocaust, partially as a result of the coming of age of the "second-generation" Holocaust survivors. For the age group born and bred in the country, the European Jewish catastrophe is not a personal memory but a disturbing specter, often left unspoken by the survivors themselves yet affecting the upbringing of their children as well as the nation's collective consciousness. Within the past two decades, the "second generation" has taken its place in the Israeli literary scene, and mainstream writers, among them David Grossman, Ruth Almog, and Savyon Liebrecht, have dealt with the Holocaust's long and disturbing shadow from the point of view of a post-Holocaust Israeli generation. Simultaneously, the works of the survivor Aharon Appelfeld, long stamped with the label "Holocaust fiction," which implied a narrow literary canvas and a marginal role in Israeli culture and society, have become the focus of a host of literary studies, uncovering in them testimony to some of the central issues of modern life.[21]

In the general culture as well, a new era in the understanding of the Holocaust experience and its integration into the Israeli psyche and the national identity has set in. The Holocaust is no longer muffled or suppressed as a tragedy of the Jewish people but is seen as necessary to understanding Israeli identity. This is reflected in the country's pedagogic efforts to assimilate Holocaust history into the curriculum and to initiate school trips to Auschwitz, as well as in the tremendous flow of memoirs and the prominence of Holocaust studies in academia. These trends have generated a new understanding of the Holocaust's role in the national identity, claiming for it a central place in contemporary literary works. The Holocaust in all its aspects—the victimization of Jews; its genocidal purpose; its "humiliating" aspect; its heroic instances; its various "uses," some people have suggested exploitation, as a political and educational tool in Israel—is now viewed as not only part of the Jewish experience but, for good or bad, an inextricable component of contemporary Israeli identity.[22]

Narrating the Self and the Collective Identity

In recent decades, the hybrid genre of "life writing" or "self-narration," retelling one's life as a form of fictional art, has gained momentum in Israeli literature. Several fictional biographies, published recently by prominent writers, were well received by the public and endorsed by the scholarly community. The search for the earlier self ties together the reconstruction of the individual's history with that of the nation and thus signifies the unique interlocking of private and collective memories in Hebrew literature.

Paradoxically, in an era of postmodern fiction, which depicts the shrinking and hollowing out of the self, the genre of life narrative proclaims the centrality of the self, even as it wrestles with questions of national and personal identities.[23] Self-narration, which strives to define one's identity by revisiting the past and attempting to reconstruct private memories, is clearly driven by early modernist insistence on individualism, not by the postmodernist temper. It appears that the postmodern or post-Zionist spirit that prevails currently in large circles of the creative and academic communities alike is certainly not the only voice or mode of thinking that drives the contemporary Israeli writer. It may be argued that some of the more important fictional works published in Israel in the past two decades are firmly ensconced, in different degrees and shadings, within the Zionist narrative.

Several critics have maintained that some writers of the younger generation, who portray the fragmentation of the Zionist identity, are not necessarily fully committed to the minority identity politics of the postmodern school.[24] Further, even with postmodern currents animating younger generations of writers and critics alike, many of the works that have captivated the Israeli public in the past fifteen years or so are still firmly rooted in Zionist history and ethos.

To illustrate how individual literary works represent the ongoing Israeli search for a firm collective self-definition, as well as the recent permutations and shifting in the understanding of what constitutes the national identity, I have chosen three of the most influential works of the past decade and a half, Amos Oz's *A Tale of Love and Darkness*, Aharon Appelfeld's *The Story of a Life*, and David Grossman's *To the End of the Land*.[25] These works have made a strong impact on the Israeli reading public and its literary scholars in the past decade and a half, touching the very nerve center of the Israeli psyche. They are also seen abroad as insightful representations of contemporary Israel. Significantly, these authors do not belong to the current young crop of postmodernist or feminist writers but to groups that had dominated the Israeli literary scene for a long while.

Amos Oz: *A Tale of Love and Darkness*

Amos Oz's memoirs, an autobiography that reads like fiction, stirred deeply the Israeli public at large and the scholarly community. The work mingles Oz's recollections of a painful childhood during the prestatehood and early statehood years with the most critical events in Israeli life: the difficulties encountered by the eastern European immigrant community in the primitive conditions of Palestine, the political morass in the waning years of the British Mandate, the United Nations' dramatic vote for partition in November 1947, and more. Oz re-creates Jerusalem of that era in colorful realism, populating it with real-life personalities from his own family as well as from the public arena. The tale follows the emotional and political transformation of Amos Klausner, of a right-wing family and great-nephew of the noted Revisionist scholar Joseph Klausner, as he becomes Amos Oz, a member of a socialist, left-wing kibbutz.

The critical appraisals of *A Tale of Love and Darkness* focused on the artistic and aesthetic elements of the book, treating this autobiography as a "novel," an "autobiographic novel," or a "family saga." A special issue of the scholarly journal *Israel* was dedicated to it, featuring essays by Israel's most prominent critics,[26] and numerous conference panels and public/academic discussions in Israel and abroad also focused on *A Tale*. The reading public responded to Oz's book with enthusiasm, making it an instant best-seller and sending letters reminiscing about the sites, facts, and public events recalled in the book and shared by Oz's readers.[27] It appears that many people read Oz's tale not so much for its art but for its sociocultural relevance, reflecting the cultural mood (zeitgeist) of the first-generation natives, or Sabras. This reception undoubtedly pointed to a collective nostalgia for an era viewed as more heroic and filled with Zionist innocence and optimism, in spite of the obvious darker moments and personal frustrations experienced by the fledgling community at the time.

For both critics and Oz's following, *A Tale* inevitably sets off a reshuffling of the writer's entire body of work, as it illuminates the origins of the many treacherous females in his works, tracks the writer's personal and political journey, and also reconstructs, both factually and lyrically, historical events of national significance, mostly through the lens of the child Amos.

Oz represents two types of reactions to the prestatehood reality encountered by European Jews in the personalities and backgrounds of his parents. His father, Yehuda Klausner, of a prominent Revisionist family, saw in the country the last stop for himself personally and for his generation in spite of his own career disappointments. His mother, Fania, sensitive and imaginative, was plagued by depression and unable to accept the shabbiness of her new circumstances or the foreign Oriental culture surrounding her. For lifelong Oz admirers, Fania is a culmination of numerous fictional women in Oz's works who betray their husbands and sons in some way. While Fania's suicide, shortly before her son's Bar Mitzvah, had long been known to the Israeli public, Oz narrates it here for the first time in his career. Fania's tragic death appears to be not only at the heart of the present autobiography but a motivating force behind Oz's entire body of work, marked by recurrent figures of neurotic mothers and their gentle, precocious sons; or hypersensitive and treacherous females; or pairs of mediocre, pedestrian males and highly imaginative, poetic females.

In Oz's treatment of the real-life woman, he masterfully blends actual events with literary art. The textual fashioning of his mother, Fania Klausner, who comes fully to life in *A Tale*, follows the same stylistic strategies manifest in Oz's fictional women, those of multiple embeddings of biblical and modern literary images and mythic archetypes, density of connotations, evasions, gaps, and the fusion of reality and fantasy. But what is of great significance is that Oz ties his mother's anguished last years to the tortured journey toward statehood of the entire *yishuv*, the prestatehood Jewish community in Palestine. Thus, the loss of the mother and the birth of the motherland become connected and loom large as a dual emotional climax in Oz's childhood years.

Another compelling element that ties Oz's private tale with the nation's search for identity is the writer's depiction of his spiritual journey, well known in a broad way but here illuminated and tied to the family drama. He explains his own choice, as a child, to align himself with his sensitive, nonpolitical, poetic mother against his father.

A Tale conforms to several paradigmatic patterns in Western autobiographies that dwell on the period of childhood.[28] In this model, a crucial event in childhood becomes life changing; in Oz's case, it is his mother's sudden disappearance from his life. Another element is a conversion, religious or otherwise, as a maturing process that moves the subject toward self-discovery. In Oz's case, the conversion is quite significant, from the right-wing nationalist fervor of his extended family to the labor movement and left-of-center ideology. We may see in Oz's personal experiences a modern, secular variation of what Alan Mintz calls "apostasy narrative" in early Hebrew autobiography.[29] Linked to conversion is the archetype of rebellion against the father, which, in the present narrative, is Amos Klausner's emotional, ideological, and finally physical estrangement from his father. To use the Talmudic phrase adopted by Mintz, Oz banished himself from his father's table by rejecting what the latter stood for, in his case not traditional-religious Judaism but his father's ideology and the entire learned ambience in Jerusalem. The death of the mother directly leads to the "killing of the father": "At the age of fourteen and a half, a couple of years after my mother's death, I killed my father and the whole of Jerusalem, changed my name, and went on my own to Kibbutz Hulda to live there over the ruins. I killed him particularly by changing my name."[30]

As much as *A Tale* is a feast for Oz's devoted following in the public and in academia, it seems that it also tugs at the collective national longings for reaffirmation of the basic Zionist creed. *A Tale* is replete with recollections of momentous events of national significance that moved the public at large, thus testifying to the national spirit in the new millennium. Among the many historical episodes that Oz re-creates is the infamous Arab massacre of the convoy of physicians and professors to Hadassah Hospital on Mount Scopus while British forces stood idly by, a scene witnessed in horror by many Jerusalemites.[31] Another recalled experience is that of the child Amos waiting anxiously, with the rest of Jerusalem, for the results of the vote for partition by the UN General Assembly in Lake Success in November 29, 1947,[32] a memorable night in the country, which Oz also narrates in his novella *Panther in the Basement* from the point of view of his fictional child protagonist, Proffy.[33]

Gershon Shaked is right in noting that in this work Oz places himself solidly within the "Zionist narrative."[34] Contrary to contemporary postcolonialist theoreticians who argue that the concept of a "nation" is a falsehood, concocted by the majority to oppress and silence minority voices, Oz's memoirs reaffirm his strong belief in the genuine validity and integrity of an Israeli/Jewish "nation" and the fundamental values of Zionism. Here, as well as in his entire body of work, Oz appears to be a humanist, respectful of the concept of individualism, compassionate toward failed people, and tolerant of the vicissitudes of the human heart. And in his geopolitical and social views, he is deeply aware of the tragedy of a dual claim to the same land, sympathetic to the plight of the Arab population, averse to the glorification of militarism and the cult of "heroism," and capable of honestly weighing issues from both sides. Oz's open criticism of Israeli society's moral and ethical failings is still within, and from the viewpoint of, the Zionist metanarrative.

Aharon Appelfeld: *The Story of a Life*

In many ways, Aharon Appelfeld's 1999 autobiography/fiction is a diametrical opposite of Oz's fictionalized memoirs. The age difference between Oz (b. 1939) and Appelfeld (b. 1932) may not be that significant, but the generational difference is. For the native-born Oz, Israel is the mother country, his spiritual and emotional habitat, in which he is the ultimate insider, a Sabra. Hebrew is not only Oz's native tongue but the storehouse of his networks of associations, the lexicon of his inner being and spirit, and the medium through which he can best exercise his creativity. Appelfeld's relationship with the country and its language has always been difficult, even though he has been granted canonical stature by Hebrew scholars. Though living in Israel since 1946 and recognized as a member of the "new wave," Appelfeld has held the paradoxical status of being mainstream and marginal, both in his own eyes and in those of the Israeli readership. *The Story of a Life*, undoubtedly the most intimate revelation of his inner being and artistic struggles, deals in large part with his estrangement from the country and the language he adopted by force of circumstances when he was fourteen. Appelfeld's fictional region is mostly pre-Holocaust Europe, a world the modern Israeli has largely tried to ignore, inhabited by assimilated, secular Jews in the throes of a colossal, tragic denial. His literary lineage is European modernism, with only thin ties to precursors from among the prestatehood Hebrew writers. In his continued insistence on themes removed from present-day Israeli life, his foreign landscapes, and ambiguity toward the Israeli culture and even Zionism, Appelfeld has thus set himself apart from the most prominent Israeli writers of his generation, whose works speak directly to the pressing geopolitical and social issues of the times. Yet, like Amos Oz, Appelfeld calls his autobiography a "tale" (*sippur*), thus mixing fact and art; and in both cases, the writer's life involves a childhood overcast by a critical trauma. Further, for both Oz and Appelfeld, the fictional works preceding the current "life story" form concentric circles that progressively narrow until they reach the point at the center, the real-life child, the subject of the current narrative, Amos and Aharon, respectively. The author as child is at the heart of all the various child figures that populate the works of each of these writers, while experiences from their own lives are interwoven into the plots and dramatic narratives in their fictional tales.

Both Oz and Appelfeld assume fluidity between art and life while addressing the question of fidelity to history versus the veracity of an imaginative tale. Thus, a life revisited is given a literary representation and becomes fiction, not in the sense of being fictitious but by being represented with the same artistic quality and narrative techniques that are unique to the aesthetics of each of these writers. Even though the term "story of a life" may promise a linear telling of events from childhood to present time, in both works there is avoidance of straight chronological lines in favor of more fractured narratives dictated by the logic of subjectivity rather than fidelity to the historical sequence of events.

While Oz writes from the comfort zone of a native-born, an "Israeli" in every way, and Appelfeld is still the "Diaspora" Jew, both chronicle childhoods of exceptional sensitivity and contemplation. In addition to narrating journeys into a stretch of recent Jewish history, both provide windows into the making of an artist, portraits of the artist as a child and a young man. As in Oz's case, the loss of a mother at an early age, though under radically different circumstances, is a crucial, life-changing tragedy for Appelfeld; and like Oz, he attributes his artistic sensitivity to his mother.[35] Both writers present an individualistic perception of their environment, insisting that it is more potent or truthful than the dictates of the national collective.

A major theme in Appelfeld's writings as well as in his present autobiography is the loss of identity in the existential sense as well as the quest for self-definition as a person, as a member of a community, and as an artist. For Appelfeld, the shedding of his Jewish identity is a necessary tool of survival in a murderous world. His happy childhood in a well-to-do, middle-class, secular family in Czernowich, Bukovina, was violently interrupted by the tumultuous events of World War II. His mother was brutally murdered, and he later became separated from his father; as a mere seven-year-old, Appelfeld found himself wandering the hinterland of war-ravaged Europe, instinctively understanding that he needed to mentally dissociate from his former self as the child who had been "enveloped . . . with so much love and warmth," as he says.[36] Appelfeld's early stories present the figure of the youngster on the run, hiding his Jewish identity for sheer survival. Indeed, the very texture of the experiences that Appelfeld shares with us in the present work has already appeared in different shades and nuances in his earlier fiction. Growing up in a secular household but exposed to Jewish tradition by his grandparents, Appelfeld describes with great sympathy both his parents and his grandparents. In his fictional works, he offers vignettes of Holocaust child survivors who grew up in assimilated families and remained forever bewildered as adults, often reflecting the delusion and ultimate tragedy of assimilated Jews, such as in *The Age of Wonders*,[37] among many other stories.

For Appelfeld, the early loss of a defined, solid selfhood as a child fugitive becomes intertwined with his struggle to develop an affinity with what was commonly held, during his first years in Israel, as the "national character." The crux of Appelfeld's present life narrative is his sense of alienation in Israel, which, at the time when he arrived, was suffused with a military, macho culture, cultivating the myth of the "new Jew," the opposite of the shtetl Jew: heroic while the shtetl Jew was cowardly, a fighter while shtetl Jews let themselves "be led like lambs to slaughter."[38] Appelfeld describes his efforts to shed his Diaspora mannerism and appearance, in an attempt to lose his old identity, flimsy and unclear to him as it had been, and improbably adopt an "Israeli" personality, alien to his nature and doomed to failure. Together with his inability to blend into the culture, he still regarded his mother's German and his grandparents' Yiddish as his mother tongues, while the Hebrew language was seen by him as a soldierly, macho language, or a "stepmother."[39] Significantly, he felt that the social club of the Holocaust survivors from his region was his only "home" in Israel and mourned its closing when the older generation disappeared and the younger found little interest in it.[40] In an especially poignant scene, displaying the blending of fiction and fact in the present life story and epitomizing the writer's total alienation from Israeli culture as a young man, Appelfeld tells of an episode when he was checked by the military physicians before his induction to the army. The military physicians "chuckled" at the skinny immigrant, with poor eyesight and a curvature in his back, who wished to become an Israeli soldier.[41]

But in a remembered scene from the 1973 war, Appelfeld provides an interesting closure to his paradoxical insider-outsider relationship with Israeli culture. On the banks of the Suez Canal, Appelfeld, now an officer in the Education Corps, succeeds in bonding with the young soldiers, some of whom are "second-generation Holocaust survivors." The soldiers, in the midst of a different Jewish predicament, display a great interest in the Holocaust and the European Jewish life that preceded it; and finally, Appelfeld, as well as the young Israelis around him, feel part of a larger Jewish experience: "As different as the struggle was here, it was, nevertheless, the same ancient curse pursuing us."[42] This scene confirms what we know about the change that occurred in Israeli culture following the explosion of the myth of Israeli invincibility caused by the Yom Kippur War. A more favorable Israeli attitude toward the Jewish historical experience ensued, resulting as well in more sympathy with Appelfeld's European landscape and also signifying the emergence of Israeli writers who carried with them the Holocaust as a secondhand experience.

These two army scenes function as bookends in the present life narrative, marking the journey that both the real/fictional Aharon and Israeli society at large have taken toward becoming more understanding of the European Jewish experience. One might argue that it is not Appelfeld who becomes more "Israeli" but that the young Israelis become more "diasporic," assimilating the Jewish historical experience into their own identity and thus implying that Israeliness and Jewishness are not contradictory. In some ways, the Yom Kippur episode marks less of a transformation in Appelfeld's journey toward becoming an "Israeli" than it does the young Israelis' journey toward becoming more "Jewish."

In fact, Appelfeld sees his works as contributing to the integration of Holocaust awareness into Israeli culture, as part of both a Jewish past that needs to be remembered and the Israeli fabric of cultural memory and national identity. His own struggles as a writer provide a window into the change that has occurred in Israeli society with regard to the Holocaust. When he began to publish his stories, Appelfeld had to contend with Israeli society's inclination to silence the Holocaust voices or to highlight instances of heroism and resistance. The latter was meant to serve as a model to the new Israeli generation and as reinforcement of the Zionist idea of *shelilat ha-golah* (negating the Diaspora). Thus, Appelfeld's stories of cowering, unglamorous victims were met with "Where were the heroes? Where were the Ghetto uprisings?"[43]

In some ways, Appelfeld's poetics is not distant from those of other modernist writers, European and Israeli; his "gray" protagonists conform to the modernist preference for a nonheroic, Leopold Bloom type of protagonist. Further, even mainstream Israeli literature of the 1960s and 1970s became engaged in puncturing the previous generation's "myth of the hero." One of the prominent examples of this trend is the disillusioned, rebellious Yonatan of Amos Oz's *A Perfect Peace*,[44] who rejects the notion that he acted with "courage under fire" and describes himself reduced to a terrified child on the battlefield. Nevertheless, Yonatan, the Israeli "antihero," is not Appelfeld's broken Holocaust survivor, nor is Yonatan's alienation from the oppressive collectivism of the kibbutz similar to that of Appelfeld's pathetic would-be soldier in a military society. Oz's Yonatan, while denying that he is a "hero" and deflating the entire notion of "heroism" on the battlefield, is still a brave Israeli soldier, good-looking and strong, the darling of the kibbutz community and the Israeli public at large. Appelfeld's antiheroes, by contrast, are shattered human beings, some confused about their identity and filled with Jewish self-hate before the war and others forever damaged emotionally and often morally after the war. Indeed, Appelfeld's persona as it comes through in the present life narrative is more reminiscent of a semicomical fictional figure in Oz's *A Perfect Peace*, Azaria, a European Jew with a diasporic mentality and unknown roots, anxious to assimilate into kibbutz society.[45]

Appelfeld also narrates his attempts to place his style of writing within the Israeli canon as well as to shape his own brand of "Zionism," explaining that his thin, minimalist style is partly a reaction to the high, rhetorical idiom of earlier Hebrew writers. As part of his search for a home in Hebrew literary tradition, Appelfeld met with the Revisionist poet U. Z. Greenberg, known for his expansive, passionate, and effusive verses, who scolded him for his supposedly anemic lexicon and lack of nationalist zeal.[46]

Even though Appelfeld has expressed an uneasy, ambivalent relationship with Zionism, in the present life narrative, he places himself within a broader, more spiritually Jewish, and more nuanced Zionist metanarrative but certainly not outside it.[47] He aligns himself with the brand of Zionism represented by the writers and scholars who had an impact on him: S. Y. Agnon, the traditionalist of a previous generation; Dov Sadan, the Yiddishist; and Gershom Scholem, the pathbreaking scholar of kabbalah.

In sum, Appelfeld's present life narrative is of great value to his readers and students of Israeli culture in three areas: the author himself offers an illumination of his poetics; he further clarifies his attitude to the Holocaust as more than a catastrophic event in recent Jewish history but as a thread in the very intricate weave that makes up the Israeli identity; and he reveals his view of the Israeli phenomenon and his preference for a Zionism that is more universal and closely tied to Jewish tradition and its storehouse of images and archetypes.

David Grossman: *To the End of the Land*

Unlike the previous works, David Grossman's novel is outright fiction, focusing on fictitious protagonists and narrating events that did not happen while transmitting authentically the essence of life in contemporary

Israel. Yet in a sense, this novel provides another twist to the genre of "life writing," as it is fiction overcast by a critical event in the author's life. In the afterword to his novel, Grossman makes clear that this tale will be forever inextricably linked to the tragic loss of his son Uri in the Second Lebanon War in 2006. The novel was received in Israel in the same spirit that it was published; the Israeli public combined its sympathy over the loss of a young son, in what many Israelis saw as a questionable military campaign, with an interest in the story as typical of Israeli life, imprinted with anxiety and sorrows.

Grossman has focused in his works on two main topics: One is the haunting presence of the Holocaust from the point of view of the "second generation," for whom the horrors of the period are secondhand, shrouded in terrifying mystery and mentally damaging. The other is the everyday life in Israel, marked by a persistent existential angst over the periodic acts of terrorism, military campaigns, and the inevitable loss of loved ones. One of Grossman's major techniques is the adoption of a child's voice or point of view as a literary mechanism or authorial strategy to represent the heartbreak of childhood when confronted with the harsh realities or horrors of adult experience, as in *See under Love* and *The Book of Intimate Grammar*.[48]

While *To the End of the Land* employs the third-person narrative, the central presence is a young soldier, Ofer, seen as a child through the recollections of his mother, Ora. The novel opens with a short prologue that takes place in a Jerusalem hospital in 1967 and introduces to us the three main protagonists—Ora; her husband, Ilan; and Ofer's biological father, Avram—all recuperating from an undisclosed illness. It then jumps thirty-three years later, to 2000, recounting a hike along the "Israel Trail" taken by Ora and Avram, while their son is engaged in a military action.

Read as a "social novel," the story is a sociopolitical and psychological portrait of contemporary Israel, where public events intrude on, transform, and also destroy private lives, as mirrored in the saga of Ora and Ilan's family. The story transmits, as well, the existential anxiety and the centrality of wars in Israeli life, reflected in the two time periods into which the novel is divided: 1967, during the Six-Day War, and 2000, the time of the Second Intifada. The Yom Kippur War is also recollected, marking a tragic turning point in the lives of the three protagonists, when Avram is captured by the Egyptians and later returns a damaged person. In the present time of the novel, Ofer voluntarily reenlists for a military campaign after having just completed his mandatory army service; his mother, apprehensive for his life, flees from her home and forces the reclusive Avram to take a trip with her. By shutting herself off from the news and not being home when the military bearers of bad news arrive, Ora, in a fit of magical thinking, believes that the feared disaster will not happen. And by telling Avram the story of Ofer's life, Ora hopes to keep Ofer alive, conjecturing that as long as he is alive in the tale, he is "protected" from getting killed. She also intends to arouse in Avram his paternal feelings toward Ofer and thus to bring Avram back to life. We also learn that Ora's own family, which includes Ilan and her other son, Adam, has just collapsed, mainly because of Ora's inability to accept that Ofer had been involved in what she considers a scandalous atrocity against an elderly Arab. In this family breakdown, as well as in other events throughout the tale, the public and the private coalesce: the teenagers' mysterious illness at the opening of the story, when the 1967 war is raging, is also metaphoric, pointing to a deeper social and spiritual malaise.

The novel further depicts the temporary, ephemeral, and illusory nature of any period of "normalcy" in life in Israel. Ora considers the relatively uneventful, happy twenty years of the family as only delaying an inevitable disaster, "until we got trapped," as she says,[49] which happens when she learns that Ofer was involved in the Hebron event. As in Grossman's other works, he is also attuned to a child's perception of reality, to what it means to be a child in a country surrounded by mortal enemies. At one point, the child Ofer decides that he does not want to be a Jew anymore, and at another, he is so overcome by dread that his mother has to take him to a military post to prove to him Israel's military strength.[50] Ora is keenly aware of the lack of private life in the country, viewing her sons' mandatory enlistment in the army as "being nationalized"; and when she gives birth, she says she has donated another soldier to the Israel Defense Forces. The sons' service is a period of "nightmare," of life suspended, until they are released and get "out of it in one piece."[51] Ora agonizes over the impact of the military service on her sons, who inevitably become hardened and even dehumanized in her eyes; both joke about shooting an Arab and treat the incident in Hebron with equanimity, and Ofer, who chose to be a vegetarian as a child, starts eating meat. Enhancing the inevitable callousness of soldiers are the tough choices that military life presents them with; for instance, in 1973, Avram's commanders decide to abandon him in a remote outpost when they know full well that he will be captured and brutally tortured.

In the figure of the family's trusted driver, the Arab Sami, Grossman exemplifies the political and psychological dilemma of a reality in which there is both suspicion and reciprocal dependency between the majority and the "other." Ora, who is horrified to learn that her son forgot to release an old Arab from a meatpacking freezer, is still insensitive enough to hire Sami to drive her son to the military depot from which he will be sent to squash the Arab uprising.

The particular Israeli tilt of the tale does not exclude, however, universal themes of general interest. Grossman explores family dynamics, especially the mother's strong intuition and deep anxieties for her "men," her position as the healer and conscience of the family, and her attempts to reverse fate by fleeing the messengers or to defeat death by repeatedly telling about her son. The solidarity of the three men in the family against the mother is, in part, distinctively Israeli—they exhibit the general cultural toughness in their attitude to the suffering of the Palestinians, while she is more sensitive and caring; yet it is also universal, the female always being considered more prone to nurturing and caring. Grossman also includes his favorite theme of the workings of a child's mind in the figure of Ofer: his sensitivity to the suffering of animals, his naïve questioning of why Israelis or Jews are hated, his childish plans to defend himself, and the strong, almost telepathic bond that he has with his brother, Adam.

The love triangle of Ora, Avram, and Ilan and the friendship of the three in spite of the sexual rivalry are also explored as a universal pattern with an Israeli twist. Avram speaks to Ora's sensitive, creative nature, and Ilan speaks to her need for a strong, steady partner. While Avram is a prisoner-of-war, Ilan and Ora become a couple, but when Avram returns a wrecked human being, Ilan deserts Ora because he cannot bear to live a normal, happy life when his friend is in the throes of suicidal depression. Ilan returns to Ora only when he learns that she has become pregnant by Avram and determines to raise the child as his own.

Underlying the sociopsychological fabric of the story is a network of mythic patterns and archetypes, Jewish (biblical and kabbalistic) and universal. The biblical is that of the story of the Akeda, the binding of Isaac, which is here anchored in the meaning of Ofer's name. In Hebrew, the noun *ofer* recalls the hart from Song of Songs 2:9; but given his father's name, Avram, it also recalls the hart from the Akeda (Genesis 22:13), especially since the novel revolves around the precariousness of Ofer's life. Ora herself suggests the biblical connection when she evokes directly Avram's biblical namesake, telling Ofer's biological father that the time has come for him to assume paternity and become Avraham, emulating the Genesis patriarch's change of name (Genesis 17:5). Ora also ties her son's name to its English meaning, "to offer,"[52] reinforcing the motif of sacrifice. The novel's mood is thus determined by the opposite biblical genres embedded in it: the love poem of Song of Songs, graphic, luxuriating in the beauty of the body and sensual pleasures, and celebrating life, and the Akeda, perhaps the grimmest tale in the Bible, puzzling, unexplained, and arousing, to quote Kierkegaard, "fear and trembling."

But there is also an undeniable mystical-magical quality to the entire narrative, enhanced by Ora's magical thinking and her attempts to defeat natural laws by all sorts of strategies, akin to the kabbalists' manipulation of nature through combinations of letters, names, and numbers. Kabbalistic symbolism is first evoked by the letter *aleph*, which unites the names Ora, Ilan, Avram, and Adam. The *aleph*, in kabbalah a potent letter and the sum of all points, suggests a symbiosis of a deep and almost metaphysical nature between the four protagonists, hinting as well at a disturbing fate of the only protagonist whose name does not start with *aleph*, Ofer. The names themselves, Ora (light), Ilan (tree), Adam (the primordial man), and Avram (the patriarch), all carry significant mystical importance in the kabbalistic system; Grossman's Hebrew is also replete with mystical concepts, such as "the hiding of the face," the exile of the soul, and more.

The kabbalistic underpinnings tighten the mystical, undying bond among the protagonists while enhancing the "magical thinking" and escape strategies behind Ora's actions. The theme of fleeing bad tidings is more than just a plot device. It is the spiritual and psychological condition of people for whom the harsh reality of life is often unbearable and who therefore devise techniques to escape reality.[53] Emulating, or adopting, kabbalistic practices, Ora hopes that the act of walking the right number of miles and traversing distances will defeat death and that the mere telling of Ofer's life story will create a world out of the words and keep her son alive.

In addition to the universal theme of man's attempt to defeat death, the novel charts an Israeli Odyssey; what Ora and Avram's hike misses in vast epic spaces it makes up in the diversity of cultures and adventures (the pack of wild dogs, hostile Arabs). And just as the mythic journey is transformative, so is this one: at the end of the novel, Avram may be on his way to healing and accepting Ofer as his son. In addition, the symbolic role of the female as land, with the men fighting over her, is also present in this tale of a love triangle.

Yet beyond the novel's complex network of images and nuanced lyrical idiom (not always translatable), it captures the spiritual and psychological conundrum of contemporary Zionism. While Ora and Avram reaffirm their bond with the Israeli terrain during their hike through the "Israel Trail," they constantly voice their concern over the precariousness of Israeli existence and its long-term chances, and Avram speaks of the possibility of "exile." Surprisingly, the tough young soldiers, Adam and Ofer, also evoke scenes of Israelis exiled from their land, and the young Adam even writes an opera about Israelis going into "exile."[54] The sons' vision of banishment from the land goes beyond their realization of the flimsy nature of the country's military security; it signifies Zionism's failure to fashion a new kind of Jew who is confident in his own territory, possesses a strong sense of roots, and is rid of Diaspora Jews' existential terror. Their disturbing vision is more than a throwback to the diasporic, pre-Zionist mentality; it is apocalyptic, revealing a post-Zionist angst.[55] Israel's powerful sovereignty, supposed to give a stable national and personal identity to Ofer and his age group, thrice removed from the Diaspora's damaging impact, ends up being hollow, an illusion, emptied of its promise. Even in Ofer's given name (meaning "young deer"), he embodies the age-old Jewish victim, the sacrificial lamb. The child Ofer's obsessive pursuit of a "safe" identity, which only results in the rejection of his Jewishness and Israeliness, is thus proven to be more than a child's naïve thinking but the beginning of a journey of search and failure. Ora's desperate resort to mystical strategies to keep her child alive is a sign of failure. Thus, the novel leaves us with the mystical option, which is an escape from history, valid as poetic enrichment but questionable in Israel of the twenty-first century.

Conclusion

The Israeli literary scene has witnessed remarkable developments in the past several decades, stemming from dramatic new trends in the national mood and in critics' understanding of the role of fiction in a society probing its geopolitical status and ideological foundations. Israeli intellectuals have introduced new paradigms to redefine the Israeli identity, reframing the debate on the nature of the Israeli self by moving away from the Zionist idea as a critical tool or a fictional subject. This ideological turn has resulted in major shifts in the scholarly evaluation of the established Hebrew literary canon and in the nature of the fictional product itself; labeling contemporary writings as Hebrew or Jewish or Israeli has thus proven to be fraught with problems. At the same time, the loosening of the parameters of the literary canon has allowed for the inclusion of minority fictional voices, hitherto marginalized or suppressed, such as women, Sephardi writers, Arab authors, chroniclers of the Holocaust or its aftermath, and Israelis who write in languages other than Hebrew.

What has not changed from the inception of Modern Hebrew literature in Europe and is still evident today is the extraordinary symbiosis between the writers and the public at large, in a culture where literary works are often considered reflections of historical processes as well as tools to uncover what ails the national psyche. The journey into the personal history or the internal life of fictional or semifictional characters is inextricably tied to the search for the meaning of the nation itself and the relevance of its Zionist underpinnings. The three works discussed here offer a window into the nation's current climate and its quest for a firm identity, illustrating that Israeli fiction cannot be separated from the broad national-ideological discourse. The works by Oz, Appelfeld, and Grossman, the former two declared to be autobiographical and the latter strongly affected by a personal experience, appear to have touched the cultural and psychological pulse of the nation at large, thus testifying to the tight interlocking of private and public histories in Israeli life.

Nevertheless, by probing into the features that made these works stir the Israeli reading public, we have seen that they were not perfectly aligned with current postnationalist or post-Zionist theories. While it is true that the cultural and literary domains have opened up to a radical reassessment of contemporary Israel's Zionist identity, the works that have had great impact have proven to be fundamentally within the larger Zionist framework. Indeed, Oz's fictional autobiography triggered in the Israeli public nostalgia for the solid Zionism of the past, not the rejection of the Zionist idea. Appelfeld's imaginative retelling of his life experiences is tied to the culture's reconsideration of its previous dissociation from a major event in recent Jewish history, the Holocaust, and to the new trend to integrate this Jewish tragedy into Israeli memory. Grossman's novel has provided a jolting reminder of Israel's precarious existence and offered glimpses of a post-Zionist apocalypse yet has also confirmed the fundamental integrity of the Israeli-Zionist self in a menacing environment. Together, these three works partake in the ongoing Israeli discourse on the national character and capture the many shadings of the contemporary Israeli zeitgeist, utilizing a broad gamut of narrative strategies in wrestling with the national identity in a changing world.

NOTES

1. For a study of the postmodern, postcolonial, and post-Zionist critique undertaken by Israeli scholars of history, sociology, and literature at the end of the millennium, see Laurence J. Silberstein, *The Postzionism Debates: Knowledge and Power in Israeli Culture* (New York: Routledge, 1999).
2. For more on these concepts, see Hannan Hever, *Producing the Modern Hebrew Canon: Nation Building and Minority Discourse* (New York: NYU Press, 2002); see also Michael Gluzman, *The Politics of Canonicity: Lines of Resistance in Modernist Hebrew Poetry* (Stanford, CA: Stanford University Press, 2003); Yerach Gover, *Zionism: The Limits of Moral Discourse in Israeli Hebrew Fiction* (Minneapolis: University of Minnesota Press, 1994). Earlier, Iris Parush studied the ideological tenets behind the formation of the canon in *Literary Canon and National Ideology: Frishman's Literary Criticism Compared with Klausner's and Brenner's* [in Hebrew] (Jerusalem: Mosad Bialik, 1992).
3. Gershon Shaked, *Hebrew Fiction* [in Hebrew] (Jerusalem: Keter, 1977).
4. On the permutations of the Zionist metanarrative in Israeli fiction, see Gershon Shaked, "Fiction and the Zionist Metanarrative: Hebrew Fiction's Dialectic Encounter with a Changing Reality" [in Hebrew], in *Independence: The First Fifty Years*, ed. Anita Shapira (Jerusalem: Zalman Shazar Center, 1998), 487–511.

5. For more on these terms, see Gershon Shaked, *Modern Hebrew Fiction*, trans. Yael Lotan (Bloomington: Indiana University Press, 2000), 139–40; and Hannan Hever, *Literature Written from Here* [in Hebrew] (Tel Aviv: Yediot Aḥaronot, Sifre Ḥemed, 1999), 8–10.
6. Yigal Schwartz, *Vantage Point* [in Hebrew] (Or Yehuda, Israel: Kinneret, 2005), 215–34.
7. See Baruch Kurzweil, *Our New Literature: Continuity or Revolution* [in Hebrew] (Tel Aviv: Schocken, 1959).
8. Dan Miron discusses the flaws in Baruch Kurzweill's and Dov Sadan's historiosophic understanding in *Continuity and Contiguity: Toward a New Jewish Literary Thinking* (Stanford, CA: Stanford University Press, 2010), 233–77.
9. Yaron Peleg, "The Critic as a Didactical Zionist," *Prooftexts* 23 (2003): 382–96.
10. Gershon Shaked, "A Memorial to the Fathers and a Signpost for the Sons," in special issue, ed. Nurit Gertz and Meir Chazan, *Israel* 7 (Spring 2005): 2.
11. For more on these writers, see Rachel Feldhay Brenner, *Inextricably Bonded* (Madison: University of Wisconsin Press, 2003).
12. Anton Shamash, *Arabesques*, trans. Vivian Eden (New York: Harper & Row, 1988), originally published in Hebrew (Tel Aviv: Am Oved and Michaelmark Books, 1986).
13. Miron, *Continuity and Contiguity*, 407.
14. Gershon Shaked, introduction to *Six Israeli Novellas* (Boston: Godine, 1999), vii.
15. Kashua's works include *Dancing Arabs*, trans. Miriam Schlesinger (New York: Grove, 2004), originally published in Hebrew (Ben-Shemen, Israel: Modan, 2002); *Let It Be Morning*, trans. Miriam Schlesinger (London: Atlantic Books, 2006), originally published in Hebrew (Jerusalem: Keter, 2004); *Second Person Singular*, trans. Mitch Ginsburg (New York: Grove, 2012), originally published in Hebrew (Jerusalem: Keter, 2010).
16. Hever, *Literature Written from Here*, 7–9.
17. For more on this development, see Nehama Aschkenasy, "Text, Nation, and Gender in Israeli Women's Fiction," in *Women and Judaism*, ed. Frederick E. Greenspahn (New York: NYU Press, 2009), 221–44; see also Nehama Aschkenasy, "Literature, Hebrew: Women Writers, 1882–2010," in *The Cambridge Dictionary of Judaism and Jewish Culture*, ed. Judith R. Baskin (Cambridge: Cambridge University Press, 2011), 385–87.
18. See Nancy Berg, "Sephardi Writing: From the Margins to the Mainstream," in *The Boom in Contemporary Israeli Fiction*, ed. Alan Mintz (Hanover, NH: Brandeis University Press, 1997), 114–42; see also Ammiel Alcalay, *Keys to the Garden* (San Francisco: City Lights, 1996). More recently, see Lital Levy, "Reorienting Hebrew Literary History: The View from the East," *Prooftexts* 29 (2009): 127–72; and Hannan Hever, "'Location, Not Identity': The Politics of Revelation in Ronit Matalon's *One Facing Us*," *Prooftexts* 30 (2010): 321–39.
19. An example in the arena of popular fiction is Naomi Ragen's novels, written in English and translated into Hebrew, some exploring the Orthodox community in Israel as well as in the United States.

20. See Anna Ronell, "Russian Israeli Literature through the Lens of Immigrant Humor," *Journal of Jewish Identities* 4 (2011): 147–69.
21. See, for instance, Yigal Schwartz, *Aharon Appelfeld*, trans. Jeffrey M. Green (Hanover, NH: Brandeis University Press, 2001; Hebrew edition, Jerusalem: Keter and Magnes Press, 1996).
22. For a review of the permutations of Holocaust awareness in Israeli intellectual and political arenas, see Anita Shapira, "The Holocaust: Private Memories, Public Memory," *Jewish Social Studies*, n.s. 4:2 (Winter 1998): 40–58; and more recently, Gulie Ne'eman Arad, "Israel and the Shoah: A Tale of Multifarious Taboos," *New German Critique* 90 (Autumn 2003): 5–26. I refer to the latter article as a good summary of a cultural process, not as an endorsement of its final conclusion.
23. For an early critical work on postmodernism in Israeli fiction, see Avraham Balaban, *A Different Wave in Israeli Fiction: Postmodernist Israeli Fiction* [in Hebrew] (Jerusalem: Keter, 1995).
24. See, for instance, Yaron Peleg, "Israeli Identity in a Post-Zionist Age," in *Arguing the Modern Jewish Canon*, ed. Justin Cammy, Dara Horn, Alyssa Quint, and Rachel Rubenstein (Cambridge, MA: Harvard University Press, 2008), 661–73.
25. Amos Oz, *A Tale of Love and Darkness*, trans. Nicholas de Lange (New York: Harcourt, 2004), originally published in Hebrew (Jerusalem: Keter, 2003); Aharon Appelfeld, *The Story of a Life*, trans. Alma Halter (New York: Schocken, 2004), originally published in Hebrew (Jerusalem: Keter, 1999); David Grossman, *To the End of the Land*, trans. Jessica Cohen (New York: Knopf, 2010), originally published in Hebrew (Tel Aviv: Ha-Kibbutz He-Me'uchad, 2008). Interestingly, Avraham Balaban notes that the novels of the postmodernist writers showed disappointing sales numbers, while the works of the more "traditional" writers, such as Oz and Yehoshua, continued to be tremendous commercial successes (*Different Wave*, 59–60).
26. Special issue, ed. Nurit Gertz and Meir Chazan, *Israel* 7 (Spring 2005).
27. For analysis of Israeli readers' reactions to Oz's autobiography, see Schwartz, *Vantage Point*, 272–304.
28. For more on these paradigmatic patterns, see Suzanne Nalbantian, *Aesthetic Autobiography* (New York: St. Martin's, 1944).
29. Alan Mintz, *Banished from Their Father's Table* (Bloomington: Indiana University Press, 1989), 5.
30. Oz, *Tale of Love and Darkness*, 464.
31. Ibid., 367.
32. Ibid., 354–57.
33. Amos Oz, *Panther in the Basement*, trans. Nicholas de Lange (New York: Harcourt Brace, 1997), originally published in Hebrew (Jerusalem: Keter, 1995).
34. Shaked, "Memorial to the Fathers," 19.
35. Appelfeld, *Story of a Life*, 136–37.
36. Ibid., 98.

37. Aharon Appelfeld, *The Age of Wonders*, trans. Dalya Bilu (Boston: D. R. Godine, 1981), originally published in Hebrew (Tel Aviv: Ha-Kibbutz Ha-Me'uchad, 1978).
38. Appelfeld, *Story of a Life*, 168.
39. Ibid., 111.
40. Ibid., 196.
41. Ibid., 126–27.
42. Ibid., 171.
43. Ibid., 188.
44. Amos Oz's *A Perfect Peace*, trans. Hillel Halkin (San Diego: Harcourt Brace Jovanovich, 1985), originally published in Hebrew (Tel Aviv: Am Oved, 1982).
45. For more on this topic, see Nehama Aschkenasy, "Deconstructing the Metanarrative: Amos Oz's Revolving Discourse with the Bible," *Symposium* 55 (Fall 2001): 123–39.
46. For more on Appelfeld's literary style and its relation to his literary forebears, see Lincoln Shlensky, "Lost and Found: Aharon Appelfeld's Hebrew Literary Affiliations and the Quest for a Home in Israeli Letters," *Prooftexts* 26 (2006): 405–48.
47. For Appelfeld's ambivalence toward Zionism, see Shai Rudin, "'Much Delusion That Is in Good Will': Aharon Appelfeld's Ambivalent Position on Zionism—in His Non-Fiction and in His Fiction," *Hebrew Studies* 50 (2009): 305–49.
48. David Grossman, *See under Love*, trans. Betsy Rosenberg (New York: Farrar, Straus and Giroux, 1989), originally published in Hebrew (Tel Aviv: Ha-Kibbutz Ha-Me'uchad, 1986); David Grossman, *The Book of Intimate Grammar*, trans. Betsy Rosenberg (New York: Riverhead Books, 1995), originally published in Hebrew (Tel Aviv: Ha-Kibbutz Ha-Me'uchad, 1991).
49. Grossman, *To the End of the Land*, 380.
50. Ibid., 373–79.
51. Ibid., 67.
52. Ibid., 293.
53. Grossman discusses the Israelis' mood of returning to the emotional patterns of the Diaspora Jew of old in his *Death as a Way of Life*, trans. Haim Watsman (New York: Farrar, 2003), 120.
54. Grossman, *To the End of the Land*, 225.
55. On the binary structure of homeland/exile in Zionist thought, see Silberstein, *Postzionism Debates*, 22.

9

Israeli Hebrew

National Identity and Language

SHMUEL BOLOZKY

The often-noted dissonance between the reality of Israel and how it is perceived—or imagined—applies to language as well. The general conception of proper Hebrew is based primarily on the notion that the only correct variety is the hybrid of biblical, Mishnaic, medieval, Enlightenment, and early modern Hebrew that has emerged as the literary norm. This attitude probably results from the combination of a conservative, puristic bent and the sense that, owing to the central role Hebrew played in building national identity, any deviation from the normative standards of formal literary Hebrew affects the nation, its culture, and its prestige.

Classical Hebrew was dead from 135 CE, when the Jews were exiled following the Bar-Kokhba revolt, to the beginning of the twentieth century, except when Jews from unrelated communities who had no common language used it to communicate. However, written Hebrew continued to develop in poetry, biblical interpretation, philosophy, ethics, science, and grammar. In the eighteenth century, a new literature began to emerge as authors of the Hebrew Enlightenment (Haskalah) began to write on secular subjects. Although they restricted themselves to biblical vocabulary, it soon became clear that this would not suffice to answer the needs of the modern period. Mendele Mokher Sefarim (Shalom Yaakov Abramovich, 1835–1917) was the first to consider all historical levels, including medieval Hebrew, which was not spoken, as legitimate sources for his writing.

When Eliezer Ben-Yehuda, who is regarded as the reviver of spoken Hebrew, arrived in Palestine in 1881–82, he insisted that his newly born son hear only Hebrew, started a major Hebrew dictionary, published a Hebrew newspaper, and, along with others such as H. N. Bialik, coined new words. But most of the revival work was done by the teachers of the *yishuv*, who made a collective decision to teach only in Hebrew. Consequently, the first modern-Hebrew-speaking children emerged between 1900 and 1910. According to a 1916–18 Jewish Agency census, 34,000 (40%) out of 85,000 Jews reported that Hebrew was the primary language at home. By 1948, that number had grown to 350,000 out of a population of 500,000 or so. Today Hebrew is used by 6–7 million Israelis. In other words, the number of speakers has increased twenty times in sixty years. However, it was not until 1957 that the first grammar of Israeli Hebrew was published,[1] even though the scientific study of Classical Hebrew had been going on uninterrupted from at least the Middle Ages.

Because language is first and foremost oral, some people ask whether a language that was not spoken for seventeen to eighteen hundred years and then suddenly revived as an oral means of communication can be regarded as the same language. For instance, Paul Wexler categorically states that modern Hebrew is not the same language, at least not genetically, as classical Hebrew.[2] Instead, he believes that Modern Hebrew is essentially Yiddish with innumerable Hebrew words and that Yiddish is, in turn, a Slavic language that had borrowed a huge German vocabulary. Hence, modern Hebrew is genetically a Slavic language.

Others respond that modern Hebrew has retained its basic Semitic character.[3] While the sounds and even sentence structures of a language can change drastically through time, the way words are formed (morphology) tends to remain stable. As we will see, even though modern Hebrew does increasingly create new words by adding suffixes, it still uses roots and patterns, which are the hallmark of Semitic languages, for word formation. Furthermore, its sentence structure and tenses connect modern Hebrew to Mishnaic Hebrew, which was also a spoken language.

To be sure, there are those who disagree. Shlomo Izreel characterizes modern Hebrew as a creole language,[4] and Ghil'ad Zuckermann considers it a hybrid, which he has renamed "Israeli."[5] Both of these are reasonable claims. But there is no doubt that it is still Hebrew and still essentially Semitic.

The notion that modern Hebrew is not a natural continuation of classical Hebrew is due to the failure of many Israelis to recognize two basic facts about any language: (a) the inevitability of change and (b) the existence of multiple levels of a language (registers) side by side.

The failure to recognize that there are different levels of usage in Hebrew, as in all languages, often leads to confusion regarding norms of acceptability. Each of these registers, ranging from the most colloquial and casual to the most elevated literary and formal style, is just as legitimate as every other. A talk at a formal setting is likely to adhere more closely to normative, prescribed grammar/usage than a conversation among friends or family. For example, one would say "my father" in a formal register but "my dad" in an informal setting. "My dad" is not in itself ungrammatical; it is perfectly acceptable in the informal, colloquial register. In other words, what might be considered an error or deviation in one register may very well be fully acceptable in another. Furthermore, colloquial structures or forms that are considered ungrammatical in the formal register may, over time, become legitimized and accepted. For instance, although English *data* is the plural of *datum*, today it is accepted as a singular noun even in the formal register; similarly, many English speakers now use *can't* in writing in lieu of the more deliberate, formal *cannot*.

Slang also does not violate normative standards per se but is simply a separate register within the broader colloquial realm, whereby speakers defy conventions of appropriateness in order to separate themselves from the general population. It can even be enormously creative and innovative, sometimes introducing new patterns and structures. By no means should it, therefore, be thought of as a corrupt form of language or an inferior mode of expression. In fact, Hebrew slang makes use of metaphors at least as much as literary Hebrew does.[6] Both registers share the desire to impress the reader/listener with originality, and one cannot think of a more effective means of achieving that than by using vivid, unexpected metaphors.

Change is natural, in fact unavoidable, and norms of acceptability change with it. If structures that were considered ungrammatical in the past are regularly used by most educated, native speakers and have a certain logic (e.g., ease of pronunciation and simplification of paradigms), then it may be time to regard them as acceptable, even if they violate the norms of "correct usage" that are learned in elementary or high school. As I will show, certain violations of formal Hebrew standards, such as the elimination of some agreement rules and the simplification of some paradigms, are natural phenomena. Even the Hebrew Language Academy, which is often regarded as an enforcer of normative standards, recognizes some of these changes as legitimate and occasionally tries to reconcile discrepancies between norm and usage. For instance, normative forms like *mizrakhan* (Orientalist) or *mishpatan* (jurist) are usually pronounced *mizrekhan* and *mishpetan*. The Academy recognized that the shift from *a* to *e* before a final accented syllable is a natural reduction that happens elsewhere in the language and therefore decreed that these are bona fide alternates.

The common complaint that the Hebrew language keeps deteriorating is, therefore, unwarranted, even by normative standards. Haiim Rosén, for instance, clearly demonstrated that today's Hebrew is markedly richer and more grammatical than Hebrew was ninety years ago.[7] Owing to an educational system that still emphasizes biblical and Mishnaic texts, the language of educated Israelis today can also be shown to be as replete with classical allusions as the language of earlier generations.

Spoken Israeli Hebrew, which is used in literature, theater, radio, television, the army, schools (including higher education), markets, and business, has also developed in leaps and bounds and is just as rich and interesting as the literary register. It is not substandard or vulgar and certainly not impoverished. It is just a different level of usage, vibrant, fast changing, and equally representative of Israeli and Jewish culture as are the norms of literary Hebrew. Thus, it deserves to be thoroughly described and linguistically analyzed. We will use several examples of the transformations it has undergone to demonstrate how the contrast between classical and contemporary forms and structure are the result of natural linguistic change.

***

Linguists describe and analyze Israeli Hebrew to discover its true nature. We will point out several phenomena to illustrate why colloquial variants are at least as interesting as the normative formal register and demonstrate that the colloquial is just as structured and logical as its normative counterpart is. Supposed violations of the norm actually present a simpler, more logical communication system that should not be dismissed but should be recognized as natural modifications that are adapted to a new linguistic reality.

Researchers usually gather data in a number of ways:

- Recording speech
- Administering tests while distracting attention from their real purpose in the hope of getting naturally produced results

- Using both multiple-choice and fill-in-the-blank questions that involve made-up words
- Comparing new dictionaries, including slang dictionaries and supplements, with older ones[8]
- Searching written texts that include considerable colloquial usage as well as direct speech

In the past few decades, many Hebrew linguists have come to realize that it is best to analyze comprehensive, representative bodies of spoken language. These should include the full variety of age groups, ethnic origins, genders, socioeconomic statuses, and educational levels, as well as possible contexts, ranging from the most formal to the most casual, and a wide variety of topics and contents. This must be done in the most natural fashion, by recording normal connected speech throughout the day. These recordings need to be planned on a sound statistical basis so as to be truly representative of the society as a whole.

This effort has paid off, providing the beginnings of a transcribed and annotated spoken corpus and a grammar that is based on it.[9] Although the sampling has only begun, it has already led to the discovery of new phonological processes and to rethinking the scope of already known phenomena. One result has been the recognition that the basic structural unit of spoken Hebrew does not always correspond to syntactic categories such as the clause or phrase, the basic units of written language. Instead, we should think of the "utterance" or "intonation unit," meaning a stretch of speech between two breaks in which the speaker pauses or shifts tone. Colloquial Hebrew also uses a whole range of abbreviated utterances that deviate widely from traditional norms for sentences and clauses,[10] for instance, elliptical sentences like *ani rak sheela* (I only [have] a question) and *láma lo madlikim* ([It's hot;] why [don't you] turn on [the air conditioner]?).

Since this approach has not yet yielded sufficient data about grammatical forms, we will begin by looking at how productivity tests and dictionary comparison show how new words are formed. We will then search written sources that incorporate colloquial usage in order to consider supposedly deviant sentence structures, before ending with an illustration that pertains to pronunciation.

New Word Formation

Languages create new words from existing ones in two ways: by adding prefixes or suffixes to a stem (linear) or by changing the stem's internal structure (discontinuous). English normally uses the first approach, creating words such as *standardize* (from *standard*), *widen* (from *wide*), and *enlarge* (from *large*); however, a small group of strong verbs demonstrate the latter (e.g., *drive, drove, driven*; *write, wrote, written*; and *ride, rode, ridden*).

Hebrew also uses the first (linear) approach, for example, *kibbutsnik* (kibbutz member) from *kibbuts*, *balaganist* (disorderly person) from *balagan* (mess), and *bankai* (banker) from *bank* (bank). However, discontinuous derivation is quite common, as it is in other Semitic languages. For example, the words for "be thrown," "inject," "syringe," "throwing" or "injection," and "neglected" (i.e., "thrown away") are *nizrak, hizrik, mazrek, zrika*, and *zaruk*—all from the root *z-r-k*. Similarly, *kalat, niklat, hiklit, maklet, klita*, and *kalut*, which mean "absorb," "be absorbed," "record" (verb), "receiver," "reception," and "absorbed," are all derived from *k-l-t*.

New verbs are often derived from existing nouns by plugging their consonants into a standard verb pattern, as in the case of *misper* (enumerate), which comes from *mispar* (number). Sometimes one of the letters is repeated in order to preserve consonant clusters, so that the source noun remains obvious; thus, the verb *fikses* (to fax) rather than *fikes* from *faks* (facsimile) and *tikhnen* (to plan) rather than *tikhen* (or *tiken*) from *tokhnit* (plan).[11]

Because the use of both suffixes (linear) and internal restructuring (discontinuous) is probably triggered by the creation of recent or new words,[12] they can be measured in three ways:

- Comparing newer with older dictionaries
- Observing how speakers invent words on the basis of given meanings or select the best choice from a variety of alternatives
- Counting the number of words that occur only once (*hapax legomena*) in large collections of authentic texts,[13] since the larger the number of common words in a particular pattern, the more productive it is as a result of the fact that spontaneous innovations tend to be unique[14]

Newer dictionaries contain several adjectives that are not found in older ones.[15] Some are formed by adding the suffix *-i*, for example, *betikhuti* (related to safety) from *betikhut* (safety), *mimsadi* (of the establishment) from *mimsad* (establishment), *tsahali* (of the Israeli army) from *tsahal* (an acronym for *tsva hagana le-yisrael*, the Israel Defense Army), *khalavi* (indecisive) from *khalav* (milk), *ovdani* (suicidal) from *ovdan* (destruction/loss), and *khadshoti* (newsworthy) from *khadashot* (news).

Others fall into one of several standard patterns, such as

meXuXaX: for example, *medupras* (depressed) from *dipres* (depress) and *dipresya* (depression); *memulkad* (booby-trapped) from *malkodet* (trap); *mevurdak* (disorganized) from the borrowed Turkish word *bardak* (brothel); *memustal* (drunk, drugged) from borrowed Arabic *mastul* (intoxicated, drunk); *memuna* (motorized) from *manoa* (motor, engine); *memudar* (compartmentalized) from *mador* (compartment); and *metusaf* (with additives) from *tosefet* (addition)

muXXaX: for example, *muashar* (enriched) from *ashir* (rich); *mushtan* (of little value) from *sheten* (urine); *mutraf* (exceptional, exciting) from *metoraf* (crazy)

XaXuX: for example, *dafuy* (flawed) from *dofi* (fault, flaw)

niXXaX: for example, *nirhav* (majestic) from *marhiv* (breathtaking)

XaXiX: for example, *hafikh* (reversible) from *hafakh* (turn over, reverse); *khatikh* (hunk) from *khatikha* (attractive girl); *rakid* (that can be danced to) from *rakad* (dance)

XaXeX: for example, *tsadek* (legitimate) from *tsadak* (be right)

Although the prevalence of a particular pattern can be measured from its frequency within the entire vocabulary, that would probably reflect the competence of only the most literate speakers. Most speakers use the patterns most relevant to their intended meaning on the basis of what they have observed. In other words, their choices tend to be based on patterns within the most recent levels of the lexicon that are available as models. We will, therefore, consider only innovations that have emerged from relatively new vocabulary.

The proportion of the 1,185 new adjectives found in all the dictionaries examined that were not listed in previous dictionaries or earlier editions of existing ones are listed in table 9.1 according to their pattern. Adding an *-i* suffix is clearly the most productive (81.6%) word formation pattern for adjectives added to recent dictionaries, followed by *meXuXaX* (9.54%).

TABLE 9.1. Patterns of New Adjectives

Pattern	Total	Proportion of total
-i	967	81.60%
meXuXaX	113	9.54%
XaXuX	48	4.05%
XaXiX	19	1.60%
muXXax	13	1.10%
meXaXeX	8	0.68%
maXXiX	7	0.59%
niXXaX	5	0.42%
XoXeX	3	0.25%
XaXeX	2	0.17%
	1,185	100%

Another way of measuring how new words are generated in Israeli Hebrew is by asking participants to create a new form for a given meaning or to choose the most appropriate form from a variety of invented (nonexistent) choices (productivity tests). For example, subjects might be asked to create an adjective meaning "equipped with an antenna" or, alternatively, to judge which of several nonexisting words would be the best way to complete the question, "Is this television *equipped with an antenna*?" (normatively, *metsuyedet be-antenna*):

Ha-televizya ha-zot ________________?

a) *antenit*
b) *antenait*
c) *meuntenet*

As it turns out, the result depends on whether the specified meaning includes a verb or only a noun. When the suggested form involves a verb (e.g., *equipped* with an antenna), participants choose the passive participle *meuntenet* 75% of the time. However, when participants are asked to create the most appropriate form to describe someone as having a "bulldog-like" face (normatively, *kmo shel buldog*, i.e., like a bulldog) or to choose the best way to complete a sentence meaning "He has a bulldog-like face," where the meaning does not include a verb, 60% of participants opted for the adjectival form that ends with the suffix *-i*, which simply means "having the quality of" (i.e., *buldogi*):

Yesh lo partsuf ____________.

a) *buldogoni*
b) *mevuldag*
c) *buldogi*
d) *buldogai*
e) *baldegani*

Moreover, when the related suffixes *-ai* and *-ani* are added (i.e., *buldogai* and *baldegani*), the total rises to 75%. In other words, the absence of a verb leads speakers to add a suffix (linear, i.e., *buldogi*, etc.), whereas the presence of a verb leads to selecting a root and pattern (discontinuous, i.e., *meuntenet*) derivation.

Considering the results from dictionary comparison and productivity tests together, it is obvious that linear derivation (adding a suffix), which is common in English, is on the increase in spoken Hebrew. Clearly it is more transparent, since the base of the word remains unchanged and the suffix is a prominent indication of the word's derivation. Nevertheless, the use of roots and patterns (discontinuous derivation) is still strong, especially when verb bases are involved, as we observed for passive participles,[16] thereby demonstrating Israeli Hebrew's continuing Semitic character.

Possessive and Existential Sentences

Modern Hebrew uses existential structures, such as "there exists to me a book" (*yesh li sefer*) and "there exists to me a problem" (*yesh li beayah*), to express possession. Note that the word *yesh* does not change regardless of whether the subject is masculine (*sefer*, "book") or feminine (*beayah*, "problem"). However, the past and future tenses use forms of the verb "to be," which must agree with the subject. For example, "I had a book" is "*hayah* li sefer" (lit., there existed [masc. sing.] to me a book), but "I had a problem" is "*haytah* li beayah" (lit., there existed [fem. sing.] to me a problem). Despite this, in everyday speech, the subject and the verb often do not agree; thus, "*hayah* li beayot" (there existed [masc. sing.] to me problems [fem. pl.], i.e., I had problems).

Although these appear to be colloquialisms, linguists know that simpler (unmarked) forms are often used when verbs precede their subject. For instance, Arabic has sentences such as *kāna lahu banūn tlēti* (he had three sons), which literally means "there *was* to him three sons." Biblical Hebrew also has such structures, as in *ve-lo hayah le-eliezer banim akherim* (lit., and-not existed [masc. sing.] to-Eliezer sons other [masc. pl.], i.e., and Eliezer had no other sons; 1 Chron. 23:17) and *ve-hayah ha-dagah rabah meod* (lit., and-was [masc. sing.] the-fish [fem. sing., collective noun] multitudinous [fem. sing.] very, i.e., and the fish was (very) multitudinous; Ezek. 47:9). Dispensing with agreement rules is a natural phenomenon called leveling, which does not signal any deterioration of the language.

Removing subject-verb agreement is optional in the preceding cases; however, it can become obligatory when the subject is definite, since it is then often perceived as a direct object.[17] For example, colloquial Hebrew hardly ever uses the normative construction *yesh li ha-sefer ha-zeh* (lit., there exists to me the-book this, i.e., I have this book) but inserts the direct object marker *et*, resulting in "yesh li *et* ha-sefer ha-zeh" (lit., there exists to me *et* the-book this). Here, the existential word *yesh* is treated as a transitive verb governing a direct object, probably under the influence of European languages, which use a verb (e.g., "have") to express possession in the present tense.

As mentioned earlier, *yesh* does not have separate forms for different numbers or genders, so it does not change to agree with other words in the sentence. However, that is not the case for possessive sentences in the past and future tense, which use the verb "to be." As a result, including the definite direct object marker *et* causes colloquial Hebrew to lose verb agreement, as in *hayah* (masc. sing.) *li kvar et ha-beayah ha-zot* (fem. sing.) (I already had this problem) and *hayah* (masc. sing.)

li kvar et ha-beayot ha-eleh (fem. pl.) (I already had these problems), rather than the normative forms *haytah* (fem. sing.) or *hayu* (pl.), which are rarely used. This happens because the possessed noun's status as subject is not obvious when it comes near the end of the sentence in a language in which subjects normally precede verbs. The fact that the noun that immediately follows the verb begins with the definite article (*ha-*), therefore, strongly "invites" the accusative marker *et*, which, in turn, leads speakers to reinterpret the original subject as a direct object, making subject-verb agreement no longer relevant.

The same is true in existential sentences, as can be seen by examining cases of direct speech in a written corpus of predominantly colloquial Hebrew. There we find sentences such as *reshit yesh et inyan ha-prasim* (First, there is *et* [direct object marker] the matter of the prizes) and *sham yesh et hats-harot ha-mas shelo* (There are *et* [direct object marker] his tax statements). The speakers have probably inserted *et* because the following word is definite ("the matter of the prizes" and "his tax statements"). In other words, the presence of the definite article *ha-* on a noun following the word *yesh* makes *et* almost automatic. Because these sentence structures are widely used by educated Israelis, they should not be characterized as ungrammatical.

Numbers

One trait of Semitic languages that has attracted linguists' attention is the "reversed gender" between numbers and the nouns they quantify: masculine nouns are preceded by numbers with feminine endings (e.g., *asara susim*, "ten [fem.] horses [masc. pl.]"), and feminine nouns by unmarked (normally masculine) forms (e.g., *eser susot*, "ten [masc.] mares [fem. pl.]").

In 1967, Robert Hetzron proposed that these forms originally had little to do with gender. Instead, unmarked forms originally referred to persons, while forms ending with *-ah* originally referred to things or smaller or derivative entities. In his view, numerals maintained that distribution even after the suffix *-ah* came to be associated with feminine gender and its absence with the masculine.[18]

In fact, the very need for gender agreement in Hebrew numerals is questionable, since they are quantifiers (like the word "many"), which precede the nouns they modify, rather than adjectives, which follow nouns. It is, therefore, not surprising that "gender" is neutralized in Hebrew numbers that precede the noun to which they refer in colloquial usage, for example, *sheva shekel* (lit., seven shekel, i.e., seven shekels) and *tesha dolar* (lit., nine dollar, i.e., nine dollars). There are even some instances in biblical Hebrew, for example, *shlosh khodashim* (three months; Gen. 38:24) instead of *shlosha khodashim*. Neutralization can also go the other way, for example, *shloshet neshey banav* (his three daughters-in-law; Gen. 7:13) instead of *shlosh neshey banav*.

Hebrew's preference for the unsuffixed form may also be due to its preference for that form when numbers occur in isolation, as in counting and after nouns in nonquantifying situations, for example, *otobus mispar khamesh* (bus number 5). In addition, unsuffixed forms fit well with the natural preference for alternating strong-weak (trochaic) stress when numbers are chanted or acquired for the first time by children: *akhát* (1), *shtáym* (2), *shalósh* (3), *arbá* (4), *xamésh* (5), *shésh* (6), *shéva* (7), *shmóne* (8), *tésha* (9), *éser* (10).[19] In sum, the so-called errors in number agreement that are common in colloquial Hebrew are, in fact, the result of simplification, which actually corrects a historical aberration.

Stress Pattern

Because Hebrew stress mostly falls on the end of a word, it shifts to added suffixes (see table 9.2). That suggests that, unlike languages such as English, Hebrew stress is not fixed, except for a number of well-defined classes of words; in other words, most Hebrew words are essentially unaccented or mobile. However, stress can make a difference for meaning. For example, the English "*pér*mit" is a noun, whereas "per*mít*" is a verb. Similarly, in Israeli Hebrew, "bi*ráh*" means "capital," but "*bí*rah" means "beer"; "ra*tsú*" means "they wanted," but "*rá*tsu" means "they ran"; and "ba*nú*" means "they built," but "*bá*nu" means "in us." The position of stress also distinguishes common nouns from proper nouns, as in the case of "rekho*vót*" (streets) and "Re*khó*vot" (a town south of Tel Aviv), "kha*yím*" (life) and "*Khá*yim" (man's name), or "pni*ná*" (pearl) and "*Pní*na" (woman's name).

Some important word classes do have fixed stress.[20] Borrowed nouns and adjectives constitute a very large example (see table 9.3). Whether or

TABLE 9.2. Hebrew Stress: Shifts to Added Suffixes

	"friend"	"white"
masc. sing.	kha*vér*	la*ván*
fem. sing.	khave*rá*	leva*ná*
masc. pl.	khave*rím*	leva*ním*
fem. pl.	khave*rót*	leva*nót*

TABLE 9.3. Hebrew Stress: Borrowed Nouns and Adjectives

	"student"	"liberal"	"objective"
masc. sing.	studént	libe*rá*li	obyek*tí*vi
fem. sing.	stu*dén*tit	libe*rá*lit	obyek*tí*vit
masc. pl.	stu*dén*tim	libe*rá*lim	obyek*tí*viyim
fem. pl.	stu*dén*tiyot	libe*rá*liyot	obyek*tí*viyot

TABLE 9.4. Hebrew Stress: Acronyms

	"publisher"	"sergeant-major"	"general manager"	Members of the first Zionist immigration to Palestine in the 1880's
masc. sing.	*MÓL* (from *MOtsi Le-or*)	Ra*SáR* (from *Rav Samal Rishon*)	MaN*KáL* (from *MeNahel KeLali*)	*BÍ*LU (from *Bet Yaakov Lekhu Ve-nelcha*)
fem. sing.	*mó*lit	ra*sá*rit	man*ká*lit	
masc. pl.	*mó*lim	ra*sá*rim	man*ká*lim	*bí*luyim
fem. pl.	*mó*liyot	ra*sá*riyot	man*ká*liyot	

not such words have their own separate grammar, as some people have argued,[21] fixed stress helps maintain transparency, in that the source, or base, can be easily identified.

Acronyms are another large class of words with fixed stress (see table 9.4).[22] Since these acronyms are native to Hebrew, they prove that where fixed stress exists, it can also be natural to the language.

Some words in the familiar, informal register also have fixed stress (see table 9.5). The same applies to many gentilic terms and residents

TABLE 9.5. Hebrew Stress: Informal Register

	"soup"	"ice cream"	"pepper"
sing.	marák	*glí*dah	*píl*pel
pl.	mar*á*kim (despite normative *merakím*)	*glí*dot	*píl*pelim

Note: *glidáh/glidót* and *pilpél/pilpelím* are attested only in extraformal speech.

TABLE 9.6. Hebrew Stress: Gentilic Terms and Residents of Cities

	Swede	Albanian	Resident of Jerusalem	Resident of Tel Aviv
masc. sing.	*shvé*di	al*bá*ni	yeru*shál*mi	tela*ví*vi
fem. sing.	*shvé*dit	al*bá*nit	yeru*shál*mit	tela*ví*vit
masc. pl.	*shvé*dim	al*bá*nim	yeru*shál*mim	tela*ví*vim
fem. pl.	*shvé*diyot	al*bá*niyot	yeru*shál*miyot	tela*ví*viyot

TABLE 9.7. Hebrew Stress: Other Gentilic Terms

	Russian	English(wo) man	German	Pole
masc. sing.	rus*í*	angl*í*	germa*ní*	pola*ní*
fem. sing.	rusi*yá*	angli*yá*	germani*yá*	polani*yá*
masc. pl.	rus*ím*	angl*ím*	germa*ním*	pola*ním*
fem. pl.	rusi*yót*	angli*yót*	germani*yót*	polani*yót*

of cities or towns in informal speech (see table 9.6). However, the stress in other gentilic names falls on the last syllable (see table 9.7). Haiim Rosén attributes the final stress in this last group to the fact that first-generation speakers of "revived" Hebrew were familiar with these countries and their cultures. As a result, they considered such terms as "rus*í*" to be native, unlike the later, less familiar countries and cultures, which they perceived as foreign.[23] However, Yishai Neuman argues that the so-called foreign accent associated with the first group (*shvédi*, etc.) is another instance of modern Hebrew's natural tendency to maximize transparency by breaking away from the bond of final stress in favor of stable stress.[24] In his view, the revivers of Hebrew around the turn of the twentieth century followed the classical model, including stress placement, which they applied to the nations and nationals they were in contact with or exposed to. They, therefore, maintained gentilic terms that they had inherited from their parents' generation but created new ones naturally, maintaining stable stress rather than shifting the stress to the suffix in a way that would have affected the words' base.

There are, then, several groups of words that maintain stable stress: borrowed stems, proper names, acronyms, gentilic terms, and residents of cities. Ora Schwarzwald regards all of these subgroups as unintegrated and, therefore, outside the mainstream system.[25] However, I believe that even though the majority of Hebrew words are unaccented, fixed accent is the language's natural word mechanism, for the following reasons:

- Loan words overwhelmingly maintain their original accent, even with suffixes. So do acronyms, which are also not perceived as foreign but used to create new native forms.
- Fixed stress helps maintain transparency, whereas moving it to the suffix causes opacity.
- Mobile stress is always associated with established morphological patterns, whereas stable accent prevails when there is no morphological pattern or the pattern is more open to variation.
- Speakers prefer to maintain stable stress when they shift into a more informal, familiar register.
- Fixed stress often coincides with strong-weak alternation of stress (trochaic rhythm), which seems to be Hebrew's natural rhythm, as can be seen in Hebrew's preference for penultimate stress and in children's rhymes and chants:[26]

    mìmromím ptsatsá yorédet ("from the sky, bomb comes down")
    éven nyár umìsparáyim ("rock, paper, and scissors")
    én den díno sóf a lá katíno (random-selection rhyme of unclear origin)
    él él yìsraél (sports chant to encourage the Israeli team)
    hàshofét ha-báyta ("referee go home!")

The trochaic rhythm is most likely a universal preference, although it may be due to Yiddish influence. Although normativists (or purists) regard these as colloquial deviations, they are not. These stress patterns form an integral part of the language and should be recognized as legitimate. Keeping stress stable helps to keep words transparent and easy to identify.

Conclusion

Hebrew is changing rapidly, with new registers continuously on the way to becoming acceptable in the mainstream. We have here noted the creation of adjectives from existing words, most often by adding a suffix *-i* (linear) but also by the use of more traditional (discontinuous) forms; changing treatment of possessive and existential sentences in which *yesh* is regarded as a (transitive) verb and *hayah* left unchanged when it precedes its subject; the neutralization of numeral gender; and the maintenance of fixed stress in certain classes of words and a gravitation toward trochaic rhythm (strong-weak alternation of stress). All of these are common patterns of language change. Some have precedents in earlier stages of Hebrew. In other words, they demonstrate that change is a natural result of modern Hebrew's being a living language, rather than evidence of its deterioration or becoming fundamentally non-Semitic.

NOTES

1. Haiim B. Rosén, *Our Hebrew Language* [in Hebrew] (Tel Aviv: Am Oved, 1957).
2. Paul Wexler, *The Schizoid Nature of Modern Hebrew: A Slavic Language in Search of a Semitic Past* (Wiesbaden, Germany: Otto Harrassowitz, 1990).
3. Shmuel Bolozky, review of *The Schizoid Nature of Modern Hebrew: A Slavic Language in Search of a Semitic Past*, by Paul Wexler, in *Critical Essays on Israeli Social Issues and Scholarship*, ed. Russell A. Stone and Walter P. Zenner (Albany: SUNY Press, 1994), 63–85; Shmuel Bolozky, "Israeli Hebrew as a Semitic Language: Genealogy and Typology" [in Hebrew], *Mekhkarim BeLashon* 7 (1995): 121–34.
4. Shlomo Izreel, "Was the Revival of the Hebrew Language a Miracle? On Pidginization and Creolization Processes in the Creation of Modern Hebrew" [in Hebrew], *Proceedings of the Ninth World Congress for Jewish Studies, Part 4, Vol. 1: Hebrew and Judaic Languages; Other Languages* (Jerusalem: World Union of Jewish Studies, 1986), 77–84.
5. Ghil'ad Zuckermann, *Israeli—A Beautiful Language* [in Hebrew] (Tel Aviv: Am Oved, 2008).
6. Shmuel Bolozky, "Metaphors in Hebrew Slang and Their Parallels in Hebrew Literature and in the Sources," *Hebrew Studies* 48 (2007): 269–90.
7. Haiim B. Rosén, "Miscellania on the Consolidation of Israeli Hebrew" [in Hebrew], *Proceedings of the Israeli Circle of the European Linguistic Society* 5 (1992): 33–39.

8. Shmuel Bolozky, *Measuring Productivity in Word Formation: The Case of Israeli Hebrew* (Leiden, Netherlands: Brill, 1999).
9. Shlomo Izreel, "The Corpus of Colloquial Hebrew in Israel: Text Samples," *Leshonenu* 64 (2002): 289–314.
10. See Esther Borochovsky Bar-Aba, *Colloquial Hebrew: Studies on Its Research and Manifestation* [in Hebrew] (Tel Aviv: Bialik Institute, 2010).
11. Shmuel Bolozky, "Word Formation Strategies in the Hebrew Verb System: Denominative Verbs," *Afroasiatic Linguistics* 5 (1978): 111–36; Bolozky, *Measuring Productivity in Word Formation*; Outi Bat-El, "Stem Modification and Cluster Transfer in Modern Hebrew," *Natural Language and Linguistic Theory* 12 (1994): 571–96.
12. Bolozky, "Word Formation Strategies in the Hebrew Verb System"; and especially Bolozky, *Measuring Productivity in Word Formation.*
13. See R. Harald Baayen, and Antoinette Renouf, "Chronicling the *Times*: Productive Lexical Innovations in an English Newspaper," *Language* 72 (1996): 69–96.
14. E.g., "headmistressly" in the *London Times* corpus used by Baayen and Renouf, which suggests that the *-ly* suffix is truly productive. This last method will not be included in the illustration later in the chapter, which describes the formation of new adjectives.
15. All the following data are from Bolozky, *Measuring Productivity in Word Formation* and are based on examples from Avraham Even-Shoshan, *The New Dictionary* [in Hebrew] (Jerusalem: Kiryat Sefer, 1963, 1970, 1980, 1983); Dan Ben-Amotz and Netiva Ben-Yehuda, *A World-Class Dictionary of Colloquial Hebrew* [in Hebrew] (vol. 1, Jerusalem: Levin-Epstein, 1972; vol. 2, Tel Aviv: Zmora, Bitan, 1982); Oded Akhiasaf and Pepi Marzel, eds., *Hebrew and Army Slang Lexicon* [in Hebrew] (Tel Aviv: Prolog, 1993); and Yaakov Choueka, Yael Zachi-Yannay, Sara Choueka, and Chagit Carmiel, *Rav Milim, A Comprehensive Dictionary of Modern Hebrew* [in Hebrew] (Tel Aviv: C.E.T., 1997).
16. See also Shmuel Bolozky and Ora Rodrigue Schwarzwald, "On the Derivation of Hebrew Forms with the *+ut* Suffix," *Hebrew Studies* 33 (1992): 51–69.
17. See Yael Ziv, "On the Reanalysis of Grammatical Terms in Hebrew Possessive Constructions," in *Studies in Modern Hebrew Syntax and Semantics; The Transformational-Generative Approach*, ed. Peter Cole (Amsterdam: North Holland, 1976), 129–52.
18. Robert Hetzron, "Agaw Numerals and Incongruence in Semitic," *Journal of Semitic Studies* 12 (1967): 169–97.
19. Although only seven through ten are trochaic on their own, the whole sequence has a general trochaic rhythm when it is recited by children. The suffixed forms created a partial iamb (weak-strong alternation) or anapest (weak-weak-strong) and therefore would not have flowed as naturally when chanted in sequence: *exád, shnáym, shloshá, arbaá, xamishá, shishá, shivá, shmoná, tishá, asará.*
20. See also Haiim B. Rosén, *Our Hebrew Language* [in Hebrew] (Tel Aviv: Am Oved, 1957); Baruch Podolsky, "Stress as a Morphological Factor in Modern Hebrew" [in

Hebrew], *Leshonenu* 45 (1981): 155–56; Baruch Podolsky, "The Problem of Word Accent in Modern Hebrew," in *Proceedings of the Fifth International Hamito-Semitic Congress*, vol. 2, ed. Hans G. Mukarovsky (Vienna: Institut für Afrikanistik und Agyptologie de Universität Wien, 1991), 277–81; Igor Melčuk and Baruch Podolsky, "Stress in Modern Hebrew Nominal Inflection," *Theoretical Linguistics* 22 (1996): 155–94; and Outi Bat-El, "Parasitic Metrification in the Modern Hebrew Stress System," *Linguistic Review* 10 (1993): 189–210.

21. E.g., Ora Rodrigue Schwarzwald, "Word Foreignness in Modern Hebrew," *Hebrew Studies* 39 (1998): 115–42.
22. Acronyms in the very formal register are an exception; see Dorit Ravid, "Internal Structure Constraints on New Word Formation Devices in Modern Hebrew," *Folia Linguistica* 24:3–4 (1990): 289–347; Outi Bat-El, "The Optimal Acronym Word in Hebrew," in *Proceedings of the 1994 Annual Conference of the Canadian Linguistic Association*, ed. Paivi Koskinen (Toronto: University of Toronto Department of Linguistics), 23–37; and Shmuel Bolozky, "On the Special Status of the Vowels *a* and *e* in Israeli Hebrew," *Hebrew Studies* 40 (1999): 233–50.
23. Rosén, *Our Hebrew Language*; Haiim B. Rosén, *Contemporary Hebrew* (The Hague, Netherlands: Mouton, 1977).
24. Yishai Neuman, "Issues Related to Phonology and Morphology" [in Hebrew] (unpublished manuscript, Ben-Gurion University, 2000).
25. Ora Rodrigue Schwarzwald, "Word Foreignness in Modern Hebrew," *Hebrew Studies* 39 (1998): 115–42.
26. Shmuel Bolozky, "Remarks on Rhythmic Stress in Modern Hebrew," *Journal of Linguistics* 18 (1982): 275–89. In the list, the grave accent indicates secondary stress, which automatically alternates with the primary one, which is marked with an acute accent, as in English "sécretàry." On numerals, child speech, chants, etc., see also Shmuel Bolozky and Adnan F. Haydar, "Colloquial Gender Neutralization in the Numeral Systems of Modern Hebrew and Lebanese Arabic," *Al-'Arabiyya* 19 (1986): 19–28.

10

The Politics of Israel

Relations with the American Jewish Community

THEODORE SASSON

Since the late 1990s, a steady stream of books, articles, and reports by social scientists have announced the "distancing" of American Jews from Israel. Researchers have described American Jews as ever less interested in Israel, less likely to give to Israeli causes, less likely to visit the country, and less likely to support Israel politically.[1] In recent years, researchers have focused especially on the younger generation and argued that distancing results from fading memory of the Holocaust and Israel's founding, the rising rate of intermarriage, and opposition to Israeli policies concerning the conflict with the Palestinians.

The social scientific claims concerning distancing have generated a great deal of popular attention. In a 2010 article published in the *New York Review of Books*, the journalism professor Peter Beinart cited a report by the sociologists Steven M. Cohen and Ari Y. Kelman as evidence of the alienation of young-adult American Jews from Israel. Beinart attributed the phenomenon to Israeli right-wing policies and the failure of American Jewish organizations to oppose them. "For several decades, the Jewish establishment has asked American Jews to check their liberalism at Zionism's door, and now, to their horror, they are finding that many young Jews have checked their Zionism instead."[2] On the opposite end of the political spectrum, Rabbi Daniel Gordis, in a 2012 book titled *The Promise of Israel*, also cites the Cohen-Kelman study to document the alleged abandonment of Israel by young-adult American Jews.[3] For Gordis, however, the fault lies not primarily with Israeli policies but rather with the failure of the younger generation to appreciate Israel's significance for world Jewry.

Unsurprisingly, the American Jewish connection to Israel has also become a leading concern of Jewish organizations and the Israeli government. Israel's Jewish Agency has reoriented its mission from promoting *aliyah* (immigration) to cultivating diaspora connections to the Jewish state. In 2012, the Israeli Knesset (parliament) held hearings on how to respond to the distancing of American Jews, and Israel's President Shimon Peres convened a conference with a plenary session devoted to the topic. In short, in recent years, the relationship of American Jewry to Israel has become a leading concern of scholars, journalists, and the political and organizational elites of the Jewish world. The dominant theme in this expansive discourse has been that the world's two largest Jewish communities are parting ways. The key challenge has been defined as what to do about it.

As in the other cases examined in this volume, the reality of American Jewish ties to Israel does not match the popular image. One difficulty with the "discourse on distancing" is that the empirical evidence for its core claims is quite dubious.[4] The first part of this chapter examines forms of American Jewish engagement with Israel that researchers have cited in their claims concerning distancing, including attitudes, donations, travel, and advocacy. Perhaps surprisingly, in each domain the evidence suggests not distancing but rather *intensifying engagement*. The relationship between American Jews and Israel, however, is not merely intensifying. It is also changing in important ways, and these may help to explain the perception of distancing. In particular, the Israeli government's policies, especially concerning the ongoing conflict with the Palestinians, are becoming more contentious in the American Jewish community. The middle section of the chapter describes the new contentiousness about Israel in the American Jewish community. Finally, the discourse on distancing is not merely erroneous; it is also potentially damaging. The final sections of the chapter explore why it has proven so attractive and why it should now be set aside.

American Jews Are Not Distancing from Israel

Researchers who allege the distancing of American Jews from Israel typically cite evidence from cross-sectional surveys. In some instances, they compare the responses to similarly worded questions on emotional attachment at two isolated points in time, documenting a decline in the proportion of respondents who report feeling connected.[5] In others, they analyze a single survey and show that attachment tends to decline across age cohorts from the oldest to the youngest.[6]

In the report mentioned in my introduction, Cohen and Kelman adopted the latter approach. They showed that in a national survey conducted in 2007, emotional attachment declined across the age cohorts from the oldest to the youngest. "We are in the midst of a massive shift in attitudes toward Israel, propelled forward by the process of cohort replacement, where the maturing younger cohorts that are the least Israel-engaged are replacing the oldest cohorts that are the most Israel-engaged." They attributed the alleged shift in attitudes to the fading memory of Israel's struggle for existence and rising incidence of intermarriage and predicted a "long-term and ongoing decline in Israel attachment" in the years to come.[7]

This interpretation, however, fails to account for the long-term trend data that are now available for analysis. The American Jewish Committee (AJC) conducts an annual telephone and Internet survey of a panel of American Jews and has done so in a fairly consistent manner since 1986. The survey asks two relevant questions, almost every year, using the same wording and response categories. One question asks respondents simply, "How close are you to Israel?" Another asks whether respondents agree or disagree with the statement "Caring about Israel is a very important part of my being a Jew."

In a 2010 paper analyzing the AJC data, Charles Kadushin, Leonard Saxe, and I reported that age-cohort differences in attachment to Israel are not a new phenomenon.[8] Rather, in almost all surveys administered since 1986, younger respondents reported less attachment to Israel than older respondents did.[9] Nonetheless, the overall level of attachment to Israel has been remarkably stable, fluctuating within a rather narrow band of about 15 percentage points for the "closeness" question and 10 percentage points for the "caring" question (figure 10.1). It is difficult to reconcile this pattern with the notion that age-cohort differences are indicative of declining attachment across the generations. If younger Jews were less attached to Israel in 1986—and if they maintained their characteristic level of attachment over the next two decades—then the overall level of attachment would necessarily have declined, but it did not.

The fact that that younger respondents have consistently reported lower levels of attachment to Israel for more than two decades, coupled with the observation that overall the level of attachment has remained

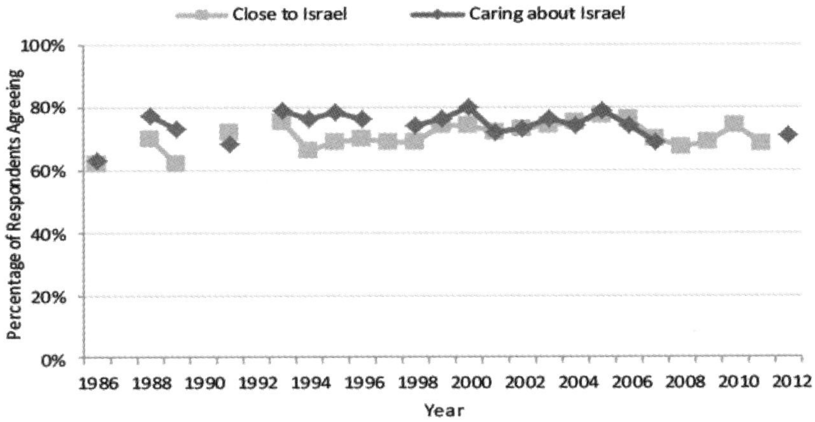

Figure 10.1. Trends in attachment to Israel: "feeling close" and "caring." Questions: "Do you agree or disagree with the statement: 'Caring about Israel is a very important part of my being a Jew'?" (figure shows "agree"); "How close do you feel to Israel?" (figure shows "very close" / "fairly close"). Source: Annual surveys of the American Jewish Committee.

stable, suggests an alternative explanation. Rather than declining across the generations, attachment to Israel has tended to increase over the life course. In other words, the age differences in attachment to Israel are not a generational phenomenon but rather a life-cycle phenomenon.

When first published, the 2010 paper was criticized for drawing on survey samples comprising exclusively "Jews by religion."[10] (The AJC surveys identify Jews with a question about religion; other surveys identify Jews through a variety of questions that tap into both religious and ethnic forms of Jewish identity.) To address this criticism and further test the "life-cycle hypothesis," we next examined pairs of surveys conducted at ten-year intervals with populations that included both Jews by religion and Jews by ethnicity. The pairs of surveys included the National Jewish Population Survey (1990 and 2000–2001) and the Jewish community surveys of Boston (1995 and 2005), Miami (1994 and 2004), and South Palm Beach (1995 and 2005). They showed that as each birth cohort (e.g., respondents born between 1960 and 1970) aged by ten years, its average level of emotional attachment to Israel tended to increase, with the largest and most consistent increases occurring as respondents who were in their thirties at Time 1 (the first survey, administered in the

1990s) matured into their forties at Time 2 (the second survey, administered in the first decade of the twenty-first century).[11]

The tendency of attachment to Israel to increase during the transition to adulthood may be related to more general life-cycle processes. It may express a subtle shift in worldview from universal to parochial that occurs when people settle down and establish families. Alternatively, it may reflect the tendency for maturing Jews to become more embedded in Jewish communal life. Whatever the explanation, the evidence from these studies contradicts the claim that today's young-adult American Jews are less attached to Israel than were their same-age counterparts ten or twenty years ago.

The point, however, may already be moot: In 2012, Steven M. Cohen reported that in a new national survey, the under-thirty-five age group was both more likely to have visited Israel and more emotionally attached than was the adjacent thirty-five to forty-four age group.[12] Cohen attributed this pattern—which departs from the stepwise decline from oldest to youngest cohorts characteristic of most surveys done in the 1990s and the first decade of the twenty-first century—to increased young-adult travel to Israel, especially through the Birthright Israel program.[13] If this new finding proves stable, then the process of "cohort replacement" that Cohen and Kelman described in their 2007 report will not lead to "ongoing decline" but rather an *ongoing increase* in Israel attachment in the years ahead.

Donations, Travel, and Advocacy

Researchers who allege the distancing of American Jews from Israel have also cited declining allocations by North American federations of Jewish charities to Israeli partner organizations, in particular, the Jewish Agency for Israel. Indeed, the federations have steadily reduced the proportion of their annual campaign revenues directed to the Jewish Agency and other Israeli organizations from 53 percent in 1985 to 41 percent in 1994 to 23 percent in 2004.[14] Throughout this period, the inflation-adjusted value of federation contributions to the Jewish Agency plummeted, from the equivalent of $520 million in 1985 to $330 million in 1994 and $169 million in 2010.[15]

American Jewish donations to causes in Israel, however, flow through a variety of channels.[16] In addition to the federations' annual campaigns, such donations flow directly to American Jewish organizations that have projects in Israel (such as Hadassah and the Jewish National Fund), to American affiliates of Israeli organizations (such as American Friends of the Hebrew University and American Friends of Magen David Adom), and to funds that allocate donations to a variety of causes (such as the New Israel Fund and the One Israel Fund). In a 2012 study, Eric Fleisch and I documented a sharp increase in the number of fundraising affiliates of Israeli organizations ("American Friends" organizations) from 265 in 1989 to 667 in 2010.[17]

Fleisch and I analyzed U.S. Internal Revenue Service documents (990 Forms) to estimate overall donations to all American Jewish organizations fundraising for causes in Israel. For the peak year 2007, donations topped \$2.1 billion; in the postrecession year 2010, they were \$1.45 billion. (Figure 10.2 shows the breakdown of these donations by the purposes they served in Israel.) By contrast, Barry Kosmin estimated total donations for 1985 of \$461 million (roughly \$934 million in 2010 dollars), and Jack Wertheimer estimated total donations for 1994 of \$774 million (roughly \$1.139 billion in 2010 dollars).[18] Notwithstanding the slide from 2007 to 2010, the overall trend in American Jewish donations to Israeli causes is therefore apparently upward.[19]

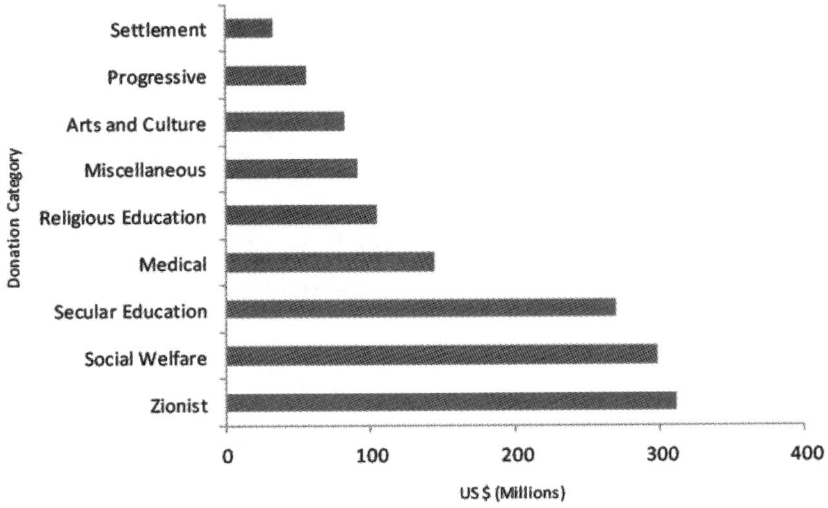

Figure 10.2. Donations to Israeli causes, by category, 2010 (millions of dollars). Source: Eric Fleisch and Theodore Sasson, *The New Philanthropy: American Jewish Giving to Israeli Organizations* (Waltham, MA: Cohen Center for Modern Jewish Studies, 2012).

The evidence regarding tourism is equally compelling. According to data assembled by the Israeli Ministry of Tourism, visits by American Jews increased from 150,000–200,000 annually in the 1990s to 200,000–250,000 annually in the later part of the first decade of the twenty-first century (figure 10.3) The biggest change, however, has been in the domain of youth travel. During the 1980s and 1990s, roughly ten to twelve thousand American Jewish high school students participated in educational programs in Israel annually. The high school programs were generally sponsored by the youth movements of the main North American denominations (Reform, Conservative, and Orthodox) and lasted four to six weeks during the summertime. In 1999, Birthright Israel was established as a private, philanthropically funded initiative to provide educational experiences in Israel to a larger number of diaspora Jews. The impetus for the program was initially not to foster ties to Israel but rather to use the Israel experience to shore up Jewish identity in the diaspora. Birthright trips are targeted at eighteen- to twenty-six-year-old travelers and last just ten days. By 2008, the program was bringing more than thirty-five thousand North American Jewish young adults to Israel annually.

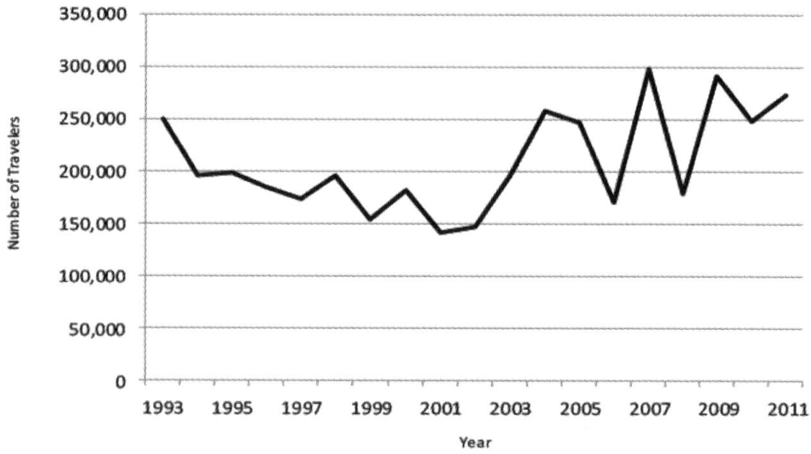

Figure 10.3. Number of American Jewish travelers to Israel by year. Source: Data supplied by the Israel Ministry of Tourism and published in its annual publication *Tayarut LeYisrael*. The estimate of Jewish travelers is derived from an annual survey conducted at border crossings.

Alongside Birthright, the field of educational tourism to Israel has expanded to include new long-term programs, organized within the framework of a Jewish Agency program known as Masa. In recent years, the number of North American participants in such programs has increased by about one-third, from four to six thousand annually. Meanwhile, the number of participants in high school programs, a category that reported diminished participation during the Second Intifada (2001–4), has returned to its previous level, with the addition of many new programs for students in Jewish day schools. The impact of these new programs in numbers alone has been remarkable. Figure 10.4 shows trends in participation. The overall increase from the late 1990s is more than 400 percent. At the current level of participation, more than half of North American Jewish young adults will eventually participate in an educational program in Israel.

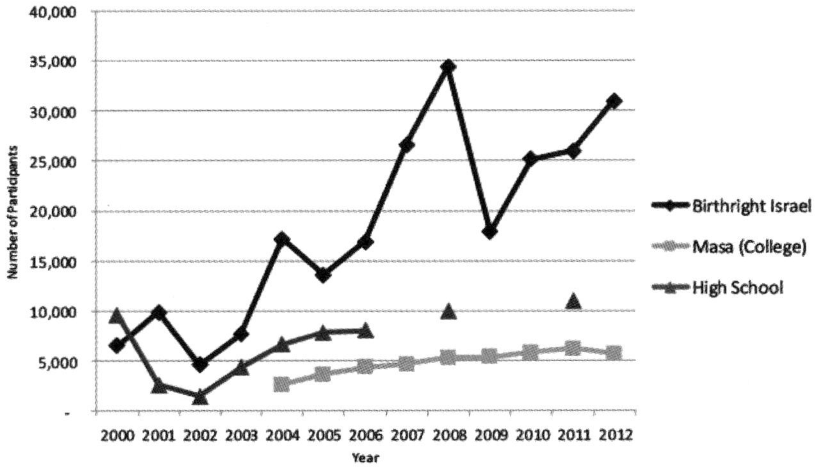

Figure 10.4. North American participation in Israel experience programs, by type. Sources: High school: For North American participation, 2000–2006, which is here estimated as 70 percent of worldwide participation, Erik H. Cohen, *Youth Tourism in Israel: Educational Experiences of the Diaspora* (Clevedon, UK: Channel View, 2008); for North America participation in 2011, Ramie Arian, *Mapping the Field of Israel Travel* (Northbrook, IL: iCenter, 2011), 2; for 2008, Ezra Kopelowitz, Minna Wolf, and Stephen Markowitz, *High School Israel Experience Programs: A Policy-Oriented Analysis of the Field* (Jerusalem: Makom/JAFI, 2009). Masa: North American participation, which is estimated as 65 percent of worldwide participation for 2004–6, is based on data supplied by Masa. Taglit: North American participation is based on data supplied by Taglit.

TABLE 10.1. The Field of Israel Advocacy

Left	Center	Right
Americans for Peace Now	American Israel Public Affairs Committee	Americans for a Safe Israel
Ameinu	American Jewish Committee	Committee for Accuracy in Middle East Reporting
Israel Policy Forum	Anti-Defamation League	David Project
J Street	Conference of Presidents	Emergency Committee for Israel
Partners for Progressive Israel	Israel Project	Jewish Institute for National Security Affairs
Jewish Voice for Peace*	Jewish Council for Public Affairs	Stand With Us
		Zionist Organization of America

* Jewish Voice for Peace does not define itself as "pro-Israel."

Finally, although the longitudinal evidence concerning Israel advocacy is the least systematic, the general trend seems to be toward higher levels of engagement. The number of advocacy organizations has certainly increased. Alongside the flagship groups the American Israel Public Affairs Committee (AIPAC) and the American Jewish Committee, which continue to dominate the field, there are new groups, albeit much smaller, representing views across the political spectrum. The new groups include, to name a few, Stand With Us on the right, the Israel Project in the center, and J Street on the left. Table 10.1 lists the larger advocacy organizations according to political orientation, as determined by the author.[20]

Although there is little longitudinal data on grassroots participation in Israel advocacy, there is some evidence of increase in the first decade of the twenty-first century:

- The number of participants attending the annual conferences of AIPAC and J Street steadily increased (figure 10.5).
- The number of college chapters increased for J Street (40), Jewish Voice for Peace (26), and the Zionist Organization of America (24). The larger organization, AIPAC, does not support campus groups.

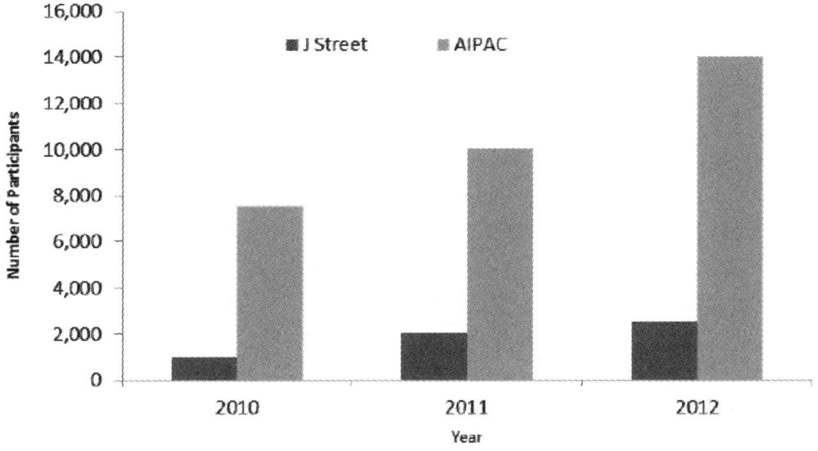

Figure 10.5. Number of participants in AIPAC and J Street annual conferences.

- Participation by college students in AIPAC's training programs increased to more than nine thousand in 2012. Other new advocacy training initiatives, including the David Project and the Hasbara Fellowship, were introduced.
- Donations to most advocacy organizations increased during the first decade of the twenty-first century (albeit unevenly, due to the 2008 recession). AIPAC's budget increased from $14.5 million in 2000 to $67 million in 2010.

On the other side of the ledger, some observers have suggested that the field of Israel advocacy is increasingly dominated by Orthodox Jews, especially in the centrist and right-wing groups. Informally, AIPAC officials dispute the claim, and there is no systematic evidence by which to assess it.

The New Contentiousness about Israeli Policies

By the measures examined in the previous section, American Jews are not distancing from Israel. There is, however, substantial evidence that American Jewish organizations are relating to Israel in new ways.

Compared to the period between the 1967 war and the 1993 Oslo Accords, the consensus framework for Israel advocacy has fractured during the most recent two decades, and organizations have pursued their own partisan agendas. At the same time, conflicts over Israeli policies and who legitimately belongs in the "pro-Israel" tent have diffused throughout American Jewish communal organizations.

During the previous period, American Jewish elites generally held to the view that advocacy organizations should follow the Israeli government's lead on policy issues and maintain a united front. The reasoning was that diaspora Jews, who choose not to live in Israel, do not have to live with the results of their political choices and should therefore defer to democratically elected Israeli leaders.[21] American Jewish elites also perceived a united front to be strategically necessary in order to maximize political impact. As a 1978 report by a leading advocacy organization put it, "Dissent ought not and should not be made public because . . . the result is to give aid and comfort to the enemy and to weaken that Jewish unity which is essential for the security of Israel."[22]

Accordingly, Israel advocacy organizations generally reached consensus on core issues, such as support for Israel's substantial package of economic and military aid and opposition to U.S. arms sales to Arab states. They also joined forces to suppress organized political dissent. The case of Breira, a liberal group that advocated peace negotiations with the Palestine Liberation Organization, is a case in point. Established in 1973 by a network of liberal rabbis and Jewish communal professionals, the group immediately became a lightning rod for harsh criticism. The Jewish community's leading figures refused all contact with the group, and several of its campus-based rabbis were threatened with dismissal. "Showing our dirty laundry in public, giving aid and comfort to Israel's enemies, is not allowed in American Jewish life," commented Arthur Samuelson, the editor of Breira's newsletter.[23] Breira's membership peaked at fifteen hundred, and the organization dissolved a few years after its launch.[24]

The consensus framework that enabled unity on core policy issues and suppression of organized dissent broke down following the signing of the Oslo Accords. Announced in 1993, the deal struck by the Israeli Labor-led government of Yitzhak Rabin and the Palestine Liberation Organization called for mutual recognition and phased Israeli withdrawal from the Gaza Strip and the West Bank with the aim—not explicit in the agreement—of eventually establishing a Palestinian state alongside Israel. Shocked by the peace deal, officials from Israel's opposition Likud party traveled to the United States to mobilize resistance. Speaking before Jewish audiences, the new Likud leader, Benjamin Netanyahu, declared, "I will lobby in Israel and American Jews will lobby in America. I think that's a good division of labor."[25] Netanyahu was joined by other prominent Likud officials, including the former minister of defense Ariel Sharon and the former prime minister Yitzhak Shamir.

The Israeli Likud politicians' appeals for action to disrupt the Oslo process were embraced by a coalition of right-wing organizations, including the Zionist Organization of America (ZOA) and the Orthodox Union. Setting their sights on Congress, the groups promoted legislation to make financial assistance to the newly established Palestinian Authority conditional on annual certification of its compliance with the treaty's Declaration of Principles. Prime Minister Rabin, with the support of AIPAC, had lobbied for the American aid, which was to supply one-quarter of a $2 billion fund. The law promoted by the ZOA and adopted the following year as the Specter-Shelby Amendment ensured that aid to the Palestinian Authority, already unpopular in Congress, would be reconsidered annually. A year later, when the renewal of aid came up for a vote, AIPAC lobbied in favor and the ZOA and the Orthodox Union lobbied against.[26]

During the 1990s and first decade of the twenty-first century, as the political pendulum swung back and forth between center-right and center-left governments in Israel, the Israel lobby in the United States repeatedly divided. During the first Netanyahu-led Likud government (1996–99), Jewish peace organizations, including Americans for Peace Now, lobbied in support of U.S. pressure on Israel to advance the Oslo process. A few years later, as the Sharon-led Kadima government prepared to withdraw from the Gaza Strip (2005), right-leaning American Jewish organizations led the opposition. Speaking at a meeting of the Presidents' Conference, ZOA leader Morton Klein denounced Sharon's plan to "throw Jews out of their home and give a terrorist regime more land."[27]

In 2008, after Netanyahu returned to the prime minister's office, J Street, an organization that advocates for a two-state solution to the Israeli-Palestinian conflict, joined the scene. Led by a seasoned Washington insider and supported by prominent Israeli politicians and public figures of the center-left, J Street rapidly emerged as the central expression of American Jewish opposition to the Netanyahu government, in particular to its policies on West Bank settlements and negotiations with the Palestinians. Notwithstanding its open criticism of Israeli government policies, J Street describes itself as "pro-Israel." However, by this phrase, the organization does not mean that it supports Israeli government policies but rather that it supports policies that will contribute to Israel's long-term flourishing as a Jewish and democratic state.

In recent years, the division of the Israel lobby into right, center, and left has become institutionalized. Each faction insists that it represents Israel's best interests and describes itself as "pro-Israel." The centrist groups, led by AIPAC, are clearly the most powerful, but the united front that enabled Jewish organizations to plausibly claim to represent the broader community has shattered. Today, as issues come to the fore, the branches of the lobby predictably take opposing positions. During the 2008 Gaza war, the centrist groups supported Israel's declared war aims, while the right-wing groups called for the destruction of Hamas and the left-leaning groups for an immediate cease-fire. In relation to the Iranian nuclear threat, the centrist groups support Israel's policy of sanctions backed up by the threat of military action, the right-wing groups urge immediate military action, and the left-wing groups urge diplomacy only. In relation to Jewish settlements on the West Bank, the centrist groups, following Israel's lead, generally try to downplay their significance. In contrast, the groups on the right promote settlement as a natural right, and the groups on the left oppose it as an obstacle to a peace deal.

Outside of Washington, DC, conflicts have roiled about who should be included in the communal tent. On college campuses, the focus has been on which advocacy organizations should be included in Jewish student communal associations. At Berkeley, the Jewish Student Union voted to exclude J Street, claiming that the organization is not truly pro-Israel. As one student leader put it, "J Street is not pro-Israel but an anti-Israel organization that, as part of the mainstream Jewish community, I could not support."[28] At Brandeis University, the Hillel association drew the line further to the left. The Brandeis Hillel accepted J Street as a member but voted to keep out Jewish Voice for Peace, a group that supports boycotts of products produced on West Bank settlements. "We are a pro-Israel organization," said the student Hillel president, "and while that can mean different things to different people, our definitions differed too much."[29]

Beyond the campuses, Jewish agencies and communal organizations have also become sites for the struggle over who can reside in the pro-Israel tent. In Washington, DC, a group calling itself Committee Opposed to Propaganda Masquerading as Art campaigned to ban Jewish Federation funding of a Jewish theatrical group, Theatre J, for staging plays deemed too critical of Israel.[30] In New York, a group calling itself JCC Watch similarly urged the New York Federation to suspend support for the Manhattan Jewish Community Center (JCC). The Manhattan JCC's offense was to host events sponsored by organizations that the group viewed as anti-Israel, including B'Tselem, an Israeli human rights organization, and Breaking the Silence, a group of Israeli army veterans opposed to the occupation.[31]

Finally, synagogues have also become sites of conflict over Israeli policies. In Newton, Massachusetts, a Reform synagogue canceled a lecture by J Street's Jeremy Ben-Ami at the last minute. The synagogue's rabbi explained that intense pressure by a few prominent members of the congregation made holding the event impossible. In New York City, the rabbis of a prominent liberal synagogue infuriated some congregants when they issued a public statement celebrating the United Nations decision to recognize Palestine as a nonmember state. As one member of the congregation commented to a *New York Times* reporter, "It's not as if we don't support a two-state solution, but to say with such embrace—it's like a high-five to the P.L.O., and that has left us numb."[32]

In sum, although not distancing from Israel, American Jews are increasingly divided over Israeli policies. The united front that characterized Israel advocacy during the 1970s and 1980s has ruptured. Today, advocacy organizations spanning the spectrum from left to right pursue partisan political programs, often in concert with Israeli allies. Meanwhile, in Jewish communities throughout the country, Israel has become a source of tension, prompting struggles over the boundaries of legitimate debate and who has the right to carry the pro-Israel mantle.

Explaining the Popularity of Distancing Claims

Why, given the paucity of evidence, have claims about distancing proven so compelling and tenacious? The new contentiousness about Israeli policies may provide at least a partial answer to the question. To many observers, the collapse of communal consensus *feels* like distancing. This is especially true with respect to how partisans on the center and right view J Street and the self-proclaimed pro-Israel left. For such individuals, lobbying the United States government to pressure Israel (for example, to freeze Jewish settlement on the West Bank) seems both disloyal and indicative of weakening diaspora ties to the homeland. Thus, the new contentiousness about Israeli policies may explain why claims about distancing seem compelling to so many observers.

A second plausible explanation may be that such claims simply express a deeply rooted and long-standing cultural pessimism about the Jewish future. As the historian Simon Rawidowicz observed, "there was hardly a generation in the Diaspora that did not consider itself the final link in Israel's chain."[33] In the contemporary context, most communal anxiety has focused on the twin phenomena of intermarriage and assimilation. Social scientists are divided over whether the master demographic trends are likely to lead to decline or growth.[34] Jewish organizational elites and most commentators, however, seem to gravitate toward the view that the American Jewish community is shrinking. The worry that American Jewry is separating from Israel fits the same pessimistic mode.

Finally, claims about distancing may also have taken hold because they can be politically useful. Peter Beinart's *New York Review of Books* essay galvanized such enormous attention not for the acuity of its critique of Israeli policies but for the damage he claimed such policies were causing American Jewry. For Beinart, the specter of the alienation of the next generation of American Jewry was an effective political weapon to wield against the Netanyahu government and big Jewish organizations that failed to criticize it. In contrast, for writers further to the political right, claims about the distancing of liberal Jews can help to neutralize the left's political critique. For example, in *The Promise of Israel*, Daniel Gordis claimed that the political disillusionment expressed by liberal Jews—and described by Beinart—does not fully account for their purported indifference. Beyond the conflict with the Palestinians, he argued, "these young Jews have also come to believe that they simply do not *need* Israel any longer. . . . American Jews are no longer marginal or subject to anti-Semitism. . . . So of what importance is a Jewish state to *them*?"[35] For Gordis, the critique of the left need not be taken at face value, since it is in reality an expression of something else, namely, a failure to understand Israel's significance for world Jewry.

Conclusion

The political divisions in Israel have spread to the diaspora in part because, in the aftermath of the Oslo Accords, Israeli politicians began recruiting diaspora supporters to their partisan causes, and they have continued doing so ever since. For better or worse, American Jews are now full participants in Israel's most important political debates. In the future, deep divisions over contentious Israeli policy issues will continue to feature prominently in American Jewish life, influencing the practice of Israel advocacy and the nature of communal relations. To be sure, such divisions will moderate in times of crisis, as during the November 2012 Gaza conflict with Hamas. For the foreseeable future, however, disagreements over core Israeli policies will surely return to the fore during periods of relative stability.

Such disagreements do not, however, indicate diminished attachment. Looking to the long term, it is certainly plausible that American Jewish attachment to Israel might diminish as a result of divergent political-cultural trends. There is certainly a palpable sense that two Jewish communities are moving in different directions, with American Jewry becoming more liberal and secular and Israeli Jewry more religious and nationalistic. But these are very slowly developing, long-term trends, and they are countervailed by other tendencies, including increased American Jewish exposure to Israel through travel, exchanges, social media, and the Internet. Whether in the long run political differences will strain the relationship or closer personal ties will strengthen it one cannot say.

In the meantime, unless researchers identify more convincing evidence, claims about the distancing of American Jews from Israel should be set aside. Such claims are not merely empirically dubious; they are also potentially damaging. The notion that liberal Jews are becoming indifferent to Israel transforms disagreements over policy issues into struggles over loyalty, thereby escalating conflicts among American Jews. The notion that American Jews, as a whole, are parting ways with Israel tends to make Israelis feel more politically and morally isolated—a stance that may reduce their readiness to take chances and make compromises for peace. Finally, the discourse on distancing threatens to produce a self-fulfilling prophecy in which the notion that American Jewish young adults have become alienated from Israel actually pushes some in that direction. It would be both more accurate and productive to describe the master trend in American Jews' relationship with Israel as one that entails increased contentiousness over policy issues rather than distancing and alienation.

NOTES

1. For example, Steven Rosenthal, *Irreconcilable Differences* (Hanover, NH: Brandeis University Press / University Press of New England, 2001); Ofira Seliktar, *Divided We Stand: America Jews, Israel, and the Peace Process* (Westport, CT: Praeger, 2002); Chaim I. Waxman, "American Jewish Philanthropy, Direct Giving, and the Unity of the Jewish Community," in *Toward a Renewed Ethic of Jewish Philanthropy*, ed. Yossi Prager (New York: Yeshiva University Press, 2010); Jack B. Ukeles, Ron Miller, and Pearl Beck, *Young Jewish Adults in the United States Today* (New York: American Jewish Committee, 2006); Steven M. Cohen and Arnold M. Eisen, *The Jew Within: Self, Family, and Community in America* (Bloomington: Indiana University Press, 2000); Steven M. Cohen and Jack Wertheimer, "Whatever Happened to the Jewish People?," *Commentary* 121:6 (June 2006): 33–37; Frank Luntz, *Israel and American Jews in the Age of Eminem* (New York: Andrea and Charles Bronfman Philanthropies, 2003).
2. Peter Beinart, "The Failure of the American Jewish Establishment," *New York Review of Books*, June 24, 2010; see also Peter Beinart, *The Crisis of Zionism* (New York: Times Books, 2012).
3. Daniel Gordis, *The Promise of Israel* (Hoboken, NJ: Wiley, 2012).
4. The phrase "discourse on distancing" is from Shmuel Rosner and Inbal Hakman, *The Challenge of Peoplehood: Strengthening the Attachment of Young American Jews to Israel in the Time of the Distancing Discourse* (Jerusalem: Jewish People Policy Institute, 2012).
5. See, for example, Cohen and Eisen, *Jew Within*; Cohen and Wertheimer, "Whatever Happened to the Jewish People?"
6. See, for example, Robert Wexler, "Israel and the Identity of American Jews," in *Israel, the Diaspora and Jewish Identity*, ed. Danny Ben Moshe and Zohar Segev (Brighton, UK: Sussex Academic Press, 2007); Ukeles, Miller, and Beck, *Young Jewish Adults in the United States Today*; Steven M. Cohen and Ari Kelman,

Beyond Distancing: Young Adult American Jews and Their Alienation from Israel (New York: Andrea and Charles Bronfman Philanthropies, 2007).

7. Cohen and Kelman, *Beyond Distancing*, 11.
8. Theodore Sasson, Charles Kadushin, and Leonard Saxe, "Trends in American Jewish Attachment to Israel: An Assessment of the 'Distancing' Hypothesis," *Contemporary Jewry* 30:2–3 (2010): 297–319.
9. For survey reports of age-cohort differences in the 1980s, see Steven M. Cohen, *Ties and Tensions: The 1986 Survey of American Jewish Attitudes towards Israel and Israelis* (New York: American Jewish Committee, 1986); Steven M. Cohen, *Content or Continuity: Alternative Bases for Commitment (the 1989 National Survey of American Jews)* (New York: American Jewish Committee, 1989).
10. See, for example, Bruce Phillips, "Splitting the Difference and Moving Forward with the Research," *Contemporary Jewry* 30:2–3 (2010): 257–61; Ron Miller and Arnold Dashefsky, "Brandeis v. Cohen et al.: The Distancing from Israel Debate," *Contemporary Jewry* 30:3 (2010): 155–64.
11. Theodore Sasson, Benjamin Phillips, Graham Wright, Charles Kadushin, and Leonard Saxe, "Understanding Young Adult Attachment to Israel: Period, Lifecycle, and Generational Dynamics," *Contemporary Jewry* 32:1 (2012): 67–84. Independently, Ira Sheskin conducted a similar study and arrived at the same conclusion. Ira Sheskin, "Attachment of American Jews to Israel: Perspectives from Local Jewish Community Studies," *Contemporary Jewry* 32:1 (2012): 27–65.
12. Simi Lampert, "Young Jews More Interested in Israel: Poll," *Forward*, July 9, 2012. In a 2010 national survey, Sasson and colleagues reported a similar finding, which they also attributed to increased travel to Israel in the youngest age group; see Theodore Sasson, Benjamin Phillips, Charles Kadushin, and Leonard Saxe, *Still Connected: American Jewish Attitudes about Israel* (Waltham, MA: Cohen Center for Modern Jewish Studies, Brandeis University, 2010).
13. Steven Cohen described the phenomenon, which entails increased young-adult attachment to Israel, as a "Birthright Bump." Lampert, "Young Jews More Interested in Israel."
14. Jewish Virtual Library, "American Jewish Contributions to Israel (1948–2004)," http://www.jewishvirtuallibrary.org/jsource/US-Israel/ujatab.html (accessed August 7, 2012).
15. The inflation adjustments for previous years are to 2010 dollars.
16. Jack Wertheimer, "Current Trends in American Jewish Philanthropy," in *American Jewish Yearbook*, ed. David Singer and Ruth Seldin (New York: American Jewish Committee, 1997), 35–40.
17. To track the number of American Friends organizations raising funds for Israeli affiliates, we examined the Guidestar database of U.S.-registered nonprofit organizations. The database includes information on year established as well as a description of philanthropic activities. See Eric Fleisch and Theodore Sasson, *The New Philanthropy: American Jewish Giving to Israeli Organizations* (Waltham, MA: Cohen Center for Modern Jewish Studies, 2012).

18. Wertheimer, "Current Trends in American Jewish Philanthropy."
19. There are no good data on trends in the number of donors to Israeli causes. It is possible that increasing donations can come from a declining donor base; however, a recent national survey reported that 32 percent of American Jews gave to a cause in Israel in the previous year. J Street, *National Survey of American Jews* (Washington, DC: Gerstein-Agne Strategic Communications, 2008).
20. See also Dov Waxman, "The Israel Lobbies: A Survey of the Pro-Israel Community in the United States," *Israel Studies Forum* 25 (2010): 5–28.
21. J. J. Goldberg, *Jewish Power: Inside the American Jewish Establishment* (New York: Addison-Wesley, 1996).
22. Annual report of the Conference of Presidents of Major American Jewish Organizations, quoted in Sol Stern, "Menachem Begin vs. the Jewish Lobby," *New York Magazine*, April 24, 1978.
23. Edward Tivnan, *The Lobby: Jewish Political Power and American Foreign Policy* (New York: Simon and Schuster, 1987), 96.
24. Jack Wertheimer, "Breaking the Taboo: Critics of Israel and the American Jewish Establishment," in *Envisioning Israel: The Changing Images and Ideals of North American Jews*, ed. Allon Gal (Detroit: Wayne State University Press, 1996), 397–419.
25. Rosenthal, *Irreconcilable Differences*, 128.
26. Seliktar, *Divided We Stand*, 137; Rosenthal, *Irreconcilable Differences*, 129.
27. The Presidents Conference was established in 1955 to ensure that Jewish organizations speak about Israel in a unified fashion. Morton Klein's comments are quoted in Stewart Ain, "Leaders Here Debate Backing Gaza Pullout," *Jewish Week*, October 22, 2004.
28. Alon Mazor, Isaiah Kirshner-Breen, Jeremy Elster, and Simone Zimmerman, "J Street U Bounced by Berkeley Group," *Forward*, December 16, 2011.
29. Peter Schworm, "Brandeis Groups Clash on Israel Stance," *Boston Globe*, March 11, 2011.
30. Nathan Guttman, "JCCs Are the New Front Line in the Culture War on Israel," *Forward*, March 23, 2011.
31. Caroline Glick, "American Jewry's Fight," *Jerusalem Post*, January 4, 2011.
32. Joseph Berger, "Rabbis Apologize for Tone of E-Mail on U.N. Vote," *New York Times*, December 6, 2012.
33. Simon Rawidowicz, *State of Israel, Diaspora, and Jewish Continuity: Essays on the "Ever-Dying People,"* ed. Benjamin C. I. Ravid (Waltham, MA: Brandeis University Press / University Press of New England, 1988), 54.
34. For two alternative perspectives, see Elizabeth Tighe, Leonard Saxe, and Charles Kadushin, *Estimating the Jewish Population of the United States: 2000–2010* (Waltham, MA: Steinhardt Social Research Institute, Brandeis University, 2011); Sergio DellaPergola, *Jewish Demographic Policies: Population Trends and Options in Israel and in the Diaspora* (Jerusalem: Jewish People Policy Institute, 2011).
35. Gordis, *Promise of Israel*, 169 (emphasis in original).

Conclusion

Imagination and Reality in Scenarios of Israel's Future

ILAN TROEN

The return to Zion has long been part of the Jewish imagination. Until the advent of Zionism, these imaginings were articulated in religious terms and rooted in biblical and rabbinic texts. They revolved around the belief that the return from exile would be the result of divine intervention, often through the agency of a messiah. In some versions, the hastening of the messianic age could be stimulated by the actions of Jews, and in others, by divine decision alone. In all cases, the end of history was not specific about the terms of the kinds of social organizations that would take place except that a society governed by halakhah was assumed. The most that could be imagined was some form of undefined theocracy.[1]

Particularly during the early years of Zionist settlement and through the creation of the state, the Jewish imagination found the prospect of thinking about ideal scenarios very inviting. Indeed, the construction of scenarios was essential. While Palestine most certainly was not an empty land—and Zionists did not imagine it as such—it was vastly underpopulated.[2] In 1800, only about 250,000 people, urban and rural Arabs, Jews, Bedouin, and others, inhabited the land between the Jordan River and the Mediterranean and between the Lebanon and the Sinai desert. By 1900, the population doubled, but that meant only 500,000 inhabitants, with an increasing number of Jews.[3] In the twentieth century, the number approached ten million. The phenomenal growth in a backward and neglected corner of the Ottoman Empire was directly related to the stimulus provided by the influx of Jewish settlers, largely from Europe but also from the Middle East and beyond. While many were poor, there were others who had capital, commercial skills, connections, and modern education.

They brought with them an appreciation for the worlds from which they came as well as a rich imagination of what might take place in a land to which they had been connected as a people and as a culture for millennia.

A Portrait of the State of the Country

To understand what took place, we should begin by appreciating that Zionist settlement was primarily an act of imagination. European Jews, like other Europeans, knew very little about the actual conditions and nature of Palestine until the mid-nineteenth century, when primarily British, French, and German explorers, scientists, adventurers, and travelers began to "discover" the Holy Land.[4] This was not, however, the same encounter that Europeans had with other distant lands with which they were largely ignorant. In the case of Palestine, they initially came to discover and confirm knowledge of the country of their religious imagination. They came to identify the sites where events in Scriptures had taken place. Their vision, in short, was directed toward re-creating and imagining the past as perceived in biblical stories.

This perspective led to disappointing comparisons. Professional and amateur travelers have left a very large literature on the topic. To quote but one famous example, Mark Twain wrote in 1867 upon his departure from Palestine,

> So ends the pilgrimage. We ought to be glad that we did not make it for the purpose of feasting our eyes upon fascinating aspects of nature, for we should have been disappointed. . . .
>
> Of all the lands there are for dismal scenery, I think Palestine must be the prince. The hills are barren, they are dull of colour, they are unpicturesque in shape. The valleys are unsightly deserts fringed with a feeble vegetation that has an expression about it of being sorrowful and despondent. . . . It is a hopeless, dreary, heart-broken land.[5]

Like that of so many other Westerners, Mark Twain's negative assessment was informed by what he believed the country had looked like in ancient times. He toured the country while quoting biblical passages and invoking biblical scenes and then comparing them with the unpleasant reality of a desolate and ruined country inhabited by an impoverished people. The exercise caused him to remark, "I must studiously and faithfully unlearn a great many things I have somehow absorbed concerning Palestine. . . . I suppose it was because I could not conceive of a small country having so large a history."[6]

Twain's account reflected the common view that Palestine had suffered decline primarily because of the ineptitude of its governments and residents. This assessment achieved the status of a "scientific" fact with "expert" reports filed by numerous professional explorers. The consensus was expressed by the view that it was the people who were at fault. Palestine, during the time of Jesus, it was claimed, had held up to three times as many people as were found in the country in 1900. It had, in fact, once been a "land flowing with milk and honey." Observers concluded that there was little to learn from the present local population. Outside ideas, technologies, funds, and even people had to be imported if the land was to be changed and improved. To illustrate this point consider the following:[7]

- There was no electricity in the country until the 1920s, when the Zionist Pinhas Ruttenberg introduced it, including a modern hydroelectric plant on the Jordan River.
- There were few roads. In the winter, when the rains came, it was easier to navigate from Jaffa/Tel Aviv to Haifa/Acre by coastal vessel than cope with unpaved mud tracks that passed for the coastal land route.
- There were not even more than half a dozen steam engines for powering industry until the British arrived at the end of World War I.
- There were no factories; the larger workshops employed perhaps only five workers and were engaged in the country's major exports: agricultural products such as soap and olive oil.
- The other major export was people, largely Christians depressed with the poverty of the country and Jews who made aliyah only to find that there was nothing for them to do.
- There was comparatively little shade in a country denuded of trees by the inhabitants in need of wood and goats looking for fodder. About a quarter billion trees have been planted by the Jewish National Fund since it was inaugurated in 1903.
- At present, the land of Israel is at least three times as populous as it ever was in the ancient world, with Jews again the dominant part of the population.

As the country leapt into the modern world, it became a setting for a diversity of plans that competed and conflicted with one another. In the course of this experience, a rich and varied country developed with modern cities integrated into the world economy, whose wealth is marked by skyscrapers and striking high-rise condominiums, attractive suburbs for people enjoying the country's wealth as well as stagnant development towns tied to older industries, a rural landscape composed of various kinds of villages based on different economic and social systems, diverse and distinctive religious communities; it is a country that runs the gamut from Tel Aviv, a world-class city on the Mediterranean, to the Negev desert's Bedouin encampments, composed of tents and ramshackle buildings that still rely at least in part on grazing animals and occasional hired labor. Nevertheless, Israel has been recognized in its totality as a first-world country.

By the first decade of the twenty-first century, Israel became the thirty-second state to be admitted into the Organization for Economic Co-operation and Development in recognition of its economic, social, and political achievements.[8] This is a remarkable transformation that was not the product of a master plan executed with precision and discipline. Rather, it was the consequence of severe competition between different and competing ideas of what that Palestinian landscape should become. Some conceptions brought by those who settled and built the land succeeded, and others failed. Most preconceptions were somehow transformed. While the contest involved competition between contending economic conceptions and social ideals, increasingly the need for successfully contending over the same land with another national group, Palestine's Arabs, has had and continues to have enormous impact on which scenarios are privileged, supported, and successful.[9]

The process of imagining, as we shall see, is far from over and remains as intense as ever. The land between the Jordan and the Mediterranean excites the imagination with its possibilities and evokes a desire for control.

Only recently, with the actual creation of a Jewish state, have more precise imaginings of the Jewish character of the state as expressed in religious terms taken on concrete form by those who previously thought solely in terms of awaiting the messiah and divine intervention. Similarly, the negation by some Arabs of Israel with alternative scenarios of what should take place and even the prescriptions of Israeli Arabs for reconstructing Israel as a binational state or a state of its citizens are complex topics that will not be treated here.[10]

What follows is a presentation of scenarios of Jewish society in secular terms. From Herzl to the builders of the kibbutz and moshav and from Dizengoff and the founders of Tel Aviv to contemporary planners of Israel's future, considerations of Jewish law have no role. These communities may accommodate religious Jews, but they are unconcerned with Judaism. Similarly, the largely political discourse by Arabs of claims for reconstituting the land as an Arab or Muslim preserve are not part of this story.[11]

What actually transpires in the rubric presented here can be set forth as follows: Zionists began by transplanting European ideas in a process of experimentation and adaptation. Initially, they planned distinctive agricultural colonies, but they soon added towns and cities to the inventory of scenarios. The balance between urban and rural colonization changed, as did the preferred models within these categories. The continuous revisions and adjustments in settlement planning were a response to the interplay of three distinct factors that determined which design concept was given priority. These factors are social and political ideologies, the need for productivity and economic independence, and the problem of ensuring security in a hostile environment.

Ideological, economic, and security objectives have competed with each other for primacy from the beginning through the present. Put another way, social values and ideas may not produce economically successful models. Also, social conceptions and financial considerations may be trumped by security needs. The relative primacy given to any one of these three factors affects the strength of the others. In sum, all scenarios are tentative. Only in Theodor Herzl's utopian novel *Altneuland* (1902) is there a conception of a Zionist society that enjoys wide appeal, is economically productive, and exists in a world without threat or hostility.[12] In the course of the decades of the growth of the *yishuv*, security concerns overtook social and economic ones and thereby distorted or at least powerfully affected all other scenarios. Only for a short time after the Oslo Accords (1993) did a large number of Zionist theoreticians consider what a society would look like in a Jewish polity that could exist in peace in the Promised Land.

Stated another way, the ever-changing history of Zionist scenarios took place within the context of the distortions caused by continuing conflict with Arabs hostile to the idea of a Jewish state. Only at rare instances do we glimpse formulations that imagine a Jewish society enjoying what can be termed "normalcy." As I shall suggest at the conclusion, it is not at all clear if, in this post-Oslo period, there is a chance for competition between only social and economic considerations. If that would ever become the case, only then could economic and social ideas confront one another on a level playing field without the distraction or intervention of security issues.

The Idea of the Nation as a Common Denominator

For all the differences among the considerable range of scenarios proposed since the beginning of the Zionist movement, all share a commitment to the collective or national character of any proposed society. This collective or national ethos was directly expressed in the manner in which the country was settled. That is, in imagining Zion's countryside from the 1880s through subsequent generations, pioneers organized and built villages rather than a multitude of individual farms that would have transformed Jews into a Middle Eastern peasantry. In the process, they established hundreds of villages, about 250 from the 1880s until independence and 400 more up to the 1967 Six-Day War, when agricultural colonization largely ended. Thus, in less than a century, from 1882 to 1967, Zionist colonizers established more than 650 communities. This is remarkable; and unlike the homesteads, latifundia, ranches, or other forms of settlement that transplanted Europeans were establishing at the same time in such venues as the United States, Australia, and Argentina, Zionism did not carve up the countryside into multiple parcels for individual pioneers. It created patterns of social organization in which the individual joined a group. There have been no "little houses on the prairie" or homesteads where individual families lived in isolation from one another. Moreover, the explicit purpose of group settlement was to serve the nation and advance its interests. The private or individualistic ethos that motivated other cultures devoted to the furtherance of the personal pursuit of happiness was absent in the case of Zionism. Even where, as I shall describe in the case of urban development, an individualistic conception of social organization was advanced, it was subservient to a national perspective.[13]

Much of this is captured in the language that permeates all early utopian scenarios. Consider the following terms: *ḥalutz* and "people." What is meant by *ḥalutz* or *ḥalutziut* in Hebrew is not captured by the usual translation "pioneer" or "pioneering."[14] That is, the pioneer in its American meaning refers to individuals. In the Hebrew or Zionist meaning of *ḥalutz*, the pioneer is one who is in service of a group; the *ḥalutz* is the avant-garde, the one who goes before the people and is in their service. The word derives from the biblical passage describing how the Israelites overcame Jericho upon entry into the Promised Land: "And he [Joshua] said unto the people, 'Pass on, and encircle the city, and let the *ḥalutz* pass on before the ark of the LORD.' And it was so, that when Joshua had spoken unto the people, the seven priests bearing the seven rams' horns before the LORD passed on and blew the horns; and the ark of the covenant and the LORD followed them. And the *ḥalutz* went before the priests that blew the horns" (Joshua 6:7–9).

The word *ḥalutz* virtually disappeared from Hebrew use through the Middle Ages. By the beginning of the twentieth century, Zionist writers recovered the word and applied it to settlers who went into the Palestinian countryside to build model Zionist societies that would be forerunners of even more settlement in the future. While these Zionist pioneers may certainly have been individualistic, they were understood by others and by themselves in terms of their mission on behalf of the nation. This is very different from the settlers of the American West, who sought out private territory in order to realize themselves and to engage in the pursuit of their individual happiness.[15] These distinctions are eminently visible should one fly over the United States west of the Alleghenies or over the State of Israel. In the former, the topography is often marked by a geometric grid with isolated farmhouses planted in the middle. In the latter, there are few freestanding buildings across the landscape. Israel is dotted by clusters of homes that form villages.

The first model for agricultural settlement was the *moshava*, a colony of independent property owners. This was superseded by the *moshav*, a farming village that blended private ownership with cooperatives and an ethos of mutualism, and then by the *kvutza* or *kibbutz*, communistic collective settlements. From the moshava to the kibbutz, the degree of individual ownership declined and the commitment to the collective enhanced. These progressions also represented the evolution from explicitly capitalistic economic conceptions through forms of socialism and communism. Whatever the particular economic and ideological basis for the village, socialist or capitalist, and whether vigorously secular or respectful of religious traditions, the distinguishing feature of all of these villages was that they were based on a strong sense of community.[16]

As with traditional Jews who remained in "holy cities" of Palestine to await the messiah, Zionist pioneers sought to live within a communal framework, a common feature of Jewish life throughout the ages and wherever Jews settled. Most founders of moshavot were traditional Jews, although they did not choose to live under an uncompromising regime supervised by religious authorities. Like religious counterparts in quarters of Jerusalem, Safed, and Tiberias, agricultural pioneers lived in communities rooted in a common tradition.

The source of this communitarian ethos has usually been traced to various streams of European cooperative, socialist, or communist ideologies. Indeed, it is possible to view socialist conceptions of "solidarity" as but a secularized form of traditional Jewish behavior and belief. It is clear that solidarity and communitarian patterns also are to be found in Jewish culture and history. They derive from the universal tradition found across time and place wherever Jews settled. The moshavot, for example, were founded with the signing of *takanot*, or the principles that established a "covenant" or bond between the members of the settlement. Such *takanot* are found throughout Jewish history well into the modern period. Even before the establishment of the "national institutions" created by the World Zionist Organization, colonies of pioneers spontaneously and without the direction of controlling institutions formed covenantal communities that expressed at once their belief in reestablishing continuity between contemporary settlers with the ancient Hebrews and a conviction that their actions were harbingers of great, national events that would soon take place.[17]

Over the early decades, the moshava gave way to the moshav, since the moshav was far more economical in settling larger numbers of potential Jewish pioneers. The change to the moshav began to take place just before the outbreak of World War I and continued until the 1930s. With the outbreak of the Arab rebellion in 1936, the kibbutz supplanted

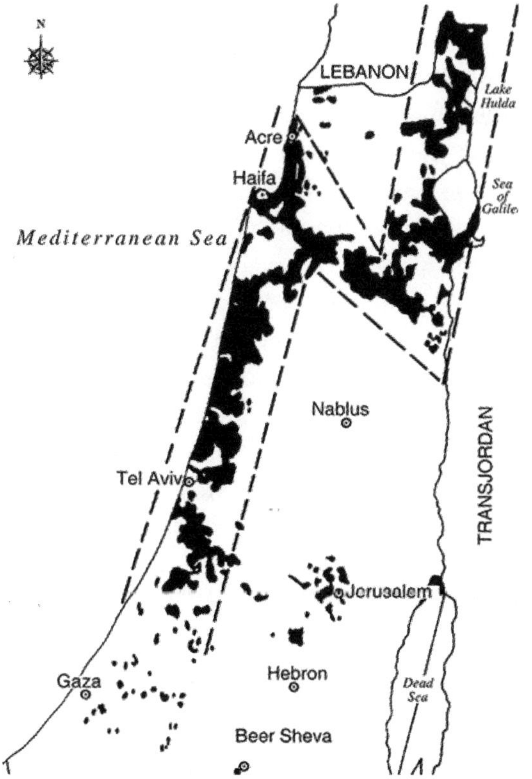

Figure C.1. The N of Zionist settlement.

the moshav, since it was a more efficient means for securing the territory for what could become a Jewish state. In effect, the primacy of ideology was replaced by the primacy of economy, to be followed by the primacy of security needs represented in the kibbutz.

A crucial marker was the outbreak of violence in 1929, when the settlement authorities made the choice of the kind of community that would be supported. It was in response to growing violence against Jewish settlements that Zionist authorities conceived of locating settlements in an N-shaped pattern across the landscape of Palestine. This concept determined that Jewish resources would be invested in the areas beginning with the northern reaches of the upper Galilee and extending to below the Sea of Galilee and then across the valley of Jezreel to where Haifa is located and then down the coast to below Tel Aviv. The high country of what we may now call Judea and Samaria or the West Bank was beyond this scenario, and minimal investment was made even in Jerusalem.

With the location determined, the crucial issue was how to place the maximum amount of Jews on the smallest allotments per person of land available. That is, there were far more potential pioneers than could readily be accommodated on a limited amount of land. This certainly ruled out private farms. Young and single pioneers were also to be preferred to families, who were the natural backbone of the moshav. Bourgeois leaders of the World Zionist Organization therefore came to support the kibbutz as the preferred engine of Jewish settlement. Only after the War of Independence, when Israel created a regular army, did the kibbutz recede as the privileged form of Jewish settlement. Indeed, after 1953, very few kibbutzim were built, but numerous moshavim were planted on the land. Thus, the Israeli countryside continued as one of villages, but the choice of village type underwent changes in new circumstances.[18]

A similar sense of community was to be found among urban pioneers, particularly those who founded and developed Tel Aviv, the first Jewish city in nearly two millennia. There were, in fact, two Tel Aviv's, one bourgeois and the other proletarian. Even the city's bourgeois founders, individuals with a commitment to private property, modern commerce, and free-enterprise, had a keen appreciation that in the sand dunes along the Mediterranean coast, they were establishing a novel community that served national purposes. Indeed, "Tel Aviv" was the Hebrew name given to Nahum Sokolov's translation of *Altneuland*, Herzl's utopian novel.[19]

Tel Aviv's founders believed that through their city they would create a vigorous Hebrew culture appropriate to a revitalized Jewish nation. It was there, rather than in Jerusalem, that the new Hebrew literature, art, music, theater, popular culture, and civil society would be established. Although the kibbutznik of the rural frontier is widely regarded as the iconic ideal of Zionist society, the reality is that by the 1930s this city, composed of middle-class or expectant bourgeois burghers, constituted one-third of the total *yishuv*. Indeed, never more than 20% of all of Zion's pioneers ever worked the land, and that was in the 1920s or just as Tel Aviv entered into a period of extraordinary growth. The essential character of the city is reflected in Tel Aviv's municipal politics. Except for several years in the mid-1920s, the city was controlled by a dominant middle-class party that often called itself *ba'alei batim* or the "home owners" party.

Even as the countryside was home to multiple scenarios, so was the city. The city's proletariat created a host of institutions that reflected markedly different conceptions of what life in the homeland should be. The most concrete example is found in colonies of working-class estates in Tel Aviv and elsewhere, particularly in the outskirts of Haifa, where a belt of such communities, the *kiryot*, was established beginning in the 1920s. These communities were urban equivalents to the moshav and the kibbutz. They were utopian communes *within* the rising metropolis, often consciously modeling themselves on the proletarian communities of "Red" Vienna, a widely imitated phenomenon that took place in that city after World War I and before the rise of Hitler.

Red Vienna featured large and imposing buildings designed as monuments to impress the power of the people on those who passed them. Indeed, they were called *Volkswohnungspaläste* (people's housing palaces) and were explicitly designed to contrast with other urban, aristocratic monuments such as royal palaces and museums. This often meant construction of very large apartment houses that contained many family units. This bias was in keeping with a tradition of utopian design that began a century earlier with Robert Owen and Charles Fourier. While the Tel Aviv version of workers' housing estates was scaled down, it did provide for community space in the form of a shared courtyard as well as libraries, kindergartens and schools, health centers, meeting halls, recreation spaces, and the like. Great care was taken to encourage a sense of community that would foster working-class solidarity and nurture the kind of individuals who would grow into and participate in proletarian societies. In Tel Aviv, Labor Zionism even produced an innovative educational system around Beit HaChinuch (the House of Education) that was similarly designed to nurture socialist personalities. These communities also organized choirs, youth groups, working-class theaters and party cells that serviced the residents of the housing estates and were often located in them or at least nearby. Moreover, most inhabitants worked within the network of companies and institutions established by the Histadrut. In other words, there was an attempt to create subuniverses of workers committed to the same culture and totally occupied within it. A prime purpose of this arrangement was to infuse this world with the *havay ha-histadruti* (Histadrut experience). This was the Labor Zionist equivalent of an idea widely disseminated in central Europe by socialists and Bauhaus architects, who advocated the design of a new *Gesamtkultur* or *Wohnkultur*. Their aim was to provide a total environment that would create and sustain collective values. It would have the added benefit of contributing to the political unity of the working class. These same principles were translated into working-class, suburban housing estates such as Shechunat Borochov and Kiryat Avoda, which was later to be called Holon.[20]

The fate of these working-class communities was the same whether located in the heart of Tel Aviv or in its suburbs. They were eventually to be engulfed and swallowed up in the ever-expanding metropolis of Tel Aviv. The point is that even though they did not enjoy the kibbutz's buffer of space, total control over community governance, strict selection of membership, and the moral and financial support of powerful institutions, they shared the common commitment to establish new communities in the relative tabula rasa of Palestine before independence.

It has been my purpose to emphasize the overriding notion of and commitment to community and nation as the prime shared characteristic of Zionist imagination and action prior to independence. The question that now arises is how and to what extent has that changed in the subsequent more than six decades. I suggest that the scenarios and experience have been one of slow decline, though still within proportions. The overarching sense of nation and community still survives, although with less fervor. One important benchmark is to examine how Israel imagined itself at independence. Even as we earlier referred to the distinction between the Zionist *ḥalutz* and the American pioneer, it is useful to compare the Israeli and American Declarations of Independence for what these societies say about themselves with regard to their justifications and and their intentions in shaping their futures.

Declarations

There is the possibility of confusion and distortion in translating the word for "people" from one language to the other, even as we have examined differences between "pioneer." The word "people," which is universally translated into Hebrew as *'am*, is problematic since the concept of "people" has different connotations in the American and the Jewish experiences. In one of the few footnotes to Yehoshua Arieli's version of the U.S. Declaration of Independence, the best and most influential of Hebrew translations of it, he is at pains to explain that "people" in the American document refers to "members of society" (*b'ney chevra*). *'Am* can and often does have a more collective sense in Hebrew. *Merriam Webster's Collegiate Dictionary* gives as the first meaning of "people" "human beings making up a group or assembly or linked by a common interest"; "persons" is offered as a synonym. A Hebrew equivalent, Reuben Alcalay's *The Complete Hebrew-English Dictionary*, renders *'am* in the following order: "nation, folk, community, populace, inhabitants, tribe, crowd, multitude, mob." The sense of the collective, and not simply of the association of individual human beings, is paramount in the Hebrew.[21]

An essay by Israel Supreme Court Justice Eliyakim Rubinstein may elucidate this point. A noted scholar of Israel's Declaration of Independence, Rubinstein compares the American and Israeli documents from an Israeli perspective. He observes that, as opposed to the American predecessor, Israel's declaration emphasizes collective or national rights rather than individual ones. An essential distinction between the two societies, he finds, is that the State of Israel is defined in ethnic, national terms and was created as an instrument for fulfilling national Jewish purposes and collective goals rather than individual liberties.[22]

The term "rights" appears seven times in Israel's declaration, and in each instance it is within a national context. For example, the document refers to the "right of the Jewish people and national renewal in its own land"; "the right [of the survivors of the Holocaust] for a life of dignity, liberty and honest labor in their nation's homeland"; the "natural right of the Jewish people to exist as all independent nations do in its own sovereign state"; and "the power of our natural and historical right." Moreover, the first set of paragraphs, fully one-half of the declaration, is devoted to reviewing Jewish history in order to establish the "rights" of the Jewish people to a state of their own in Palestine. Such an assertion of collective, national rights would have been premature in the U.S. Declaration of Independence, and it probably is still unthinkable in the American experience. Israel's declaration also claims that Israelis are endowed with individual rights, but this assertion comes only toward the end of the document in a section that echoes formulations of human rights promulgated by the United Nations, the international body that granted legitimacy to the "Jewish state."

Postindependence Scenarios

There is a significant and growing body of scholarship interested in exploring how and when the commitment to group diminished within the framework of a "Jewish" state and without considering such ideas as "binationalism" or a "state of all its citizens." Recent studies such as Orit Rozin's work on Tel Aviv in the first decade of independence reflect on "the rise of the individual in 1950s Israel" as "a challenge to collectivism."[23] In Rozin's remarkable study of popular behavior of ordinary citizens, housewives, politicians, judges, black-market profiteers, immigrants in transit camps, and rural settlements, one can readily discern the erosion of a collectivist ethos into one in which an unprecedented privileging of individualism emerges.

If one were to review a host of new scholarship, a similar observation would emerge through examining various phenomena in subsequent decades, ranging from the ways in which fallen soldiers were commemorated (not only as willing sacrifices for the nation but as individuals with their own history) to the erosion of the power of the Histadrut and its institutions (the most manifest symbol of the power of group solidarity) to the revolution in the national economy, where a liberal capitalism has become dominant. Perhaps the most significant iconic change is in the transformation of the kibbutz from an egalitarian economy based in agriculture to one in which there are marked differentials in income, a reliance on industry and new technologies for prosperity, and the return of the family unit as the prime instrument and locus of the socialization of the child rather than the kibbutz community at large.[24] Moreover, in reviewing the political history of the country, the electoral revolution of 1977 brought about the end of Labor Zionist hegemony and the rise of new possibilities for government that are significantly to the right and pluralistic in both economic and social ideals.[25]

Changes in education of the young reflect the same trend. Zionist education from the earliest years of the *yishuv* through much of the history of Israel emphasized preparing the young with a large dose of collective principles and values. The invention of the position of *mechaneych* (educator) assigned to each classroom was a reflection of the intent of inculcating desired norms that emphasized collective values. By the 1990s, new trends viewed this and similar phenomena as suffocating and compromising individual freedoms.[26] The Ministry of Education's 1994 Shenhar Report reflects a growing demand to move toward an appreciation of individualism with the formal adoption of the idea of "pluralism" and new conceptions on how to inculcate "identity." Pluralism suggests choice and a direction not previously considered. It was suggested that the child and youth decide what he or she is to become from a range of choices offered by the school. Only English and quantitative skills remain from a traditional set of examinations that had previously included Bible and Hebrew literature as essential elements of the national culture that should be acquired by Israel's youth. For many Israelis, this change reflected a desire for openness that has been expressed in terms of greater individual freedom of the kind Americans enjoy. Indeed, the quest for "Americanization" or "globalization" enters into academic and popular discourse. Some welcomed the possibility and desirability of such change as a move toward "normality."[27]

Scenarios of "Normality" for Israel's Second Century

At the same time, in the period of the 1993 Oslo Accords, when peace appeared to be possible between Israel and its Palestinian neighbors and when Jordan and Israel signed a peace agreement (1993) and the Vatican finally recognized the Jewish state (1994), it appeared possible that normality, that is, an absence of war, could produce new scenarios of what Israel could look like in another generation or so. One important set of such views is found in a new national "master plan": "Israel 2020." This is an extraordinarily ambitious, systematic analysis of Israel in the twenty-first century that replaces the primacy of security with ideology and economics. Since 1993, when the first projections were published, more than 250 experts from a wide variety of academic disciplines as well as professionals and public officials have produced more than two hundred overviews, scenarios, and specific plans. The urgency behind this remarkable effort is that much of Israel (with the exception of the lightly populated Negev and Galilee) is already the fifth most densely populated country in the world (after Singapore, Malta, Bangladesh, and Bahrain) and could become the most densely populated by 2020. At the same time, Israel's rapidly expanding, high value-added, and increasingly high-tech economy could push its per capita wealth to the levels of advanced western European countries. "Israel 2020" argues that future plans must incorporate and confront the problem of an advanced industrial state organized on a modern capitalistic basis in the turbulent Middle East.[28]

"Israel 2020" postulates that there will be two political entities between the Jordan River and the Mediterranean: a Jewish and a Palestinian one. Moreover, it anticipates that the Palestinian entity may federate or confederate with Jordan, that it will be autonomous, and that it will conduct its own affairs with the exception of military and security matters. The borders with the Palestinian entity as well as with the neighboring Arab states are expected to be open for the controlled movement of people and goods but closed to migration into Israeli territory. This also implies that the demand of the PLO for a return to pre-1967 Israel will be rejected and lapse. While acknowledging that this scenario will take time to accomplish and that there will be numerous setbacks, planners predict that the principles outlined in the document may be achieved by people of goodwill on all sides and through the pressure of the world community. In sum, they expect the military conflict to be defused and a regional framework for economic cooperation to be established. With this prospect, there is much that national planners could do.

Perhaps such optimism is necessary since, in the doomsday vision with an all-out attack using unconventional weapons, imagining scenarios is pointless. The prime actors shaping the context in which Israel would be imagined should be diplomats, politicians, and economists rather than the security specialists.

The scenario for Israel's future is one of unprecedented concentrations of population and industry. Tel Aviv will continue to develop as Israel's primary city with a population of millions. Haifa, further north on the Mediterranean coast, will be the country's second metropolis and closely related to Tel Aviv. Jerusalem is expected to radiate out, particularly toward the coastal plain and the Tel Aviv region. As anyone who has driven from Jerusalem to Haifa knows, it is possible to view all three metropolises as essentially contiguous, forming one large megalopolis. Contemporary planners find this blueprint attractive because of its economic advantages and appropriateness to a new moment in the evolution of Zionist thought. The new, national economic ethos endorses bringing skilled labor and high value-added industries, such as those associated with advanced technologies, in close proximity to one another. It willingly submits to the power of large cities to attract population. Competition and free choice are viewed as the most serviceable and efficient methods of advancing the prosperity of individuals and society. These concepts are familiar in western Europe, where experts advocate enhancing a few selected metropolitan nodes rather than artificially supporting diffusion. The countryside, including the kibbutz, is no longer a matter of national concern or support. The farmer as pioneer is replaced by the high-tech inventor and entrepreneur.[29]

This rose-tinted vision also represents a significant change from the ideologies that shaped the first century of Zionist imagination, which had the collective rather than the individual at the center of its purposes and value system. Israel was established as the "Jewish state" to serve the needs and interests of the Jewish people. An interesting and revealing index of this change is the emergence of a new attitude toward control over land. Unlike many Western societies, where access to land is identified with *individual* liberty, in Zionist thought, land has been identified with *national* independence and freedom. The centrality of collective rights to territory has also been true for Palestinian nationalists, who have threatened and even murdered Arabs who have sold their land to Jews. Altering the rules to liberalize the acquisition of land is therefore a prime indicator of how far Israel has moved or can move to a civil and perhaps less nationalistic state. On the one hand, this opens up land to Arab citizens of Israel. On the other, it means that land becomes a resource for the benefit of individuals rather than the Jewish people. Should this become the path Israel chooses, Israel would be an even greater anomaly in a region where states and societies are rooted in ethnic, national, or religious identities rather than the primacy of the individual. In sum, normalcy could mean adopting Western models rather than conforming to the values of Israel's Middle Eastern neighbors.

Recent cases adjudicated by Israel Supreme Court indicate a willingness to place individual rights alongside the state's obligation to defend collective Jewish interests. American legal theory, in addition to the growing power of human rights discourse, has clearly affected Israeli judicial thought as well as popular discourse. If the possibility of peaceful coexistence with Arab neighbors somewhat alleviates security anxieties, the state will likely come under increasing pressure to acknowledge the rights of individual citizens without reference to the community with which they are associated. This is an indication of Israel redefining itself with the attributes of a civil society. It is a significant step taken in a society that is apparently still consciously struggling to become "normal" within a rubric associated with Western democracies.[30]

Only a small minority of "post-Zionist" Israelis claim that their country should become a "state of all its citizens" or an imitation of a de-ethnicized and individualistic American civil society. The covenantal and collective base of Israel as a Jewish state remains intact. Indeed, the great majority of Israeli citizens and scholars emphasize that democracy in Israel can be and must be derived from Jewish sources and historical experience. For the foreseeable future, there is likely to be considerable residual power in the founding collective ideals and traditions even among secular and outward-looking Jewish intellectuals.[31]

Yet change is visible in such a basic area as the relationship to land as a national resource. What once passed for ecology was only nature preservation. This coincided with a romantic nationalism that sought to rediscover the country as it had been in the ancient world and the need to familiarize an essentially immigrant population with the ancient homeland and to nurture a sense of rootedness in it. Generations of Israeli youth have hiked across the country, becoming intimately familiar with the natural and historic treasures present in the landscape. At the same time, this nurtured intimacy with the land was expected to enhance their willingness and ability to defend it and what could be located on it.[32]

As in other countries that have undergone rapid development and pursued a higher standard of living, in Israel, too, much of the natural environment has been abused. Affluence and industry place enormous demands on the scarce resources of a small country. The tenfold increase in population over this past century has resulted in growing competition between agricultural, industrial, and residential needs and between these and the need to preserve the country's landscape, air, and water. Struggles loom over choices of means of transportation and land and water usage. So, too, there are debates over whether to encourage private-home ownership through suburban development or to maintain land reserves by allowing for greater urban densities. Still other points of dispute concern the disposition of Israel's very limited littoral areas and the few remaining vacant interior lands. The terms of debate in these and a host of other issues emphasize the public versus the private interest. This challenge by individual citizens and nongovernmental organizations against the "official" version of the public good is a striking new phenomenon.[33]

A host of citizens' organizations are springing up to advocate interests and positions as they have in America, which provides the model for many activists in patterns of organization and identification of issues. In the debates over Israel's future, a cacophony of voices clamor for attention. The efflorescence of issues and parties to controversy so reminiscent of debates in the United States and other modern societies reflects the new way in which Israelis imagine "normalization." The erosion of exceptionalism based on the rationale for the exigencies of building a Jewish state is clearly part of this trend.[34]

I have outlined here a trend that is obviously growing. However, it is far from certain how radical and far-reaching the transformation may be. At the same time that these changes are taking place, there is great continuity. It is far from certain that the scenarios of "Israel 2020" will come to pass. The forces among Palestinians and in the Arab world against reconciliation with Israel are powerful. On the Israeli side, there are many people who now doubt that the essential component of "Israel 2020," a permanent accommodation with the Palestinians, can be achieved. Others conceive of Israel in a way in which accommodation with Palestinians and the Arabs would be difficult, if not impossible.

"Israel 2020," then, was drafted at a moment in Israeli history when, after a century of sustained effort, enterprise, and strife, it was possible to begin to see a way out of an Israel distorted by conflict and a future that could and should be different. The imaginable differences go beyond the end of conflict. "Israel 2020" assumes a new national ideology that favors privatism and the capitalism that usually accompanies it.

Should Israel be able to imagine its future in an environment of peace, it would do so, for the first time, without the burdens of organizing a fortress society. "Israel 2020" ultimately tries to imagine scenarios of rational decisions based on values shared with advanced and progressive societies that enjoy prestige and admiration. Whatever the actual future, it is nevertheless likely that the tensions between normalcy and exceptionalism will grow and color the debate of how a Jewish state should be imagined and realized.

NOTES

1. See Aviezer Ravitzky, *Messianism, Zionism, and Jewish Religious Radicalism* (Chicago: University of Chicago Press, 1996). For Zionism generally, see Walter Laqueur, *A History of Zionism* (New York: Schocken Books, 2003); and Gideon Shimoni, *The Zionist Ideology* (Hanover, NH: University Press of New England, 1995).
2. Adam M. Garfinkle, "On the Origin, Meaning, Use and Abuse of a Phrase," *Middle Eastern Studies* 27 (1991): 539–50.
3. Justin McCarthy, *The Population of Palestine: Population History and Statistics of the Late Ottoman Period and the Mandate* (New York: Columbia University Press, 1990).
4. There is a large literature of travelers' accounts. A good beginning is Yehoshua Ben-Arieh, *The Rediscovery of the Holy Land in the Nineteenth Century* (Detroit: Wayne State University Press, 1979).
5. Mark Twain (Samuel Clemens), *Innocents Abroad; or, The New Pilgrim's Progress* (London: Chatto & Windus, 1916), 449.
6. Ibid.
7. There are numerous reports, official and unofficial, about the economic state of the country. A convenient review of statistics, social and political data and their interpretations in Palestine, is to be found in ESCO Foundation for Palestine, *Palestine: A Study of Jewish, Arab, and British Policies*, 2 vols. (New Haven, CT: Yale University Press, 1947).
8. For the portal of the Organization for Economic Co-operation and Development, see http://www.oecd.org/israel/.
9. S. Ilan Troen, *Imagining Zion: Dreams, Designs, and Realities in a Century of Jewish Settlement* (New Haven, CT: Yale University Press, 2003).
10. The best of the large literature on the subject is Asher Susser, *Israel, Jordan, and Palestine: The Two-State Imperative* (Waltham, MA: Brandeis University Press, 2011).
11. A large-scale synthesis of competing Jewish and Arab views is found in Jacob Lassner and S. Ilan Troen, *Jews and Muslims in the Arab World: Haunted by Pasts Real and Imagined* (Lanham, MD: Rowman & Littlefield, 2007).
12. Theodor Herzl, *Altneuland = Old-New Land: Novel*, trans. Paula Arnold (Haifa, Israel: Haifa Publishing, 1960).

13. S. Ilan Troen, "Frontier Myths and Their Applications in America and Israel: A Transnational Perspective," *Journal of American History* (1999): 1209–30.
14. Henry Near, *Frontiersmen and Halutzim: The Image of the Pioneer in North America and Pre-State Jewish Palestine* (Haifa, Israel: University of Haifa, 1987).
15. Charles M. Haar, *Land-Use Planning: A Casebook on the Use, Misuse, and Re-use of Urban Land* (Boston: Little, Brown, 1959), 28–29.
16. See Emanuel Yalan, *Private and Cooperative Agricultural Settlement: Physical Planning* (Haifa, Israel: Ha-Makhpil, 1962); and Dov Weintraub, Moshe Lissak, and Yael Azmon, *Moshava, Kibbutz, and Moshav: Patterns of Jewish Rural Settlement and Development in Palestine* (Ithaca, NY: Cornell University Press, 1969). Valuable for the tradition of Jewish communal self-government are Daniel Elazar, *People and Polity: The Organizational Dynamics of World Jewry* (Detroit: Wayne State University Press, 1989); and Alan Dowty, *The Jewish State: A Century Later* (Berkeley: University of California Press, 1998).
17. Troen, *Imagining Zion*, chap. 1; Alter Druyanov, ed., *Documents on the History of Hibbat-Zion and the Settlement of Eretz-Israel* [in Hebrew], new ed. by Shulamit Laskov, 7 vols. (Tel Aviv: Tel Aviv University, 1982–93).
18. Elwood Mead et al., *Reports of the Experts Submitted to the Joint Palestine Survey Commission* (Boston: Daniels, 1928).
19. For a recent, comprehensive volume of new scholarship on the founding and shaping of Tel Aviv, see Maoz Azaryahu and S. Ilan Troen, ed., *Tel-Aviv, the First Century: Visions, Designs, Actualities* (Bloomington: Indiana University Press, 2012).
20. Troen, *Imagining Zion*, chap. 5.
21. S. Ilan Troen, "The Hebrew Translation of the Declaration of Independence," in "Interpreting the Declaration of Independence by Translation: A Round Table," *Journal of American History* 85 (1999): 1380–84.
22. Elyakim Rubinstein, "The Declaration of Independence as a Basic Document of the State of Israel," *Israel Studies* 3 (1998): 195–210.
23. Orit Rozin, *The Rise of the Individual in 1950s Israel: A Challenge to Collectivism* (Waltham, MA: Brandeis University Press, 2011).
24. Representative of scholarship analyzing the transformation of the kibbutz is Eliezer Ben-Rafael, *Crisis and Transformation: The Kibbutz at Century's End* (Albany: SUNY Press, 1997). See, too, for a recent review of the literature, M. Naor, "The Kibbutz at 100: But Does It Have a Future?," *Haaretz*, January 23, 2011, http://www.haaretz.com/jewish/books/the-kibbutz-at-100-but-does-it-have-a-future-1.338704.
25. Social and political changes as measured by success in elections are charted regularly in a series titled *Israel at the Polls* by the Jerusalem Center for Public Affairs. For a summary of the trends indicated here, see Daniel J. Elazar and Ben Mollov, eds., *Israel at the Polls, 1999* (Portland, OR: F. Cass, 2001).
26. A good example of this trend is found in Yaron Ezrahi, *Rubber Bullets: Power and Conscience in Modern Israel* (New York: Farrar, Straus & Giroux, 1997).

27. See Walter Ackerman, "Making Jews: An Enduring Challenge in Education," *Israel Studies* 2 (1997): 1–20; S. Ilan Troen, "The Construction of a Secular Jewish Identity: European and American Influences on Israeli Education," in *Divergent Jewish Cultures; Israel and America*, ed. Deborah D. Moore and S. Ilan Troen (New Haven, CT: Yale University Press, 2001), 27–52.
28. Troen, *Imagining Zion*, 181–92.
29. See Dan Senor and Saul Singer, *Start-Up Nation: The Story of Israel's Economic Miracle* (New York: Twelve, 2009).
30. *Bagatz* (Israel Supreme Court Decision) 6698/95, *Quaadan vs. Israel Lands Authority, et al.* For a review of the comments on this case, see Gerald M. Steinberg, "'The Poor in Your Own City Shall Have Precedence': A New Zionist Critique of the Katzir-Qaadan Decision," *Jerusalem Viewpoints* (Jerusalem Center for Public Affairs) 445 (January 1, 2001).
31. For a fascinating and central debate on these issues, see a series of articles published under "Zionist Dialectics" in *Israel Studies*: Sammy Smooha, "Ethnic Democracy: Israel as an Archetype," *Israel Studies* 2 (1997): 198–241; As'ad Ganim, Nadim N. Rouhana, and Oren Yiftachel, "Questioning 'Ethnic Democracy': A Response to Sammy Smooha," *Israel Studies* 3 (1998): 253–67; Ruth Gavison, "Jewish and Democratic? A Rejoinder to the 'Ethnic Democracy' Debate," *Israel Studies* 4 (1999): 44–72; Alan Dowty, "Is Israel Democratic? Substance and Semantics in the 'Ethnic Democracy' Debate," *Israel Studies* 4 (1999): 1–15; Allan Arkush, "Ethnocracy Land and Identity Politics in Israel/Palestine (review)," *Israel Studies* 12 (2007): 161–67.
32. A recent volume that recovers the feelings and emotions of those who engage with "the Land" is Boaz Neumann, *Land and Desire in Early Zionism* (Waltham, MA: Brandeis University Press, 2011).
33. Examples of this new discussion are found in Alon Tal, Daniel Orenstein, and Char Miller, eds., *Between Ruin and Restoration: An Environmental History of Israel* (Pittsburgh: University of Pittsburgh Press, 2012); Alon Tal and Alfred Abed Rabbo, eds., *Water Wisdom: Preparing the Groundwork for Cooperative and Sustainable Water Management in the Middle East* (New Brunswick, NJ: Rutgers University Press, 2010).
34. Theodore Sasson and Eric Fleisch, *The New Philanthropy: American Jewish Giving to Israeli Organizations* (Waltham, MA: Cohen Center for Modern Jewish Studies, 2012).

ABOUT THE CONTRIBUTORS

Nehama Aschkenasy is Professor of Comparative Literary and Cultural Studies at the University of Connecticut and founding director of its Stamford campus Center for Judaic and Middle Eastern Studies. She is the author of four books, including the award-winning *Eve's Journey: Feminine Images in Hebraic Literary Tradition* (1986) and *Woman at the Window: Biblical Tales of Oppression and Escape* (1998).

Paula J. Birnbaum is Associate Professor of Art History/Arts Management and Academic Director of the Museum Studies Masters program at the University of San Francisco. She is the author of *Women Artists in Interwar France: Framing Femininities* (2011) and is completing a monograph on Chana Orloff (1888–1968), a prolific sculptor who made her career in France and Israel.

Shmuel Bolozky is Professor of Hebrew in the Department of Judaic and Near Eastern Studies at the University of Massachusetts–Amherst and past president of the National Association of Professors of Hebrew. His major publications include *Measuring Productivity in Word Formation: The Case of Israeli Hebrew* (1999), *501 Hebrew Verbs* (1996/2008), and *A Reference Grammar of Modern Hebrew* (coauthor, 2005).

Michael Feige is a sociologist at the Ben-Gurion Research Institute, Ben-Gurion University of the Negev. His book *Settling in the Hearts: Jewish Fundamentalism in the Occupied Territories* (2009) won the Shapiro Award for best book in Israel studies.

Calvin Goldscheider is Scholar in Residence at American University and Professor Emeritus at Brown University. From 1969 to 1985, he was Professor of Sociology and Demography at the Hebrew University of Jerusalem. He is the author or coauthor of several books on Jewish and

Israel-related themes, including *The Population of Israel* (1979), *The Transformation of the Jews* (1984), *Israel's Changing Society: Population, Ethnicity, and Development* (2002), *The Arab-Israeli Conflict* (2002), *Studying the Jewish Future* (2004), and *Israeli Society in the 21st Century* (2015).

Frederick E. Greenspahn is Gimelstob Eminent Scholar of Judaic Studies at Florida Atlantic University. He is the author/editor of numerous other titles and past president of the National Association of Professors of Hebrew and editor of its journal *Hebrew Studies*.

Nadim N. Rouhana is Professor of International Affairs and Conflict Studies at the Fletcher School of Law and Diplomacy at Tufts University. He is also Founding Director of Mada al-Carmel—The Arab Center for Applied Social Research in Haifa. He has held various academic positions in Palestinian, Israeli, and American universities. His publications include *Palestinian Citizens in an Ethnic Jewish State: Identities in Conflict* (1997) and numerous academic articles on collective identity, settler colonialism, multiethnic states, democratic citizenship, Palestinians in Israel, and other topics.

Raymond Russell is Professor of Sociology at the University of California, Riverside. His works on Israel include *Utopia in Zion: The Israeli Experience with Worker Cooperatives* (1995) and *The Renewal of the Kibbutz: From Reform to Transformation* (with Robert Hanneman and Shlomo Getz, 2013).

Areej Sabbagh-Khoury received her Ph.D. from Tel Aviv University. She is a research associate at Mada al-Carmel—Arab Center for Applied Social Research and the academic coordinator of the Political Participation of the Palestinians in Israel. She is also the coeditor of *The Palestinians in Israel: A Guide to History, Politics, and Society* (with Nadim N. Rouhana).

Arieh Saposnik is Associate Professor at the Ben-Gurion Institute for the Study of Israel and Zionism at Ben-Gurion University of the Negev. He is the author of *Becoming Hebrew: The Creation of a Jewish National Cul-*

ture in Ottoman Palestine (2008) and has held positions at the Hebrew University in Jerusalem, the University of Florida, the University of Wisconsin, Arizona State University, and UCLA, where he was founding director of the Younes and Soraya Nazarian Center for Israel Studies.

Theodore Sasson is Professor of Jewish Studies at Middlebury College and Senior Research Scientist at the Cohen Center for Modern Jewish Studies. He is also Visiting Research Professor of Sociology at Brandeis University and a consultant to the Mandel Foundation. He is the author most recently of *The New American Zionism* (2014).

Ilan Troen is the Stoll Family Professor in Israel Studies at Brandeis University and founding director of its Schusterman Center for Israel Studies. He is also the founding editor of the journal *Israel Studies*. His most recent books are *Jews and Muslims in the Arab World: Haunted by Pasts Real and Imagined* (with Jacob Lassner, 2007) and *Tel-Aviv, the First Century: Visions, Designs, Actualities* (coedited with Maoz Azaryahu, 2012).

Patricia J. Woods is Associate Professor of Political Science and Jewish Studies at the University of Florida. She is the author of *Judicial Power and National Politics: Courts and Gender in the Religious-Secular Conflict in Israel* (2008) and of articles in *Droit et Société, Field Methods, Political Research Quarterly, Studies in Law, Politics, and Society*, and *Israel Studies Forum*.

INDEX